Sacraments of Memory

UNIVERSITY PRESS OF FLORIDA

Florida A&M University, Tallahassee
Florida Atlantic University, Boca Raton
Florida Gulf Coast University, Ft. Myers
Florida International University, Miami
Florida State University, Tallahassee
New College of Florida, Sarasota
University of Central Florida, Orlando
University of Florida, Gainesville
University of North Florida, Jacksonville
University of South Florida, Tampa
University of West Florida, Pensacola

SACRAMENTS OF MEMORY

Catholicism and Slavery in Contemporary African American Literature

Erin Michael Salius

UNIVERSITY PRESS OF FLORIDA

Gainesville / Tallahassee / Tampa / Boca Raton

Pensacola / Orlando / Miami / Jacksonville / Ft. Myers / Sarasota

Publication of this paperback edition made possible by a Sustaining the Humanities through the American Rescue Plan grant from the National Endowment for the Humanities.

COPYRIGHT 2018 BY ERIN MICHAEL SALIUS
All rights reserved
Printed in the United States of America

First cloth printing, 2018
First paperback printing, 2022

27 26 25 24 23 22   6 5 4 3 2 1

Library of Congress Cataloging-in-Publication Data
Names: Salius, Erin Michael, author.
Title: Sacraments of memory : Catholicism and slavery in contemporary African American literature / Erin Michael Salius.
Description: Gainesville : University Press of Florida, 2018. | Includes bibliographical references and index.
Identifiers: LCCN 2017033921 | ISBN 9780813056890 (cloth) | ISBN 9780813068893 (pbk.)
Subjects: LCSH: Slavery and the church—Catholic Church. | American literature—African American authors—History. | Slavery in literature. | Catholics in literature. | African Americans in literature.
Classification: LCC PS508.N3 S25 2018 | DDC 810.9/3828208996073—dc23
LC record available at https://lccn.loc.gov/2017033921

The University Press of Florida is the scholarly publishing agency for the State University System of Florida, comprising Florida A&M University, Florida Atlantic University, Florida Gulf Coast University, Florida International University, Florida State University, New College of Florida, University of Central Florida, University of Florida, University of North Florida, University of South Florida, and University of West Florida.

UNIVERSITY PRESS OF FLORIDA
2046 NE Waldo Road
Suite 2100
Gainesville, FL 32609
http://upress.ufl.edu

Contents

ACKNOWLEDGMENTS vii

Introduction: Toward a Reading of the Catholic Margin in Contemporary Narratives of Slavery 1

1. Toni Morrison's Sacramental Rememory 13

2. A Sacred Communion: The Catholic Side of Possession in *The Autobiography of Miss Jane Pittman* and *Two Wings to Veil My Face* 67

3. Catholicism and Narrative Time: Transcending the Past and the Present in *Stigmata* and *Oxherding Tale* 109

4. Catholicism and Narrative Time, Continued: Divine Prescience in Edward P. Jones's *The Known World* 160

Coda 193

NOTES 195
BIBLIOGRAPHY 209
INDEX 217

Acknowledgments

THIS BOOK BEGAN as many books do: with a question that nagged at me and wouldn't let go. At the time, I was engaged in another project, about literary representations of racial violence in works by contemporary African American authors. It seemed to me that Christian imagery was being deployed in these representations in remarkable ways, and I had set out to document what I expected to be a sharp critique of the religious justification for slavery and racial oppression in the United States. Because slaveholding in this country was an overwhelmingly Protestant enterprise (with some notable exceptions) and because the characters in the works I was reading were also overwhelmingly Protestant, my assumption was that evangelical Protestantism would inform their representations of violence and would constitute their primary object of critique. But what I found instead—first in one or two texts and then in many, many more—was that the Christian imagery I encountered had a distinctively *Catholic* cast. Why, I asked, in a novel set in a town where the only churches are Protestant, would scenes of racial brutality be informed by images of saints or transubstantiation? How to explain finding Catholicism at the margins of these works?

Susan Mizruchi encouraged those early questions and spurred me to ask even more challenging ones. Susan's advice has always been invaluable to me, and I wish to thank her for the extraordinary intellectual guidance she's given as well as the personal support. In my view, she sets the bar for what a scholar and a mentor can be, and I could not imagine a better model. I am exceedingly grateful, too, to Gene Jarrett, who took an early interest in the project and helped to shape it into what it has become. His insightful feedback and wealth of knowledge pushed me to take the analysis in a different direction than I had originally planned—and the book benefited significantly as a result.

My work has also benefited from conversations with a number of other faculty from the Boston University English Department, including Maurice Lee, Laura Korobkin, Laurence Breiner, Robert Chodat, Joseph Rezek, Bill Carroll, Jack Matthews, and Erin Murphy. I was fortunate enough to participate with the latter two in the Fellows' Seminar, run through the BU Center for the Humanities. The BUCH afforded the opportunity to meet regularly with scholars working on an array of interesting projects that inspired my own. I want to express my gratitude to all the BUCH Fellows and to James Winn, former director of the BUCH, for their generosity.

During the many years I have spent at BU, I have had the opportunity to collaborate with people from diverse disciplines on a range of endeavors that stoked—and broadened in valuable ways—my investment in literary studies. My colleagues at the Writing Program and the Educational Resource Center, especially Gin Schaffer, provided a warm, welcoming space in which to develop my approach to literature. My colleagues at Summer Term have taught me important lessons about teamwork and communication. I feel fortunate to learn from them every day. And I am appreciative, too, of my students from BU and MIT who challenged me with insightful queries about the texts we studied together.

The wonderful team at University Press of Florida, including Sian Hunter, Ali Sundook, and Eleanor Deumens, has provided invaluable support and guidance from start to finish. I also want to thank Ann Marlowe and Rachel Lyon for their contributions, as well as Sheldon George and another anonymous reader, who offered crucial feedback.

On a personal note, I would like to acknowledge the friends and family members who have contributed to this work both directly and indirectly over the years. There are, in fact, too many to list, including my relatives on the Salius and Ruwet sides who have been cheering me on for as long as I can remember. A special debt of gratitude goes to the Michigan crew, in particular to my mother-in-law, Leslie, whose strength and perseverance have taught me a great deal. Thanks are also due to Sarah, Sara, Kristen, Lauren, and, of course, to Mikaela, who never doubted and has been there through it all.

Finally, the opportunity to devote myself to this project day in and day out was granted to me by three people who worked together seamlessly to ensure that my girls never noticed how many hours I spent behind the computer screen. To my mother and father: thank you for creating such a magical world for Sadie and Emeline to grow up in. As I did as a child, they are learning from you the stuff that really matters, and nothing makes me happier than to witness the joy you bring them. To my daughters: you have given me the greatest gift, and I can't believe you're mine. To Matthew, my partner in all things: words fail, but you never do; I am forever grateful. This is for you.

Introduction

Toward a Reading of the Catholic Margin
in Contemporary Narratives of Slavery

IN 1992, PAUL GILES PUBLISHED his broad and ambitious account of Roman Catholicism "as a residual cultural determinant" within American literature from the early part of the nineteenth century to the present (1). Focusing on writers who grew up Catholic or were exposed to Catholic practices as children, he argues that even for nonbelievers and apostates, the rituals they performed and the doctrines they studied in their youth can affect aesthetic production "in some circuitous or unconscious fashion long after the forces of rationality have deconstructed and rejected" such irrational precepts (2). The range of Giles's analysis is extensive, and he examines the work of authors from a variety of socioeconomic and ethnic contexts as well as from nearly two centuries of U.S. history. Yet at the end of the book he acknowledges that there remains at least one key aspect of contemporary Catholic culture that his inquiry barely touches upon: he calls in his conclusion for a fuller consideration of how artists who have been historically disenfranchised by racial segregation within the church— and African Americans specifically—deploy discourses of Catholicism in their fiction. Fewer than four pages of his 531-page book are devoted to nonwhite authors, and so by way of atoning for this imbalance, Giles invites further consideration of a literature that reflects the "distinctly . . . oppositional cultural perspective" through which African American writers "filter" Catholic "themes" (518).

Now, almost a quarter century after Giles's *American Catholic Arts and Fictions* highlighted the dearth of scholarship on Catholicism in African American literature, we find ourselves still awaiting the start of the conversation. While a handful of articles and book chapters have addressed the religious content of texts by individuals with clear ties to Catholic culture, such as Alice Dunbar-Nelson, whose Creole heritage features prominently in her fiction, and Claude McKay, who wrote extensively about converting to Catholicism, no major study of the topic has yet been undertaken.[1] My project thus inaugurates what I hope will become a far-reaching, multidirectional effort among critics to identify and contextualize how the African American literary tradition engages Catholic ideology, theology, and social practices. For when we look closely, Catholicism appears at the margins of a significant number of significant works throughout the canon of African American literature—including those written by authors who were never practicing Catholics. From some of the earliest published texts in the tradition (fugitive slave narratives by Frederick Douglass and Harriet Jacobs, for example)[2] to some of the most recent (plays such as *The Death of the Last Black Man in the Whole Entire World* by Suzan-Lori Parks),[3] Catholicism operates in various ways, all of which warrant extended reflection. Indeed, given the conspicuous lack of scholarly attention to this Catholic margin and its implications, an examination of the subject in virtually any historical period or generic categorization would contribute materially to a more complete portrait of African American literary history.

This book focuses on contemporary narratives of slavery in particular because the genre developed at a time when there was growing interest in how religion and religious discourses determine our collective "memory" of the slave experience in the United States. Contemporary narratives of slavery—also called neo-slave narratives[4]—first emerged in the late 1960s and 1970s, during the height of national conversations about the way we remember that "peculiar institution," conversations that defined the legacy of racial oppression that persisted well past Emancipation and persists still.[5] In the wake of the civil rights and Black Power movements, academics from newly established Black Studies programs across the nation were advocating for a revision of the traditional historiography of slavery. Their calls were echoed by African American artists and writers, many of them affiliated with the Black Arts Movement whose founder, Amiri Baraka, made explicit his aesthetic compulsion to expose the lies that sustained white America's view of the past. As Ashraf Rushdy has contended, chief among those lies was the suggestion, prominent in white-authored texts like William Styron's 1967 novel *The Confessions of Nat Turner*, that slaves possessed neither the knowledge nor the intellectual capacity to successfully resist the conditions of their enslavement—that they were, in effect, largely unthinking victims of the abuses perpetrated against them. In part to dispel these erroneous claims, historians and other academics invested in revising the historical record aimed to demonstrate the extraordinary lengths to which slaves often went to challenge the ideology of the system that made them chattel.

With regard to religion specifically, important work by Eugene Genovese, Lawrence Levine, and Albert Raboteau revealed how slaves manipulated the fundamentalist Protestant ideals imposed on them by southern slave owners seeking to cultivate an atmosphere of obedience. Their scholarship charted multiple courses of resistance, making the case that even the most apparently devout—and obedient—Christians were subtly defying their masters' power by using church meetings and religious gatherings for their own (sometimes revolutionary) purposes. Along similar lines, literary scholars began during this period to consider the canny ways that slave autobiographers negotiated Christianity in their writing, showing how they appealed to the abolitionist sympathies of an evangelical readership in the North by condemning the "ungodly" behavior of white Protestants in the South. But while this criticism brought awareness to the strategic use of religion in autobiographies by fugitive slave authors and helped to establish their autobiographies as "legitimate" works of literature, it also confirmed the tenuousness of their theological positions. In other words: by emphasizing the thoughtfulness and purpose with which the antebellum autobiographers wrote about Christian theology, studies such as John Blassingame's *The Slave Community* simultaneously drew attention to the religious conventions they were forced to uphold in the quest to gain northern sympathizers. Collectively, then, these studies made clear how much the political strategy of the fugitive slave authors depended on their ability to market themselves as spiritually saved and God-fearing Christians, whom white evangelicals in the North would deem "worthy" of liberation.

As a result of this burgeoning field of scholarship, which outlined both the advantages and the limitations of religious discourses of resistance for slaves, there was intense scrutiny in the post-civil-rights period on the way that antebellum narratives of slavery were shaped by Christianity—

and specifically on what the autobiographers had to withhold from their testimonies for fear of offending their readers or otherwise jeopardizing the abolitionist cause. Thus, at almost the same moment when academics were establishing the historical legitimacy and literary value of these first-person accounts of enslavement, new questions surfaced about the silences and obfuscations that pervade them.[6] If fugitive slave authors knew their political aims were contingent upon "proof" of Christian salvation, then what might they have chosen to leave out or to forget about their past? How could they possibly be expected to communicate the full truth of their experience to an audience looking for any reason to condemn them? The frustration implicit in entertaining such questions is, of course, that no satisfactory answers can ever be given, since—as Toni Morrison reminds us in her 1987 essay "The Site of Memory"—it would be impossible to separate the texts from the milieu in which they were written. According to Morrison, "whatever the level of eloquence" of a slave's autobiography, "popular taste" determined its style and its content, forcing the excision of any detail that might appear "sordid" or "excessive" (69). Morrison's analysis reflects the rising tide of skepticism that tempered early claims about the authenticity or truth-value of fugitive slave narratives from historians eager to legitimize their version of events. Rather than joining the chorus of those who celebrated unequivocally the autobiographers' capacity for accurately representing history from the slave's point of view, she sought to understand the social, political—and, yes, religious—forces that "dictated" what they wrote and the way they wrote it.

While skepticism of the kind that Morrison expresses might be thought to lessen interest in the form, what most critics argue is that it actually had the exact opposite effect: that the explosion of novels about slavery in the second half of the twentieth century was driven, not dampened, by studies exposing how dramatically the fugitive slave narratives were influenced by the values of their white readership. To put this in other terms: the criticism tends to correlate the genre's emergence in the decades following the movements for racial equality in the United States with a widespread effort of imagination on the part of contemporary African American authors to "fill the gaps" in the historical record of slavery—gaps left by antebellum autobiographers who had no choice but to relate their memories according to discursive conventions that would appeal to a white, evangelical audience in the North. And, in many respects, the correlation these critics are making is based on the same premise that Morrison herself used to describe her "job" as a writer working in a "very different" historical context, "more than a hundred years after Emancipation." To her, "any person who is black, or who belongs to any marginalized category," has a responsibility to imaginatively recover that which the fugitive slaves could not remember, as a consequence of the "climate in which they wrote." Thus Morrison regards her own fiction about slavery as a concerted attempt "to rip that veil aside" that was drawn over their autobiographies by a set of discourses they "were seldom invited to participate in . . . even when [they] were its topic" ("Site" 70).

As Madhu Dubey has demonstrated, the particular set of discourses that contemporary narratives of slavery sought to undermine were informed by "Enlightenment modernity" as well as the realist and rationalist imperatives that characterized writing produced "during an era when slaves were relegated to subhuman status because they were believed to be innately incapable of reason" (340). With that in mind, Dubey and other literary scholars working on the genre have stressed the range of techniques that authors deploy to confound the rationalizing impulse of antebellum texts, arguing that by disrupting realism in their narratives, they are effectively "reclaiming" those portions of the slave experience that were "suppressed by the modern legacy" and consequently excised from the traditional historiography of slavery ("Neo-Slave" 342).[7] The more unrealistic or supernatural aspects of the genre that proliferate especially in contemporary slave narratives written after 1970 have therefore been interpreted as a reaction against Enlightenment rationalism—and the values of the Protestant Reformation with which, in the United States as in Europe, the Age of Enlightenment was inexorably connected. Following Paul Gilroy's brilliant and hugely influential study *The Black Atlantic*, the vast majority of criticism on these novels links their radical breaks with realism to a "counterculture" of modernity that "defiantly reconstructs its own critical, intellectual, and moral genealogy" in terms categorically opposed to the Western model (37–38). This is how critics have explained, for example, the frequent appearance of alternative belief structures and non-Western religions in contemporary narratives of slavery: as a tool for destabilizing the religious strictures placed on the antebellum slave autobiographers by the evangelical Protestant audiences who constituted their primary readership.

There can be no doubt that the African and African-derived spiritual practices found in so many contemporary narratives of slavery promote radically different ways of remembering the slave experience that challenge the conventions of the form—conventions determined by the autobiographers' need to proclaim their own clear and rational faith in a Christian God and to disaffiliate completely from what were perceived as the irrational beliefs of Africa. (Think of the famous footnote from Frederick Douglass's *Narrative* in which he characterizes Sandy's rootwork as ignorant superstition.) And so, through the textual reclamation of these suppressed and disparaged spiritualities, post-civil-rights novels about slavery engage in what Gilroy has called "a politics of transfiguration": a striving toward new modes of representation "that are consequent on the overcoming of the racial oppression on which modernity and its antinomy of rational, western progress as excessive barbarity relied" (38). In other words, the disruptions in formal structure and narrative content that such non-Western belief systems enact in the texts are political, as well as narratological, acts of revision. Thus the genre's overwhelming antirealist (alternately termed "speculative" or "postmodern") orientation is almost always associated in the criticism with a push away from the constraints imposed by "Western Christianity" on the fugitive slave writers.

While I agree in a general sense with arguments linking antirealism to a politics of historical revision, my study will complicate the prevailing understanding of the mechanisms by which contemporary slave narratives disrupt the antebellum discourse of slavery. For, as I argue, non-Western belief systems alone do not account for all the ways that the novels considered here "transfigure" the conventions of Enlightenment rationalism. More to the point, they do not account for the striking presence of Catholicism at the margins of these texts, nor for how the Catholic margin imaginatively intervenes in and shapes their revisionist aims. Indeed, by teasing out the moments where the authors in this study critically engage Catholicism as part of the effort to revise the traditional historiography of slavery, I propose a new framework for reading the alternative spiritualities emergent in their novels, suggesting that along with the African and African-derived practices they are consciously reclaiming, they also marshal Catholic themes and images in the service of the radical "counterculture" the writing sustains. On the one hand, their recourse to Catholicism makes sense, since historically the religion has been associated with the very irrationality and aberrant supernaturalism that the Enlightenment endeavored to stamp out. Therefore it seems logical to assume that the anti-Enlightenment resonances of Catholic theology contribute to the contemporary slave narrative's critique of rationalist modernity. On the other hand, Catholicism and the institutions of the American Catholic Church have been complicit not only in slavery itself but also in the systemic racial segregation and oppression that persisted in the United States well into the civil rights period. So what would incline African American authors to imaginatively deploy Catholicism in their attempts to change how slavery is remembered—especially during a time characterized by a deep suspicion of the cultural traditions that supported the rise of slave societies in the West?

Answering this question brings to light a host of startling inconsistencies and ambiguities that are, in a way, the subject of my inquiry. That is because to acknowledge how contemporary narratives of slavery use Catholicism to challenge the realist and rationalist imperatives of fugitive slave autobiographies is to acknowledge—simultaneously—the profound ambivalence with which these novels are engaging the religion's disruptive potential. The Catholic margin constitutes a territory of deep internal conflict, wherein the texts negotiate their imaginative attraction to the "irrational" language of sacraments and saints with their very real concerns about the historical and social policies of the church. One representative instance occurs in Leon Forrest's 1983 novel *Two Wings to Veil My Face* when, just as the protagonist, Nathaniel Witherspoon, starts to imagine the story his grandmother tells him as a Eucharistic celebration through which he might actually commune with the spirits of his slave ancestors, he finds himself remembering a disturbing event from his childhood: the burning down of his local Catholic church by its white congregants, who destroyed the building "rather than see it be turned over to the coloreds; starting the fire with the cloth that lined the Communion rail; and seven [black] children perished" (65). Nathaniel's memory of this horrific act of racism (as well as his memories of other atrocities committed in the name of Catholicism, such as Mussolini's invasion of Ethiopia)[8] effectively interrupts his desire to associate his family in any way with the religion—even in imaginary terms. The hesitation Nathaniel experiences at this moment in the novel, as he seeks a mode of representation that will adequately represent the past, is indicative, I argue, of how the authors in my study approach Catholic discourse. For although they were not all raised in Catholicism as Nathaniel and his creator were, their works display an intimate awareness of the racist history that undergirds institutions run and supported by church hierarchy—an awareness gained either through their education in Catholic schools (Ernest Gaines, Edward P. Jones, Phyllis Alesia Perry), through their conversion to Catholicism (Toni Morrison), or through their academic study of the religion (Charles Johnson).

...

The book's chapters trace the ambivalence with which these authors deploy the anti-Enlightenment orientation of Catholicism to disrupt the conventional historiography of American slavery and to imagine radically different means of remembering the past. Chapter 1, "Toni Morrison's Sacramental Rememory," discovers this ambivalence in the margins of two novels that are widely celebrated for undermining Enlightenment rationalism: *Beloved* (1987) and *A Mercy* (2008). As critics often note, Morrison's concept of rememory—an antirealist trope premised on the supernatural irruption of the past in the present—destabilizes rationalist discourse by imagining an alternative history of slavery. Rememory thus promotes a kind of redemption: a means of redressing the formulaic way that the antebellum slave autobiographers were forced to remember their personal history. But because the criticism has not yet acknowledged how thoroughly the concept is informed by Catholic theology and, in particular, by a Catholic conception of grace, it tends to overlook its redemptive potential. A complete picture of these novels requires an account of the way that Morrison structures rememory—quite remarkably and with palpable historical reservations—as a Catholic sacrament. The chapter therefore addresses a significant gap in scholarship on Morrison, who identifies as Catholic, but never does it imply that her religious vision is uncritical or pure. Rather, throughout my analysis, I suggest that the sacramental aspects of rememory are in constant tension with the sharp critique of Catholicism evident in both novels. That critique, I contend, builds upon the sociological study of slave religion that Orlando Patterson developed in *Slavery and Social Death*, particularly his pioneering claim that "the special version of Protestantism" that arose in the American slave South was, in key respects, theologically "identical" to Catholicism (ix).

Chapter 2, "A Sacred Communion," considers another trope that upsets the realist and rationalist discourse of slavery: spirit possession. In contemporary narratives of slavery, spirit possession signals a connection between the text's present and slave history, as the ancestral spirit communicates the trauma of enslavement through a living mediator who embodies the experience. Whereas existing scholarship has stressed the postmodernist resonances of this trope, I argue that the two novels I consider each depict their radical breaks with realism through the discourse of Catholicism. In other words, the Catholic margin of these two texts serves to frame—and even to facilitate—the antirealist effect that the trope of spirit possession has on their narratives. I turn first to Ernest Gaines's *The Autobiography of Miss Jane Pittman* (1971), which is one of the earliest examples of the genre. By highlighting where Jane's narrative voice is possessed by other speakers, I document how the Catholic characters in the novel enable it to engage radically antirealist views about history without ultimately endorsing them. The second part of the chapter focuses on Leon Forrest's critically acclaimed but insufficiently studied novel *Two Wings to Veil My Face*, which also figures storytelling as a kind of spirit possession. In contrast to Gaines's text, Forrest foregrounds the supernatural, as his narrator learns about his family's past from a community of long-dead slaves who inhabit the body of his grandmother. Despite its obvious skepticism toward organized religion, the novel depicts these spiritual intercessions as Catholic sacraments: rituals of eating and drinking that recall the Eucharist. Catholicism is implicated in the way the narrator remembers slavery and in the parts of his history that are "beyond understanding."

The third and fourth chapters both consider the trope of temporal disjuncture, or the abrupt and often inexplicable ways that texts destabilize conventions of linear time. In chapter 3, I argue that Phyllis Alesia Perry's *Stigmata* (1998) and Charles Johnson's *Oxherding Tale* (1982) manipulate past and present modalities, respectively, to contradict the Enlightenment-era principle that history moves forward progressively and linearly. Chapter 4 examines the flash-forward technique in Edward P. Jones's *The Known World* (2003), showing how that novel uses conceptions of future time to similarly disrupt the linearity of the narrative. In all three cases, temporal disjuncture serves as the means by which these contemporary narratives of slavery contend with the persistent trauma of the slave experience, for it creates an imaginative space outside the limits of Western temporality, suggesting a way to transcend the cycle of racial suffering and oppression. As these texts demonstrate, art that self-consciously interrupts standard chronologies has the advantage not only of upsetting the traditional historiography of slavery but also of promoting non-Western approaches to time, which have been delegitimized in the West since the Age of Enlightenment. What is striking about the non-Western temporal modes that each of the novels privileges is how dramatically they are informed by Catholicism. Specifically, as I suggest, the alternative temporalities they imagine reveal a strange and often disconcerting faithfulness to the theology of time that Augustine of Hippo laid out in some of his most canonical works. Since Augustinian theology has had such formative, lasting consequences for Western Christianity, and Catholicism in particular, it might appear contradictory to insist upon its relevance here, in all three novels I consider, which very plainly reject Western conceptions of chronological progress. However, I endeavor to show that theological contradictions of this sort in the Catholic margin of these three novels actually sustain the way they revise the historiography of slavery.

. . .

In focusing on the contradictions and tensions that Catholicism engenders in the novels under consideration, my approach throughout the book does not rely on—or offer—a static definition of the religion, nor indeed a rigid formula for how it operates in these works of fiction. Although I highlight in individual chapters the various means by which the Catholic margin disrupts Enlightenment rationality, I resist aligning it with a single discursive strategy or way of looking at the world. Quite simply, Catholicism functions differently in each of the texts examined here. For some, it refers to a set of ritualistic practices and beliefs that fall outside the bounds of rational thought; for others, it signifies a social history fraught with racial segregation and oppression; for others still, it indicates a potentially enabling theology of salvation. And to make matters even more complicated, Catholicism often sustains multiple—and conflicting—modes of articulation within the same work of literature. By bringing attention to the multiplicity inherent in the various ways that these novels deploy Catholicism, my study draws methodologically on the vital work of scholars such as Thomas J. Ferraro, Susan L. Mizruchi, Robert A. Orsi, and Jonathan Z. Smith, all of whom have stressed the importance of viewing religion as a dynamic and perpetually shifting category of discourse, through which it is possible to negotiate a variety of other, non-religious, aspects of culture.[9] More specifically, following Jenny Franchot, I regard the Catholic margin of these novels as a contested imaginative space that simultaneously "serve[s] many masters" (xxii). In other words, depending on the context, Catholicism in the novels I consider might be deployed in what Franchot calls "strategically confused" terms—to both legitimize and condemn the salvific meaning of suffering, for instance—and the efforts of my analysis are directed toward teasing out "the cultural and literary power of such taxonomic confusions," according to their functionality in the text (xxii, xxiii).

To that end, my methodology in the following chapters involves placing each contemporary slave narrative in conversation with the set of ideas, ideologies, and rituals it encompasses that are coded "Catholic." Attentive to the uniquely dynamic constitution and operation of Catholicism in every novel, I utilize a disciplinarily diverse range of germane texts, from doctrinal Catholic theology to poststructuralist theory, to frame the genre's complex engagement with the religion. My reading of *Beloved* and *A Mercy* in chapter 1, for example, turns to a work of social history, Patterson's *Slavery and Social Death*, that underpins Morrison's own literary and historical scholarship on antebellum texts to argue that the excessiveness of her fiction often evokes Catholicism's anti-Enlightenment orientation. I show how her critique of Enlightenment rationality in both novels depends, in fact, on reinserting "irrational" expressions of fear and anger into the historiography of slavery through the language of a Catholic sacramentality. In chapter 2, I put cultural studies of religious syncretism by Colin Dayan and Leslie Desmangles in dialogue with a Thomist theology of atemporality to demonstrate how the trope of spirit possession in novels by Ernest Gaines and Leon Forrest is linked to Catholicism. My third and fourth chapters, which connect the temporal disjuncture of *Stigmata*, *Oxherding Tale*, and *The Known World* to Augustine's famous theological musings on time, apply a deconstructionist reading of presence via Cixous and Derrida to account for the strange appearance of Catholic characters and iconography at the margins of these texts.

By uncovering the multiple and conflicting—and, to this point, unexamined—ways Catholicism functions in contemporary narratives of slavery, this book contributes to the recent push to rethink how religion operates in African American literature. Along with studies by Katherine Clay Bassard, Joanna Brooks, and Tuire Valkeakari that reveal the ingenious means by which so-called minority writers manipulate religious forms and idioms to suit their purposes, my project aims ultimately to offer a new perspective on the relationship between Christianity and representations of the slave experience.

1

Toni Morrison's Sacramental Rememory

NEAR THE START of Toni Morrison's *Beloved*, in the quiet that follows Paul D's violent expulsion of the baby ghost from 124 Bluestone Road, the narrative rests briefly on Denver and her curious reaction to what has just occurred. Four short paragraphs describe the girl's motions as she "wander[s] through the silence" of her upturned house, unhurriedly collecting food for a midday meal that she will eat alone (22). By contrast to the confusion of the preceding moments, her actions appear rehearsed, even ritualistic—a sense that is communicated by the spare prose, as well as by the particularization of every gesture:

> She ashed over the fire and pulled the pan of biscuits from the oven. The jelly cupboard was on its back, its contents lying in a heap in the corner of the bottom shelf. She took out a jar, and, looking around for a plate, found half of one by the door. These things she carried out to the porch steps, where she sat down.
> . . . She pried the wire from the top of the jar and then the lid. Under it was cloth and under that a thin cake of wax. She removed it all and coaxed the jelly onto one half of the half a plate. She took a biscuit and pulled off its black top. Smoke curled from the soft white insides. . . .
> . . . Denver dipped a bit of bread into the jelly. Slowly, methodically, miserably she ate it. (22–23)

In response to losing "the only other company she had"—the spirit of her dead sister, who haunted the house she lived in with her mother and who drove everyone else away—Denver resorts to the familiar act of preparing and eating her meal as a means of coping with the loss (23).

In fact, there is a significant body of criticism on *Beloved* that associates consumption, both in this passage and elsewhere, with the desire to repress an unspeakable trauma.[1] Critics making this claim point out that Morrison regularly conflates eating and forgetting. They tend to read much of her food-related imagery, such as the "chewing laughter" that will "swallow" Beloved "all away" at the end of the novel, as exemplary of this theme.[2] But, with respect to the passage quoted above, I want to shift the focus from what Denver's meal allows her to forget—because it seems to me that the language of the scene is actually cultivating a way to remember. Specifically, I contend that by describing in such exacting terms how Denver prepares and consumes her food, Morrison's writing takes a sacramental turn, effectively transforming the paltry snack of biscuits and jelly into a rite of remembrance that recalls the Catholic Eucharist.

The simple subject-predicate construction of the sentences and succession of dynamic verbs places particular emphasis on Denver's physical movements, what she *does* instead of what she tries to avoid ("She took"; "She pried"; "She removed"). With our attention drawn to Denver in this way, the Eucharistic resonances of her actions become apparent. Not only does the bread itself have clear associations with the Communion host, but the way that Denver presides over it—"slowly" and "methodically"—follows the distinctive structure of the Roman Mass. First there is the preparation of the gifts: the part of the Mass during which the priest transfers the offerings from tabernacle (jelly cupboard) to altar (porch steps) and arranges them deliberately before him. Then there is the fraction of the bread, wherein the priest breaks apart the Eucharist in a gesture reminiscent of Christ's at the Last Supper. (Denver's version even includes smoke curling heavenward, like that of the incense that some priests burn over the gifts to signify the church's prayer.) Finally there is the act of intinction: the ceremonial dipping of broken bread in wine (jelly) that immediately precedes its consumption.[3] All of this means that by the time Denver eats the biscuit in the last sentence of the scene, she has performed virtually the complete celebration of the Liturgy of the Eucharist just as it has been done for centuries by Catholic priests.

Of course, Denver is not a priest. Nor does the novel give any indication that she is Catholic or that she has ever witnessed a Roman Mass. Like the vast majority of African Americans born in the United States after the Second Great Awakening,[4] Denver's experience of Christianity is overwhelmingly Protestant. The ex-slaves she lives among in Cincinnati are "AME's and Baptists, Holinesses and Sanctifieds, [members of] the Church of the Redeemer and the Redeemed" (102). It is, therefore, the sacred practices of these sects that would be most familiar to Denver. Apart from the "unchurched" woodland sermons of her grandmother that she attended as a child and the occasional Africanist rituals she observed while growing up, Protestantism constitutes the extent of her religious knowledge and, by extension, everything she could possibly know about the Communion rite. But, as I have been arguing, the ritualistic overtones in Morrison's depiction of Denver align more closely with Catholicism than either of the Protestant variations practiced in her hometown. (Both the tabernacle and incense, for example, are exclusive to the Roman Mass; they are not present in Baptist or Methodist services.) Moreover, this scene does not mark the only time in the novel where Denver appears to demonstrate an uncanny predilection for Catholic ceremonials. Whenever she visits the "emerald closet" (123)—a circle of boxwood trees described as her private "temple" (60)—Denver anoints herself and the space with a "Christmas cologne" (34) in the same way that a Catholic priest would administer the holy oils while bestowing a sacrament. Notably, her character's response to the anointing is properly sacramental as well: Morrison writes that in the perfumed chamber, "closed off from the hurt of the hurt world," Denver "felt ripe and clear, and salvation was as easy as a wish" (35).

So what is it that drives Denver to turn during these moments of profound sorrow and isolation to Catholicism? How do we explain why a character with no known exposure to that religion performs its sacraments with such ritualistic precision? What, if anything, can she gain from the performance? And are we meant to take the performance seriously? In other words, to what extent is Morrison's representation of Catholic sacramentality in *Beloved* ironic or intentionally subversive? To what extent does it differ from her representation of other (Protestant) kinds of Christianity? These are questions worth asking, I contend, because of their implications for one of the most widely considered and vexed areas of scholarship on the novel: its use of Christian scripture and conspicuous Pauline orientation. Beyond that, they also promote a fuller understanding of the way religion informs Morrison's revision of the classic slave narrative form and, in particular, her original concept of rememory.

Almost from the moment *Beloved* appeared in 1987, critics have been locked in a contentious debate over how to interpret its frequent allusions to the New Testament, especially those to the epistles of Saint Paul. On one hand, Morrison's narrative reflects a deep suspicion of Christianity and the support it provided for race-based slavery in the United States. She routinely characterizes the cruelest slaveholders as the most devout Christians and suggests that Pauline theology was responsible, at least in part, for accommodating slaves to their mistreatment. For example, the woodland sermons of Baby Suggs—whose religious perspective scholars tend to align with the author's own—plainly reject the portions of Saint Paul's teachings that venerate suffering and divine enslavement. This sort of pointed critique has been taken by some, such as Ann-Janine Morey, as a "latter day judgment upon Christianity" that discloses "the failure of Christian promise" (499). On the other hand, the novel stops short of a wholesale rejection of Christianity, and there are many instances in which its religious allusiveness is more difficult to characterize. The novel's epigraph as well as its title, both drawn from Paul's Letter to the Romans, and the fact that three of its most sympathetic characters (brothers Paul D, Paul A, and Paul F) share a first name with the apostle imply that its Pauline subtext is not purely subversive. These things, along with other aspects of Baby Suggs's sermons that are less openly hostile to the epistles, have inclined critics such as Ágnes Surányi to argue something else entirely. Surányi sees "the ideology of St. Paul's letters" as the inspiration not only for "Morrison's concept of Christianity" but also "the generous love that [she] advocates" in her novels (127).

That *Beloved* supports two such diametrically opposed interpretations of Christian scripture is, by now, a well-recognized feature of Morrison's work. For this reason, a recent study of religious idiom in African American literature by Tuire Valkeakari places the author firmly within a long "history of African Americans" who present "Christianity as a double-edged sword" in their fiction (15). But even that study, which accounts for the presence of a Catholic sacramentality in Morrison's other novels, does not consider how Catholicism informs the way Christianity is depicted in *Beloved*.[5] Indeed, until this point, there has been virtually no critical interest in the Catholic thematics of *Beloved*, nor in Morrison's subsequent slave narrative, *A Mercy*, published twenty-one years later. When it comes to the topic of slavery in her writing, critics prove reluctant to acknowledge any serious engagement with Catholicism. To a certain extent, the reluctance makes sense: unlike slave societies elsewhere in the Americas, slavery in the United States has been perceived historically as a Protestant institution without significant influence from Catholic theology or culture.[6] Accordingly, the criticism takes for granted that in reconstructing the world of the antebellum American South in her fiction, Morrison likewise minimizes the significance of Catholicism for its slaves. As this chapter demonstrates, however, that critical trend obscures the relevance of Catholicism to Morrison's imaginative retelling of slave history in both novels.

The lack of attention to Catholic themes in *Beloved* and *A Mercy* is surprising, given Morrison's biography. Her mother, whom she describes as "highly religious," brought her up with a thoroughgoing education in Protestantism (Jones and Vinson 179). Outside the home, however, she attended Catholic schools where she studied the catechism in detail and became "fascinated by the rituals" that bolster it (Monda 117). This fascination ran so deep that at the age of twelve she converted from Protestantism and continues to this day to identify as Catholic.[7] While Morrison's church affiliation should not be taken as a statement of belief or—even less so—an endorsement of orthodox Catholicism (in some interviews she has implied that belief for her is incompatible with organized religion; see Monda 117–19), her conversion does indicate a profound personal awareness of what distinguishes these two major branches of Christianity. For that reason, in contrast to the prevailing scholarship on Morrison's contemporary slave narratives, with its tendency to conflate any specifically Catholic reference with references to Christianity (a decidedly *Protestant* Christianity) more generally, my reading places the distinction between Protestantism and Catholicism at the center of her fictional project.

More to the point, I argue that this distinction informs the way her novels *remember* slavery, both in terms of *what* they remember (their representation of the historical experience of slaves) and *how* they remember it (their distinctive narrative style and form). The first part of the chapter makes the case that Morrison uses the groundbreaking analysis of sociologist Orlando Patterson to challenge conventional accounts of slave religion. Patterson remains one of the only scholars of U.S. slavery to recognize the extent to which Catholicism helped shape its religious culture. Indeed, taken together, *Beloved* and *A Mercy* constitute an extended imaginative amplification of his claim that the "special version of Protestantism that triumphed" in the slaveholding American South was far more Catholic than ever previously acknowledged (ix). Catholicism thus emerges in these novels as a crucial but often overlooked feature of the history of slavery in the United States—one with insidious and lasting consequences for generations of African Americans who were enslaved by nominally Protestant masters. Acknowledging this feature is vital, I suggest, if we hope to make sense of the ambivalence with which Morrison approaches New Testament scripture. For, as I will demonstrate, it is a specifically Catholic interpretation of the Pauline epistles that her novels associate with the development of institutionalized racism in the American South and the legacy of racial suffering that endured in its wake.

At the margins of *Beloved* and *A Mercy*, then, we find subtle yet persistent references to Catholicism that undermine the idea of the U.S. slave system as a fundamentally Protestant institution. The Catholic margin of these two novels therefore contributes in important ways to Morrison's widely documented compulsion to disrupt how slavery was rationalized in the antebellum South—as well as the Enlightenment-era discourses that supported such rationalization. Specifically, it has been shown that Morrison "deliberately confounds" the Enlightenment period's "[p]seudo-scientific claims about the biological inferiority of peoples of African descent [which] served to disqualify them from human status and thereby ... sanction their enslavement" (Dubey, "Neo-Slave" 343). Her work subverts not only these racist ideologies themselves but also the consequences they had for the slaves who escaped bondage and wrote about their experiences to promote abolition. Morrison has been especially critical of the formulaic way that slave autobiographers were forced to remember their past as well as the sentiments they had to excise. The distinctive narrative style and form of her novels are the means she developed to redress these strictures, and her concept of rememory informs them both. As I will argue in the second part of the chapter, these narratological features—rememory, in particular—also reveal the influence of Catholicism. Indeed, I will demonstrate that Morrison structures memory in *Beloved* and *A Mercy* like a Catholic sacrament.

I. Toward a Catholic History of Slavery in the United States

In *Playing in the Dark*, her highly acclaimed book of literary criticism from 1992, Morrison makes a passing reference to the work of Orlando Patterson. The reference comes in the middle of a chapter on canonical early

American literature, where she develops her now-famous argument about "a dark and abiding presence" that lurks at the margins of these works (33). Specifically, Morrison is trying to show that white writers such as Poe and Melville deployed images of suffering, enslaved black people to highlight their own freedom and the freedom of the New World from "Europe's moral and social disorder." But rather than dissociating the burgeoning American style from an Old World aesthetic, she argues that the "gothic" quality of these images paradoxically reproduced "the typology of diabolism it wanted to leave behind," exposing how inexorably the concept of liberty was yoked to racial slavery in the United States (36). For this reason Morrison implicates the literature of young America in the critique of Enlightenment rationalism that Patterson and other scholars of the Black Atlantic were proposing around the same time. She recognizes a profound generative link between Enlightenment-era ideologies about "the rights of man" and the "conveniently bound and violently silenced black bodies" that sustained them. Her reference to Patterson lays bare the connection: "As the sociologist Orlando Patterson has noted," she writes, "we should not be surprised that the Enlightenment could accommodate slavery; we should be surprised if it had not" (38).

Although she does not provide a source text for the citation, Morrison is almost certainly referring to Patterson's *Slavery and Social Death: A Comparative Study*, which was published ten years earlier. There, in the original preface to his book, Patterson makes exactly the point that Morrison ascribes to him: that the "joint rise of slavery and the cultivation of freedom was no accident. It was . . . a sociohistorical necessity" (ix). This premise is borne out consistently in the study and especially in its analysis of modern slaveholding societies emerging during the Age of Enlightenment. With regard to the antebellum U.S. South in particular, Patterson documents how the master class rationalized the system by way of an elaborate and self-contradictory discourse of liberation and enslavement that perversely confirmed the slaves' submission. The discourse that concerns him is what he calls fundamentalist Christianity: that "special version of Protestantism that triumphed in the South" in the late eighteenth and nineteenth centuries (73).[8] According to Patterson, it was the large-scale expansion of fundamentalist Christianity that provided the "reform" needed to institutionalize plantation slavery and to make it "function effectively" for generations of U.S. farmers. He describes the religion itself as a "major development" in modern slaveholding practice because—for the first time since the Reformation—a Protestant form of Christianity came to be "used by the master class as an agent of social control" (73–74).

Prior to the Second Great Awakening in the United States, Protestantism was generally deemed incompatible with slavery. Its classical form emphasized values like individual liberty and antiauthoritarianism that masters did not want to promote in their chattel, and so Protestant slaveholders in the New World tended either to curtail religious expression or forbid it altogether.[9] In this way they differed markedly from their Catholic counterparts, who not only continued to worship as they always had but also mandated the conversion of their slaves. Patterson attributes the falloff in religious practice among Protestant slaveholders to a decisive theological divergence from the traditional, Catholic interpretation of the epistles of Saint Paul.

As Patterson points out, the Pauline epistles regularly exploit the language of slavery "as a metaphoric source" for the Crucifixion. Historically, Catholics have stressed the "profoundly conservative spiritual and social implications" of Paul's metaphor, claiming that in dying for their sins, Jesus did not "emancipate" the spiritually enslaved sinner but rather reenslaved him in Christ, who "became his new master." Because Catholicism perceived "Christianity as a transmutation of the order of slavery," it was therefore possible for "faithful" slaveholders to reconcile their religious beliefs with the suppression of their slaves' freedom. The Protestant reformers took a more liberating view of Pauline theology, maintaining that Jesus's death ultimately "annulled the condition of slavery" so that all believers "may live and be free" (71). With its "emphasis on personal choice and freedom," this interpretation underscores the well-documented affinity between Protestantism and Enlightenment conceptions of liberty (73). However, as Patterson explains further, it also suggests how problematic it was for Protestants of this period to justify their slaveholding interests. Not until the emergence of fundamentalist Christianity in the American South, he says, were they able to discover a means for doing so. Once the master class recognized the extent to which this new version of Protestantism would bolster their authority, in a move exceptional among Protestant slaveholding societies, they encouraged—and in some cases required—the conversion of their slaves.[10]

Patterson's analysis of fundamentalist Christianity represents a significant departure from the way that historians of slavery had previously understood the impact of the Second Great Awakening on its converts. Before the publication of *Slavery and Social Death*, Protestant conversion was generally thought enabling for the slaves, since it afforded them the opportunity to practice religion on their own terms. Earlier studies in the field, such as Eugene Genovese's, focus on the way that slaves "reshaped the Christianity they embraced" to fit their specific needs and, ultimately, "turned" the slaveholders' Protestantism "into a weapon of personal and community survival" (212). But Patterson was unwilling to accept this assessment. While his study acknowledges that fundamentalist Christianity did offer the enslaved masses some "relief from the agonies of thralldom, and . . . some room for a sense of dignity before God and before each other," he regards even these spiritual rewards as a form of accommodation to the system (74). In a move that definitively separates his analysis from the prevailing scholarship on slave religion, Patterson argues that the slaves' exposure to the "liberating" aspects of Protestantism perversely rendered them better servants and more reliable field hands by defining freedom in terms of total submission to their masters.

This bleak appraisal of fundamentalist Christianity conforms to Patterson's broader argument about Enlightenment-era discourses, particularly the idea that Morrison cites in *Playing in the Dark*: that in the modern Western imagination conceptions of slavery and freedom "are intimately connected" (Patterson ix). In fact, we might say that Patterson's claims have become something of a mainstay for Morrison. As early as 1987, in a critical essay called "The Site of Memory," she was already indicating the ways that the Enlightenment determined how early American authors represented the slave experience. In that essay, the authors that concern her are black, not white; they are the fugitive and ex-slave autobiographers, whose narratives portray the struggle to escape from enslavement. However, as Morrison explains, the racial orientation of these authors made them no less susceptible than Melville or Poe to the ideologies of the period. "One has to remember," she cautions, that the original narratives of slavery "reflected not only the Age of Enlightenment but its twin, born at the same time, the Age of Scientific Racism" (69). What she is suggesting is that despite impressive efforts to expose the horrors of their situation, the slave narrators were as "conveniently bound" and "silenced" as the "black bodies" depicted elsewhere in antebellum U.S. literature. For these authors, this meant they had to excise the "more sordid details of their experience" for fear that "dwelling too long or too carefully" on the horror would indelibly link them in the minds of the audience to the very diabolism they hoped to eradicate (69). Thus, as opposed to the literature of their white contemporaries, it is in the silences that occupy their writing—in the resolute unwillingness of the slave narrators "to offend the reader by being too angry, or by showing too much outrage" (67)—that Morrison locates the impact of Enlightenment ideals of freedom on the black author. She points out that unlike Melville and Poe, who used gothic depictions of suffering and enslavement to define their own liberty, those writers who actually suffered and were enslaved could not do the same. Rather, in order to convey rationality, they had to expunge from their narratives any detail that might be perceived as gruesome or impassioned.

Part of Morrison's objective in "The Site of Memory" for documenting the way ideologies of the Enlightenment "dictated the purpose and style" of slave autobiography is to account for her own approach to writing about slavery (69). The essay was published the same year as *Beloved*—Morrison's first attempt at the neo-slave narrative form—and it provides valuable context for many of the distinctive features of that novel, particularly for those that undermine the rationalist imperative of Enlightenment ideals. Morrison explains that in reimagining the true story of escaped slave Margaret Garner from a twentieth-century perspective, she felt compelled to answer for what had to go unwritten in the original discourse of slavery: that she was "trying to fill in the blanks that the slave narratives left—to part the veil that was so frequently drawn" over their less palatable, less rational articulations. This, she understands, exposes her work to charges of stylistic excessiveness—acceding that, yes, "it may be excessive" (72). But given how attuned she is to the strictures placed on antebellum black authors by the milieu in which they wrote, Morrison makes clear that all the "excess" in her novel has a purpose. Namely, it enables her to expose and ultimately to disrupt the modern ideologies of freedom, which—via Patterson—she correlates with the rise of racialized slavery in the United States.

The excessiveness of Morrison's fiction has received a great deal of attention in the critical press. And, as she anticipated, there were early reviewers of *Beloved* who objected to her impassioned depiction of slavery. Stanley Crouch is the most notorious example. Seemingly unaware that he is reiterating the rationalist imperative that kept the original slave autobiographers from fully articulating the horror of their experience, Crouch accuses Morrison of reveling in "portentous melodrama" so that she "loses control" of her narrative (29). In particular he chides her for "[t]oo many . . . attempts at biblical grandeur, run through by Negro folk rhythms," which he says "stymie a book that might have been important" (30). The complaint is a hollow one, to be sure, indicative of Crouch's failure to comprehend the relationship between *Beloved*'s excessive style and its critique of Enlightenment rationalism.[11] If we look beyond the hollowness, though, his remark does imply something significant about the way the novel structures that critique. By underscoring how frequently Morrison alludes in these moments of stylistic excess to the Bible, Crouch reveals (albeit inadvertently) the extent to which New Testament scripture is itself implicated in the Enlightenment-era discourses that *Beloved* disrupts. In this regard his review indeed enables a fuller understanding of the influence that Patterson's analysis has had on her fiction.

To demonstrate what I mean, we can examine one of those "attempts at biblical grandeur" to which Crouch objects. In this passage, presented as a flashback, Sethe is remembering the famous woodland sermons of her mother-in-law, Baby Suggs, an ex-slave who preached for a short time to a community of her peers:

> She told them that the only grace they could have was the grace they could imagine. That if they could not see it, they would not have it.
>
> "Here," she said, "in this here place, we flesh; flesh that weeps, laughs; flesh that dances on bare feet in grass. Love it. Love it hard. Yonder they do not love your flesh. They despise it. They don't love your eyes; they'd just as soon pick em out. No more do they love the skin on your back. Yonder they flay it. And O my people they do not love your hands. Those they only use, tie, bind, chop off and leave empty. Love your hands! Love them. Raise them up and kiss them. Touch others with them, pat them together, stroke them on your face 'cause they don't love that either. . . . *You* got to love it. This is flesh I'm talking about here. Flesh that needs to be loved. . . . And O my people, out yonder, hear me, they do not love your neck unnoosed and straight. So love your neck; put a hand on it, grace it, stroke it and hold it up. And all your inside parts that they'd just as soon slop for hogs, you got to love them." (103–4)

Here we find examples of the gothic or excessive elements that Morrison claims were excised from the original narratives of slavery: graphic descriptions of horror (flayed skin, picked-out eyes, tied-up and chopped-off hands) as well as an unapologetic sense of outrage ("This is flesh I'm talking about here. Flesh that needs to be loved."). Notably, both the horror and the outrage are filtered through Baby Suggs's idiosyncratic preaching style, which draws heavily from the language of the Bible. There are familiar constructions ("O my people"; "out yonder"; "Raise them up") peppered throughout that lend her speech the general tenor of scripture. And there are also explicit allusions to the New Testament, particularly to the eighth chapter of the Letter to the Romans, where Paul explores what it means to "live according to the flesh" (8.5).[12] These biblical components do undoubtedly, as Crouch suggests, contribute to the "grandeur" of Baby Suggs's message. But to regard them as mere decoration or stylized rhetoric is to neglect how purposefully their content is disrupted.

For example, in telling her congregants "that the only grace they could have was the grace they could imagine" and "if they could not see it, they would not have it," Baby Suggs does not just invoke verse from Romans 8; she inverts its meaning. Specifically, her words allude to Paul's proclamation that "hope which is seen is not hope" and to the rhetorical question he asks just after: "For who hopes for what he sees?" (8.24). The point Paul endeavors to make is that true followers of Christ will set their sights on the unseen spiritual reward made possible by the Crucifixion, not on the fleshly rewards of material existence. Living under God's law, he explains, requires man to accept subjugation and pain "with patience" in this world, so that he might be glorified after death (8.25). Baby Suggs rejects this premise outright, imploring her fellow ex-slaves to discover ("see") redemption *in the flesh*, through the way their bodies interact with and take pleasure from the living world. Her entire speech, in fact, should be understood as a denunciation of the image of the suffering servant that is celebrated in Romans. She does not buy into Paul's claim that physical agony brings one closer to Christ, nor that humans suffer in slavery because God loves them. As she perceives it, slaveholding always indicates hate ("Yonder they do not love your flesh. They despise it."), and her sermon underscores the peril of believing otherwise—the peril of believing, as Paul writes, that enslavement is theologically justified and divine.

Implicit in Baby Suggs's allusions to Romans 8, then, is her awareness of its complicity in the experience of slavery that she and her community have recently endured. What's more, she maintains that they must abandon the Pauline concept of divine enslavement if they want to be truly free from bondage. This is important for two reasons. First, it suggests that despite spending most of their lives on U.S. plantations where Protestantism was the rule, the ex-slaves in Baby Suggs's audience were exposed to a traditionally Catholic interpretation of Paul's epistles, one that sanctified their suffering and demanded their obedience to God's law. Second, it suggests that this exposure to Catholic doctrine contributed to their subjugation in ways that even they were not aware of, rendering them less likely to challenge the slaveholders' authority. These are, of course, the very same arguments that Patterson develops in *Slavery and Social Death*. Indeed, his analysis of slaveholding culture in the United States rests on the groundbreaking idea that fundamentalist Christianity was actually, with regard to Pauline theology at least, "identical" to Catholicism—and that this was what transformed the nominally Protestant religion into an efficient means of social control.[13]

To be exact, Patterson argues that fundamentalist Christianity supported the aims of slaveholders in the American South by restoring the conservative ethic of "law, judgment and obedience" that classic Protestantism had eliminated from its teachings on Paul (76). Therefore, all those who converted (or were forcibly converted) during the Second Great Awakening studied a version of the epistles that was historically aligned with Catholicism. Slaves were taught to accept their suffering "with patience" and to obey the rightful law of their Master/masters according to the same theological rationale that Catholic slave owners had been using for centuries. But, significantly, this did not mean that fundamentalist Christianity abandoned the other, more liberating pole of Pauline theology. Rather, as Patterson goes on to say, what distinguished the religion and helped it create the "most perfectly articulated slave culture since the fall of the Roman empire" was its doctrinal dualism: the "contextual shifting" it permitted from a Catholic interpretation of Paul's letters to a Protestant one (74).

As Patterson describes it,

> Both masters and slaves adhered to Pauline ethical dualism, with its sustained "eschatological dissonance." And in exactly the same way

> that Paul and the early Christians shifted from one pole of their doctrinal dualism to another as occasion and context demanded, so did the masters and their slaves. Thus the masters, among themselves, could find both spiritual and personal dignity and salvation in the ethic of the justified and redeemed sinner. The crucified Jesus as redeemer and liberator from enslavement to sin supported a proud, free group of people with a highly developed sense of their own dignity and worth. Similarly, the slaves in the silence of their souls and among themselves *with their own preachers*, could find salvation and dignity in this same interpretation of the crucified Lord. (75)

The result of this doctrinal dualism was that for the first time in the history of Protestant slaveholding societies in the Americas, enslaved blacks in the U.S. South had the "freedom" to gather together outside the boundaries of their master's plantation and to listen to the Word of God. But, as with other Enlightenment-era discourses, Patterson insists that the freedom associated with fundamentalist Christianity was deeply perilous for the slaves, since it served primarily to accommodate them to enslavement. In other words, the "salvation and dignity" inspired by the liberating pole of Pauline theology only made them more susceptible to the other, Catholic pole which effectively confirmed their subjugation.

By describing fundamentalist Christianity in these doctrinally dualistic terms, Patterson explains that it "provided the slave South with the perfect creed, one . . . with a built-in flexibility that made it possible for emperor and slave to worship the same god without threatening the system, but also without denying all dignity to the oppressed" (72). His study identified the specter of Catholicism in a culture historically perceived to be dominated by Protestantism—a culture that rationalized its own slaveholding interests according to its *difference from* an old, unenlightened European system of slavery. I am suggesting that Morrison makes an analogous move in *Beloved*. Not only does her excessive style underscore the "gothic" nature of the U.S. system, but the subtle references she makes to Catholicism throughout the novel affirm the ways an Old World religion came to define slave experience in a New World context. Thus a character like Denver, who was raised firmly within a Protestant tradition and without a Catholic church in sight, displays an uncanny and inexplicable knowledge of the Roman Mass.

Along similar lines, there is the following scene, which also insinuates the pervasive—yet unacknowledged—presence of Catholicism in the antebellum American South. In it, Sethe recounts one of her only memories of her mother from the plantation where they both were enslaved:

> " . . . She picked me up and carried me behind the smokehouse. Back there she opened up her dress front and lifted her breast and pointed under it. Right on her rib was a circle and a cross burnt right in the skin. She said, 'This is your ma'am. This,' and she pointed. 'I am the only one got this mark now. The rest dead. If something happens to me and you can't tell me by my face, you can know me by this mark.' Scared me so. All I could think of was how important this was and how I needed to have something important to say back, but I couldn't think of anything so I just said what I thought. 'Yes, Ma'am,' I said. 'But how will you know me? How will you know me? Mark me, too,' I said. 'Mark the mark on me too.' . . .
>
> "She slapped my face. . . .
>
> "I didn't understand it then. Not till I had a mark of my own." (72–73)

Most readers of *Beloved* will quickly understand what Sethe could not as a child: that the mark on her mother's skin came from a slave owner's branding iron and was burned there—into the flesh—to designate his property. Here again Morrison's narrative takes a gothic turn, when the image of another suffering black body emerges from the margins of the story, and the recesses of Sethe's memory, to reveal the horrors of slavery. And as with the graphic descriptions of fleshly torment that Baby Suggs offers up in her sermon, this image reveals a specifically Catholic understanding of the relationship between master and slave.

The cross, an archetypal symbol of Christ's sacrifice, not only signifies the pain that Sethe's mother endured and confirms her enslavement, but it also implies (as the slave owner who placed it there undoubtedly intended it to imply) that she suffers righteously, as Jesus did and in his name. This reflects an interpretation of the Crucifixion that aligns with the way that Catholics have traditionally understood it—as a "transmutation of the order of slavery" (Patterson 71). Moreover, the fact that this particular cross is depicted inside a circle suggests a visual link between the wound and Catholic iconography.[14] In Catholicism the encircled cross represents the body of Jesus in the community; it is a symbolic depiction of the sacrament of Holy Communion, in which the faithful believe they become Christ by consuming him. For that reason, the icon is commonly found on the wafers distributed during the Catholic Eucharist as well as on the pendants worn around the neck of Eucharistic ministers. It is a much less prevalent symbol in Protestantism, however, where the doctrine of transubstantiation is minimized if not abandoned altogether.[15] Therefore, the image appears noticeably out of place on the skin of a slave owned by a Protestant master. Since we never learn the precise origins of Sethe's mother or anything about her previous owners, it is possible that the burn was made by a Catholic owner who came into possession of her prior to her arrival on the southern plantation where Sethe was raised. Just as likely, it might have been branded on her by a Protestant who was either ignorant of or unconcerned with its Catholic resonances. In either case, whichever way Morrison intended readers to understand its genesis, the wound—and Sethe's reaction to it—hints at the insidious role that Patterson claims Catholicism played in the religious culture of the slaveholding South.

Even as a child, Sethe seems to understand the awesome power conveyed by the religious symbol. Yet because she was still fairly well insulated from the devastating physical and emotional traumas of slavery at the time the mark was revealed to her, she does not view it in the context of her mother's agony. Instead her little-girl eyes perceive the wound reverentially, enviously: how one might look upon stigmata or another sign of divine selection. Years later, remembering the interaction after having experienced the torment of slavery herself—including a brutal whipping that left her with stigmatic markings of her own[16]—Sethe feels "something privately shameful" for failing to empathize with her mother's pain (73). But in the moment she could not help being impressed by, and covetous of, the circled cross that represents such suffering. The reverence Sethe shows for this most Catholic symbol is therefore indicative of the way that fundamentalist Christianity helped to psychologically accommodate slaves to the system. It reveals how the embodied horror of slavery could be rebranded as "salvation and dignity" in the image of the crucified Lord.

Again and again *Beloved* underscores the devastating impact that this kind of psychological accommodation had on the slaves. In fact, the novel's ultimate tragedy—Sethe's gruesome act of infanticide—is cast as a theologically appropriate response to Pauline dualism. Sethe justifies the murder by telling Paul D that rather than resigning her children to a life of slavery, she "took and put my babies where they'd be safe" (193). The emphasis she places on personal choice and freedom is consistent with the Protestant interpretation of the Crucifixion. She believes that by turning her children over to God, she effectively guarantees their salvation and sets them free. But at the same time, the freedom to which she delivers them is decidedly not of this world; they must die in order to realize it. Moreover, as Morrison's vivid description of the scene in the woodshed makes clear, those deaths are neither easy nor painless. Their bodies suffer violently in order to be redeemed, as Sethe sacrifices her own flesh and blood for the promise of a spiritual reward. So, in this sense, the murderous act also fulfills the Catholic pole of Pauline theology—particularly the passage from Romans 8 that Baby Suggs denounced in her sermon. By setting her sights on an unseen, heavenly idea of freedom, Sethe does exactly what her mother-in-law warned against: she places her faith in something she cannot see. Thus, Morrison writes, while cutting up her children's bodies, she "looked like she didn't have any [eyes]. . . . she looked blind" (177). This description not only confirms how thoroughly Sethe has defied Baby Suggs but it also alludes yet again to the conservative teachings of Saint Paul—teachings that repeatedly equate blindness with spiritual glory.[17]

As the novel suggests, everything that Baby Suggs represents—"Her authority in the pulpit, her dance in the Clearing, her powerful Call"—was "mocked and rebuked by the bloodspill in her backyard" (208). She was, then, finally unsuccessful in her attempt to dispel the Catholic interpretation of suffering from her community. Even on the northern side of the Ohio River, ex-slaves remain bound by what Patterson calls the "theologically dualistic" religion that said they must suffer in order to be free. It is this self-destructive theology, derived from Catholicism, that *Beloved* blames for "the Misery" that took place in the woodshed as well as for the circumstances that precipitated it. Significantly, Sethe was not the only member of Baby Suggs's congregation who believed her family should suffer. A group of congregants also tacitly affirmed Sethe's sacrifice when they failed to warn her about the slavecatchers' approach. This detail, which proves to be the principal devastation of Baby Suggs's life, implies just how subtle and invasive the Catholic ethic could be. Morrison explains that the ex-slaves collectively turned their backs on Baby Suggs because "they were angry" about the feast at her home the night before, a feast of biblical proportions that felt "too much" for them (163). In other words, the community cannot accept that one of their own possesses the power to create such a meal, nor that they themselves have taken pleasure in such "reckless generosity" (162). Their experience of slavery, and specifically the conservative pole of Pauline theology to which they were exposed, has conditioned them to reject this sort of fleshly indulgence; it has conditioned them to be "offended . . . by excess" (163). And so they respond in a way that bears out the fundamentally Catholic idea that God's slaves are simply "sheep to be slaughtered" (Romans 8.36).

Read in these terms, Sethe's infanticidal act and her community's complicity in it indicate that Morrison perceives Catholicism to be even more invasive in the American South than Patterson's analysis contends. Where *Slavery and Social Death* stops short of considering the legacy of the theologically dualistic religion that it describes, *Beloved* implies that the Catholic pole of Pauline theology continued to determine the behavior of slaves long after they became free. This is what ultimately silences Baby Suggs and resigns her to "quit the Word" (209). She comes to believe that she will never be successful in convincing the ex-slaves to renounce suffering. Furthermore, the novel hints that she too succumbs at the end of her life to the conservative interpretation of Saint Paul that she previously condemned. When Stamp Paid accuses her of punishing the Lord for the Misery her family has endured, Baby Suggs replies, "Not like He punish me" (211). The response recalls the Pauline concept of divine enslavement to which her sermon also referred. Except that now, after witnessing the murder of her granddaughter and the callousness of her own people, she no longer denies that the pain she feels has been mandated by God. Rather, she appears to accept the traditional Catholic view that sorrow and subjugation are the slave's crosses to bear, adding that she has abandoned all plans to challenge her condition. For the rest of her life, she will be "looking for what I was put here to look for: the back door," which insinuates her total resignation to servitude (211).

By way of the tragic conclusion to the story of Baby Suggs, then, the novel articulates the enduring consequences of slavery for those who have managed to outlive it. And, as I have been suggesting, Morrison consistently imagines those consequences as a theological capitulation to Catholicism. Not only does Baby Suggs stop preaching the sermons that represent her opposition to a Catholic ethic, but she also sends herself to bed to "fix on something harmless in this world" (211). What she means is that she will spend her remaining days and "the little energy left her . . . pondering color" instead of railing against the injustice of her family's isolation or trying to keep her grandsons from running away (4). This decision might seem to indicate a loss of faith on her part (and at first that is how Stamp Paid perceives it), but it becomes clear that Baby Suggs is actually atoning. In the aftermath of the murder, she does not reject God. She asks Him for forgiveness: "I beg your pardon. Lord, I beg your pardon. I sure do" (180). As she sees it, her "sin" has been to believe that she and the other former slaves in her community could be truly free—that they could escape suffering and find redemption in this world. The scene in the woodshed proved her wrong; it proved that her sermons "didn't count" because whitefolks "came in her yard anyway" to remind her that, following divine law, her people would always be enslaved. Accordingly, the choice to give up preaching and confine herself to bed must be read as an act of penance in the Catholic sense, as a final submission to the conservative theology that said the slavecatchers were doing God's work. It is therefore worth noting that the colors she asks for just before she dies—lavender "if you got any" and pink "if you don't"—are used twice a year in the Roman Catholic Mass to signify periods of solemnity and atonement that precede the coming of the Lord.[18] The fact that these are the colors Baby Suggs ponders while preparing for death—a death she knows will mean "anything but forgetfulness"—underscores how completely Catholicism has revised her views of redemption (4).

Even after the slaves' manumission and on the free side of the Ohio River where they reside during the years the novel takes place, *Beloved* thus suggests that Catholicism has remained a pervasive, if marginal, presence in the lives of its characters. This is the way Morrison characterizes the legacy of Patterson's analysis. In *A Mercy* she takes Patterson's analysis a step further. Rather than considering the legacy of U.S. slavery as *Beloved* does, Morrison's more recent novel considers the origins of the colonial slave system at a time prior to its racialization. Set in the late seventeenth century, *A Mercy* predates the historical period that Patterson analyzed by more than a hundred years, well before the theologically dualistic religion he calls fundamentalist Christianity transformed the religious culture of the slaveholding South. And yet, despite its earlier setting, I will show that in this novel Morrison still relies on the basic tenets of Patterson's study—specifically, the way he attributes the insidious power of slave religion to a "contextual shifting" between classical Protestantism and Catholicism (74). In this fashion she once again exposes the inherently irrational and gothic nature of New World slavery. Moreover, as we shall see, by remapping Patterson's argument onto a narrative about the beginning of institutionalized racism in what will become the United States, Morrison imaginatively aligns the racialization of the American slave system with Catholic slaveholding practice.

. . .

A Mercy tracks the rise of race-based slavery through the experience of some of its earliest participants: the Vaark family and the ad hoc, racially diverse collection of unpaid laborers who work on their farm in northeastern colonial America. It recounts the transformation of the Vaark property from a relatively equitable system of labor, in which work and benefits are dispensed equally regardless of race, to a fledgling slave economy premised on strict racial hierarchies. I argue that, through a canny recontextualization of Patterson's analysis, Morrison attributes the Vaark family's descent into institutionalized racism to Catholicism—or, more specifically, to the Catholic ethic of slavery that Patterson describes in his study. She accomplishes this through her portrayal of the Vaark patriarch's seminal trip to Maryland, where he makes the financial arrangements that turn him from a landowner with a few well-cared-for, if monetarily uncompensated, laborers into an active participant in the slave system. As I will show, Morrison depicts the way Jacob rationalizes his decision as a theological struggle between the liberal Protestant beliefs he was brought up with and the Catholic ethic of slaveholding that he encounters for the first time on his trip to the D'Ortega plantation in Maryland.

Everything we know about Jacob Vaark prior to the deal he makes to purchase Florens suggests a fundamental opposition to slavery and the set of principles on which the institution depends. In the few pages that precede the scene of his arrival at the D'Ortega plantation, Morrison takes an unusually heavy-handed approach to establish Jacob as a moral character. First there is the description of his views on Bacon's Rebellion and its aftermath. Upon crossing over into Virginia on his way to Maryland, Jacob braces himself for the possibility of attack by "a family of runaways . . . or an armed felon" (11). He attributes the increased risk of violence to the "mess" that followed the war waged by "an army of blacks, natives, whites, mulattoes—freedmen, slaves and indentured" against the "local gentry"—presumably Bacon's Rebellion.[19] But rather than blaming the rebels for the aggression, Jacob cites "a thicket of new laws" spawned in the wake of the conflict for "authorizing chaos in defense of order." He is referring, of course, to the set of regulations designed by the ruling class to solidify the racial cast of slavery, thereby diminishing the likelihood that poor whites would ever again unite with blacks and Native Americans in opposition to the gentry. Historians often associate these regulations, which eliminated "manumission, gatherings, travel and bearing arms for black people" and gave "license to any white to kill any black for any reason" (10), with the rise of the race-based slave system in the United States.[20] Morrison plainly seeks to dissociate her character from this kind of institutionalized racism: "In Jacob Vaark's view," she writes, "these were lawless laws encouraging cruelty in exchange for common cause, if not common virtue" (10–11). Jacob takes no pleasure in the "relative safety" that his skin color provides him; instead, his brand of morality causes him to sympathize with the racial other, whose basic freedoms he recognizes as increasingly under threat.

In fact, the sympathy that Jacob feels for the disenfranchised runs so deep that it extends to animals as well as humans. Twice in this chapter Morrison highlights his natural tendency to protect the vulnerable from excessive pain or subjugation. She notes that in the midst of his arduous journey, Jacob takes the time to dismount in order to gently "free the bloody hindleg of a young raccoon stuck in a tree break" (11). Later on, after he decides to accept D'Ortega's offer and profit from the slave trade, the "faint trace of coon's blood" (35) that remains on Jacob's hand from this encounter will take on new meaning and come to suggest the myriad ways he compromises his morality, but here Morrison uses the interaction to communicate his unwillingness to abide the suffering of any sentient being. That same aversion to cruelty is again on display just a few hours later when, on his way home from the plantation, he observes a man beating a horse to its knees. Although a group of sailors come to the animal's aid before Jacob has a chance to get involved, the moment affords yet another opportunity for Morrison to emphasize his compassionate nature:

> Few things angered Jacob more than the brutal handling of domesticated animals. He did not know what the sailors were objecting to, but his own fury was not only because of the pain it inflicted on the horse, but because of the mute, unprotesting surrender glazing its eyes. (28)

This passage pointedly recalls an earlier occurrence on the D'Ortega property, as Jacob inspected for purchase—"at his host's insistence"—an assemblage of slaves.

> The women's eyes looked shockproof, gazing beyond place and time as though they were not actually there. The men looked at the ground....
> Suddenly Jacob felt his stomach seize.... he couldn't stay there surrounded by a passel of slaves whose silence made him imagine an avalanche seen from a great distance. No sound, just the knowledge of a roar he could not hear. (22)

In both of these instances, the eyes of the tormented, subjugated beings cause Jacob the greatest distress: he cannot bear to witness, to be complicit in, their wordless acceptance of domination.

As Morrison makes clear, the antiauthoritarian streak in Jacob is strong. Despite being of European extraction himself and having profited from a variety of British and Dutch colonial ventures, his allegiances frequently align with the colonized instead of the colonizer. For example, when riding through the contested coastal territories on his way to Maryland, Jacob refuses to refer to these areas by the names bestowed on them by a constantly changing cast of brutal white colonizers—"Fort Orange; Cape Henry; Nieuw Amsterdam; Wiltwyck" (13)—preferring to think of the land in terms of the Native American tribes who first inhabited it and "to whom it all [still] belonged," in his opinion (12). Though the force of his defiance is mitigated to a great extent by the relative passivity of its expression (spoken only in the solitude of Jacob's own thoughts, the censure remains private, discreet), it is remarkable for how resolutely it undermines the European theory of divine right. For Jacob, "there had never been much point in knowing who claimed this or that terrain," since as he sees it, the Indians possess the sole legitimate rights to the land (12). He rejects as absurd the notion that God somehow sanctioned the authority of the Christian colonizers to declare the American territories their own and to subject the native peoples to tyranny and enslavement.

Although in an early nineteenth-century context these plainly democratic leanings—predispositions against institutionalized racism, oppression, cruelty, and European claims of divine authority—would associate Jacob with an abolitionist agenda, here in Morrison's representation of colonial America they are not incompatible with a generalized acceptance of slavery. Conspicuously, despite all his internal musings on man's treatment of man during his travels to the D'Ortega plantation, Jacob never once thinks to question the morality of his own slaveholding practices. Throughout he maintains "his good opinion of himself" and the particular brand of slavery his farm participates in, believing that he treats his unpaid labor justly and does not discriminate among them based on race or any other characteristic beyond their control (27). The fact that Jacob can legitimize his possession of slaves on the grounds that they are neither abused nor oppressed—he prefers to think "the acquisition of both [young ones] could be seen as rescue," for their enslavement denotes protection, comfort even (34)—means that it is not the ownership of another human being that makes his stomach seize, but rather how that ownership is managed. As long as he is able to discriminate between moral and immoral approaches to slaveholding, he can justify the small collection of slaves who work on the Vaark property. Fortunately for him, his travels provide ample opportunity to observe and critique alternative kinds of enslavement. Jacob's principal means of comparison and the measure by which he assesses his own righteousness is the Catholic version of slavery he beholds in the "palatinate" of Maryland, which "was Romish to the core" (13). He feels "offended by the lax, flashy cunning of the Papists" (14); for him, Roman Catholics represent the worst of slaveholders because of the way they disguise their cruelty behind extravagant displays of wealth and sanctimonious religious expression.

It is significant that Morrison associates Jacob's reviling of Catholics with his Protestant upbringing. The revulsion he experiences is a direct consequence of the religious education he received as a boy "in the children's quarter of the poorhouse" in England where he was raised. There he memorized the lines from a Protestant primer that run through his head as he travels through the streets of Maryland, disparaging its Papist excesses: "Abhor that arrant whore of Rome / And all her blasphemies / Drink not of her cursed cup / Obey not her decrees" (14).[21] These lines constitute the foundation of his attitude toward Catholics in general and the D'Ortegas in particular.[22] Not only do they explain his reluctance at sharing an afternoon meal with a family "of the Roman faith" and his finding everything about the "heavily seasoned dishes" and sweet wine served at the D'Ortega table "intolerable" (17), but they also provide context for his denunciation of Senhor D'Ortega's business practices and perspective on slaveholding. Jacob has been conditioned from a young age to regard the Catholics as brutal enforcers of a strict hierarchical order that places immoral limits on personal freedom and dignity. Brought up in a culture of Protestantism, which certainly would have privileged the liberating pole of Pauline theology that Patterson describes in *Slavery and Social Death*, Jacob is predisposed toward a total rejection of the principles on which D'Ortega's livelihood is based, and he "sneer[s] at wealth dependent on a captured workforce that required more work to maintain. Thin as they were, the dregs of [Jacob's] kind of Protestantism recoiled at whips, chains and armed overseers" (28).

As the reference to Protestant morality in the above passage indicates, Jacob's critique of D'Ortega is rooted in the historical theological dispute between Christian denominations over Paul's contrasting interpretations of Christ's crucifixion. Toeing the line of classical Protestantism, Jacob uses what Patterson calls the "ethic of the justified person" (74) to condemn the Catholic planter's more conservative—and hence, as he sees it, more systematic and oppressive—version of slavery. Notably, however, the condemnation is not generalized to include all forms of slaveholding. Like the majority of Protestants in the New World who owned slaves, Jacob's religious orientation does not preclude him from buying and selling human beings; it simply inclines him toward viewing Christian morality as distinct from the practice of slavery. This perspective aligns exactly with that of other Protestant masters in the Americas that Patterson documents in his study; as opposed to Catholics, who tended to apply their theological beliefs as a means of justifying their harsh treatment of the slaves, Protestants generally subscribed to an emancipatory interpretation of Pauline theology and sought to separate their religion and their slaveholding because of the inconsistency it implied.[23] Thus Morrison portrays Jacob as particularly troubled by the way that the D'Ortegas employ the Catholic "ethic of judgment and obedience" to sanctify their actions. Listening to the Senhor and Senhora speak of the organization of their plantation,

> it seemed to Jacob that nothing transpired in the conversation that had footing in the real world. They both spoke of the gravity, the unique responsibility, this untamed world offered them; its unbreakable connection to God's work and the difficulties they endured on His behalf. Caring for ill or recalcitrant labor was enough, they said, for canonization. (19)

The idea that a Christian God would consecrate slaveholding is preposterous to Jacob because his liberating conception of Pauline theology could never accommodate such a position.

In a novel as invested in the religious topology of colonial America as *A Mercy*, it comes as no surprise that Morrison would want to articulate so clear a theological distinction between the Catholic and Protestant justifications of slavery. But, since her narrative's main focus is the Vaark property's descent into institutionalized racism, perhaps the most significant aspect of the distinction she draws is the way it disintegrates throughout the work. The flashback to Jacob's experience on the D'Ortega plantation establishes more than just his theological resistance to the principles that supported the institutionalization of a race-based slave system in the United States; it also anticipates how that resistance will ultimately collapse under the burden of increasing his wealth and gaining a foothold in the burgeoning economy of the New World. It is, after all, during his visit to the D'Ortegas that Jacob makes two decisions that indicate his assimilation of his host's attitudes toward racialized slavery: first, to avoid financial loss, he agrees to accept Florens, an African slave, as partial payment for a debt; second, he initiates a plan to invest in the sugar trade, an industry that, like D'Ortega's, contributes to the degradation of thousands of enslaved Africans in the Caribbean. Together these actions set in motion a chain of events that results in his farm's abandonment of the egalitarian values on which it was founded. What's more, because they are both made expressly to "amass the fortune, the station, D'Ortega claimed," Jacob's decisions also signify the extent to which he is willing to compromise "his kind of Protestantism" in order to achieve the level of prosperity that he comes to believe a Catholic ethic can beget (28). Despite a healthy dose of native anti-Catholicism,[24] and a characteristic inclination toward kindness, Jacob chooses to pursue the path that gives him the best chance of realizing his dream of "a grand house of many rooms rising on a hill above the fog" (35), a path carved out for him by Senhor D'Ortega.

In depicting the way that Jacob, an "honest free-thinking" Protestant (58), comes to relinquish the theologically inscribed principles that most clearly distinguished his method of slaveholding from the Catholics,' Morrison is effectively retracing Patterson's argument about the religious transformation of American slave society—but doing so in a seventeenth-century context. Jacob's journey to and from the Catholic enclave of Maryland offers a geographical interpretation of Patterson's original claim that the "theology of slavery" that developed in the United States was premised upon a restoration of the conservative pole of Pauline theology. His trip literally maps out the theological accommodations that southern masters made in order to simultaneously justify their own freedom and the oppression of their slaves, the way they "shifted from one pole of their doctrinal dualism to another as occasion and context demanded" (Patterson 75). As Jacob travels through the Romish palatinate, his perspective on slaveholding shifts in a similar fashion; whereas he began the expedition in fervent denial of the possibility of sanctioning the horrible conditions under which slaves on tobacco and sugar plantations live, the new desire for luxury inspired by his experience with the D'Ortegas encourages him to accept the deplorable situation of "a remote labor force in Barbados" because of the prosperity it is certain to bring him (35).

Like the American slaveholders whom Patterson describes in his study, Jacob modifies his liberating theology *just enough* to rationalize the suffering of thousands of Caribbean slaves. For instance, on his last night of his journey, when considering the slaves' plight and what they will have to endure in order to help him turn a profit, he calls upon a recognizably Catholic ethic of judgment and obedience to declare the path forward "[c]lear and right." Morrison shows him gazing up to the heavens at this moment, toward "a sky vulgar with stars," as if discovering justification for his "sweet" plan in the righteous design of the universe (35). Doing exactly what he has previously condemned the Catholics for, Jacob regards the promise of his own fortune—and the dignity that he believes his future wealth will provide him—as God's way of consecrating his decision to invest in the Barbadian sugar trade and, by extension, the slave trade.

In the time it took to pass through Maryland and collect his debt from D'Ortega, Jacob has, in a manner of speaking, been converted. Though he continues to perceive himself as a Protestant and would undoubtedly recoil at any implication to the contrary, the flashback directly correlates Jacob's revised stance on slavery with his brush with Catholicism. After witnessing the riches that an enterprise like D'Ortega's can bring, Jacob adopts a theologically dualistic attitude toward the practice of slaveholding: the liberating Protestant ethic still justifies his dignity and redeems him from sin while the adoption of a conservative Catholic ethic sanctifies the suffering of his slaves and rewards his righteous authority. The oscillation between the two poles of Pauline dualism that his rationalization of slavery requires represents a radically new theology for Jacob, but one that he feels compelled to embrace if he wishes to achieve a level of success comparable to D'Ortega's. The fact that this theology is identical to the description of fundamentalist Christianity that Patterson puts forth in his study signals how thoroughly Morrison has recontextualized the argument for her purposes. She transposes Patterson's idea about the Catholic influence on Protestant slaveholders from the period of the Second Great Awakening to a time in American history when the racialized approach to slavery was first developing. This move, as I will explain, enables her to establish an imaginative link between the racialization of the American slave system and Catholic attitudes toward slaveholding.

What I am suggesting is that by rearticulating Patterson's claims in a seventeenth-century context, Morrison endeavors to undermine traditional narratives about the rise of race-based slavery in colonial America—narratives developed during the Age of Enlightenment as a means of rationalizing institutionalized racism. As she makes clear in "The Site of Memory," Morrison is attuned to the way that the Enlightenment's prioritization of human reason and scientific objectivity was used to excuse the enslavement of African peoples, who were deemed incapable of rational thought. Madhu Dubey has shown how this critique of "the dehumanizing racial logic" of the Enlightenment translates to *A Mercy*. Rather than "demonstrating the slave's possession of reason," the novel, Dubey argues, "indicts" the prevailing discourses of the day by exposing their very irrationality. She cites, in particular, the way Morrison uses "the simple and powerful" testimony of slaves to underscore the "Unreason" of slavery; by depicting the absurdity of the auction block or the language of the bill of sale from their point of view, Morrison is able, Dubey contends, to destabilize the legitimacy of the logic that supported these enterprises ("Neo-Slave" 341).

I am proposing that the depiction of Jacob in the opening scenes of the novel promotes a similar effect. Instead of launching her critique from the slaves' perspective, though, Morrison uses Jacob's own words to indicate the extent to which the rationalization of slavery relied upon a categorically *irrational* premise—namely Catholic theology. In other words, by aligning Jacob's descent into institutionalized racism with his theological assimilation of a Catholic ethic, Morrison insinuates a fundamental affinity between Catholicism and the racialized logic of the Enlightenment. Undoubtedly, any suggestion of an affinity of this sort would have been antithetical to the foundational precepts of Enlightenment rationality, which were diametrically opposed to Catholicism and its superstitious associations. But, as her portrayal of Jacob implies, Morrison means to demonstrate that these apparently competing discourses were not nearly as hostile to one another as the Enlightenment thinkers would have liked to believe. In her fictional reconstruction of colonial America, it is the Protestant's encounter with his "irrational" Catholic other that supplies the theological rationale for the enslavement of Africans and ultimately facilitates the transition to a race-based slave economy.

Although the racialization of slave labor on the Vaark property happens some time after Jacob's visit with the D'Ortegas and only following his death, Morrison establishes a clear connection between the theological transformation he experienced while in Maryland and the final outcome for his slaves. The earliest manifestation of this connection is the new house he starts building immediately upon returning from his trip: a massive residence his wife views as "befitting not a farmer, not even a trader, but a squire" (88). It is an undertaking that no one except Jacob endorses and, as the feudal overtones of Rebekka's description of the project imply, the construction will dramatically revise the relatively equitable division of labor that the farmworkers had previously enjoyed.[25] Lina, a Native American slave who helped Jacob build the first two homes on the property, believes her master's third house, his "profane monument to himself," courts "malfortune" because of the unnecessary killing of trees that its building requires (44). Her criticism calls attention to how completely Jacob's values were affected by the time he spent with Senhor D'Ortega. Whereas his exposure to the Catholic slave owner's mansion provided the impetus for the plans "to build a house that size on his own property," initially Jacob intended to make his version "[n]ot as ornate as D'Ortega's. None of that pagan excess, . . . but fair. And pure, noble even, because it would not be compromised" (27). However, as Lina notes, those intentions quickly collapse. In addition to the excessive number of trees he fells during the construction, Jacob surprises everyone by hiring a blacksmith to fashion an ironwork masterpiece out front that glitters "like a gate to heaven" (89). The biblical imagery carved into the gate baldly contradicts his Protestant predisposition toward iconoclasm; its "gilded vines were actually serpents, scales and all," that make the house into a kind of American Eden, rivaling even a Catholic's taste for "graven idols" (150, 16).[26]

For the workers on the Vaark farm, though, what is more upsetting than Jacob's sudden appreciation for religious iconography is that the new house destabilizes the balanced way he has always managed his labor force. Before the construction began, farmwork was divided fairly among the laborers, regardless of race or status. Rebekka and he worked side by side with their racially diverse collection of slaves and indentured servants, sharing with them both the hardships and the rewards of farming in the harsh wilderness. While not entirely without hierarchical designations, the community they formed did not regard race as the principal designator of social worth. Rather, what mattered was one's ability to contribute productively to the enterprise of the land. As a result of the Vaarks' equitable management of farmwork, Morrison portrays the relationship that developed between the unpaid laborers and their owners as mutually beneficial and nurturing. Throughout the novel, the workers repeatedly characterize their arrangement as "a kind of family" (155). Willard and Scully, white indentured servants whose time Jacob rents from a neighbor, go so far as to describe the community in terms that completely elide racial distinctions. For them, the interaction among the farm's inhabitants suggested bonds of real kinship; instead of as a labor collective, they chose to regard the group as a "good-hearted couple (parents), and three female servants (sisters, say) and them helpful sons" (144). But with the transformation inspired by Jacob's trip to Maryland, the familial quality of their arrangement cannot be sustained, as differences of race and class become increasingly difficult to ignore.

The white servants are among the first to recognize how the construction of the new house affects the social order of the farm. At first the changes do not appear to be in their favor: Willard and Scully feel scandalized by Jacob's decision to pay a free black man for his labor on the gate, while they continue to be forced to work without financial compensation. Though they have never previously objected to performing the same duties as African and Native American slaves and indentured laborers, once Willard and Scully learn that "the blacksmith was being paid for his work, like the [white] men who delivered building materials," their racial pride is piqued, and they suddenly refuse to accept an inferior status (150). Fortunately for them, the canny blacksmith identifies the source of their discomfort and compensates by treating them with excessive deference. He even starts referring to Willard as "Mr. Bond"—a "courtesy" that, however comic in its misapplication, nonetheless serves to restore the white man's sense of innate superiority: "Although he was still rankled by the status of a free African versus himself, there was nothing he could do about it. No law existed to defend indentured labor against them. Yet the smithy had charm and he did so enjoy being called mister" (151). The blacksmith's humbling gesture lays the groundwork for the imminent reorganization of the farm's labor force along racial lines. Beyond the psychological "lift" it gives to Willard, it anticipates how, in a matter of just a few months, all of the Vaarks' white laborers will be granted official advantage over their African and Native American slaves.

Jacob does not live long enough to witness the racialization of his farm. And perhaps, if he had not died before the construction of his house was finished, he might have successfully staved off the practice for a while longer. As it was never his objective to institute a slave system on the order of D'Ortega's—he simply intended to make his property *appear* like a feudal manor, not necessarily to function like one—Morrison gives no indication that Jacob would have approved of the changes that ultimately occur in his labor force. But because her novel is poised right at the moment in American colonial history when slavery was about to be institutionalized and legally coupled with racism, there is a strong sense of historical inevitability. Morrison's unique take on the progress of history, then, is how intimately she associates the development of a race-based slave system with Jacob's plans for the new house—plans initiated and funded as a direct result of the theological "conversion" he underwent in Maryland. Not only are the materials and labor financed by the investments he has made in the Barbadian sugar and rum trade, but also his death is presented as a consequence of its construction. Rebekka blames the "fever of building" for killing him, or at least for masking the signs of his sickness from her until it was too late to find a cure (89); Lina correlates the onset of his disease with the "malfortune" stirred up by the indiscriminate murder of trees (44). Since Jacob's demise serves as the immediate catalyst for the farm's descent into racialized slavery, its connection to his house relates all that follows to his irrational attempts to replicate the Catholic standard of wealth on his own property.

The "ravages of Vaark's death" are carried out by his widow, whose grief and anxiety over the prospects of the farm result in her increasingly cruel treatment of the slaves (155). She beats Sorrow for even minor infractions; forces Lina to sleep in the toolshed, a modified slave quarters; and puts Florens up for sale. These changes not only bring an abrupt end to the principle of shared and equitable labor that all of the group have taken pride in, but they also signal the community's new racial hierarchy. The only characters whose status improves in the wake of Jacob's passing are white. After her husband's death, Rebekka, who once labored alongside the other women, "laundered nothing, planted nothing, weeded never. She cooked and mended. Otherwise her time was spent reading a Bible or entertaining one or two people from the village" (145). The domestication of her daily tasks confirms her privileged position on the property; having fully assumed the role of a slaveholding mistress, she relegates the field labor to her racially designated servants. And although the white indentured servants continue to "fell sixty-foot trees, build pens, repair saddles, slaughter or butcher beef, shoe a horse or hunt" (155), Rebekka's reordering of the labor structure now provides Willard and Scully with payment for their work. The final pages of the novel anticipate a not-too-distant future in which the two men will have earned enough wages from the Mistress to purchase their own freedom, leaving only nonwhite slaves to work the land (at least until such time as they are sold into the open slave market) and thus completing the farm's capitulation to a race-based system of enslavement.

It turns out, then, that the house "befitting . . . a squire" that Jacob constructs on his property more than just resembles the plantation mansion he saw and envied in Catholic Maryland; it effectively re-creates its social order. Jacob's encounter with Catholicism spawned the transformations that take his farm from a diverse collective of workers into a traditional slave economy in which whites alone profit from the degradation of a racially stratified, unpaid labor force. In order to secure her financial prospects, Rebekka realizes almost immediately after the passing of her husband that she must accede to a racialized approach to slavery if she hopes to retain the property and protect herself from ruin. Once again, the realization gets figured in the novel as a kind of religious conversion. This time, though, instead of Catholicism, it is Rebekka's association with a separatist branch of Protestantism that triggers the modification of slaveholding practices. She understands that the only way to maintain the land that she labored so painstakingly to cultivate is to marry one of the men from the neighboring Anabaptist community who would be able to provide her with legal rights to it. Triggered by practical concerns, Rebekka's sudden desire to seek refuge among the Separatists leads her to fully accommodate their religious values—including the racist belief that redemption is a possibility "open to most . . . except the children of Ham" (92). For these reasons, Rebekka's swift assumption of another faith could be interpreted as the principal motivation for the racial divisions she draws on the farm. However, even though Rebekka adopts the racialized approach to slavery that "she believes her piety demands," as one of the victims of the Mistress's conversion suspects, the cruelty she shows them exceeds what she learns in the church services. "Her church-going alters her," Florens concedes, "but I don't believe they tell her to behave that way. These rules are her own and she is not the same" (159). The way that Florens qualifies the Anabaptists' influence on Rebekka emphasizes the personal rather than the theological motivations for restructuring her relationship with the slaves. By dissociating herself from her African and Native servants through a series of arbitrary "rules" whose purpose seems only to flaunt their subjugation—she "requires [Lina's] company on the way to church but sits her by the road in all weather because she cannot enter" (160), and she forbids the slaves to enter the grand house for any reason other than to clean it—Rebekka could no longer be accused of sharing an affinity with her racial other. In line with the new standard of living that Jacob brought to the farm, she remakes herself in the image of a plantation mistress so as to attract the kind of husband who would be able to support one. Whether or not she succeeds is beyond the scope—and the concerns—of the novel; Morrison has already established the link between Jacob's exposure to Catholicism and the racialization of his labor force.

II. Redeeming History and Sacramentalizing Memory

Between *Beloved* and *A Mercy*, Morrison imagines the historical implications of Catholic theology as devastating for American slaves and their descendants. As with so much of her work, however, this damning portrait of Catholicism is not the whole story. In the final part of the chapter, I will show how Morrison's engagement with the religion exceeds its dangerously conservative repercussions. Specifically, I contend that Catholicism informs not only how these two novels remember slavery but also, foundationally, Morrison's original concept of "rememory," which indeed determines the narrative style and form of both texts. In my reading, Morrison uses a definitively Catholic idea of sacramentality to create a new approach for remembering the traumatic past. Somewhat paradoxically, even as this approach recalls the destructive consequences of Catholicism for American slaves, it also opens up the possibility of—in Morrison's view—redeeming this legacy.

The term "rememory" appears for the first time in *Beloved*, when Sethe invents it to describe how she experiences the past:

> Someday you be walking down the road and you hear something or see something going on. So clear. And you think it's you thinking it up. A thought picture. But no. It's when you bump into a rememory that belongs to somebody else. Where I was before I came here, that place is real. It's never going away. Even if the whole farm—every tree and grass blade of it dies. The picture is still there and what's more, if you go there—you who never was there—if you go there and stand in the place where it was, it will happen again; it will be there for you, waiting for you. (43–44)

What emerges here is a way of remembering that is simultaneously phenomenal, atemporal, and communal. At any point and without warning, Sethe explains, someone else's memories will erupt in the present moment with a force that is perceptible to her senses. She will see, hear, smell—or "bump into"—the past before knowing what she has encountered. Sethe's sensory experience in fact determines the extent to which knowledge is even possible, since it is all that remains of the person to whom that memory "belongs."

Critics have long recognized a connection between Sethe's description of rememory and the way Morrison herself remembers slavery—the way she imaginatively represents a lost or inaccessible slave history in her fiction. Consider, for example, the following account of the opening lines of *Beloved*, where Morrison expresses a desire to confound rather than to explicate:

> The reader is snatched, yanked, thrown into an environment completely foreign, and I want it as the first stroke of the shared experience that might be possible between the reader and the novel's population. Snatched just as the slaves were from one place to another, from any place to another, without preparation and without defense. No lobby, no door, no entrance—a gangplank, perhaps (but a very short one). And the house into which this snatching—this kidnapping—propels one, changes from spiteful to loud to quiet, as the sounds in the body of the ship itself may have changed. ("Unspeakable" 32)

Like Sethe, Morrison's reader will be plunged "without preparation and without defense" into the past. There is no narrative exposition, no written record of where we are or how we got there—only the sensation of being lost and unmoored, as slaves "in the body of the ship" may have felt. And it is important to note that Morrison intends this "shared experience" of feeling "snatched, yanked, thrown" to extend beyond the first few lines of the novel. Because even after the basic elements of the story become clear—that readers have entered a house, not a slave ship, occupied by free women who survived both slavery and Emancipation—*Beloved* still shifts relentlessly among temporal modes and types of focalization. The result is a narratological strategy that foregrounds disruption and privileges sense impression over other, more conventional means of narrative progression, such as chronological time.

For example, in an early scene in the novel, when Paul D and Sethe lie silently together in bed, Morrison's narration weaves almost imperceptibly in and out of each character's consciousness as they grapple with what has just happened between them. Their thoughts move, in turn, to moments from the past—their life together on the Garner plantation, when Sethe was married to Halle and, out of respect for them both, Paul D stifled his desire for her. These recollections, however, do not manifest in chronological order or with any clear designation of narrative time. Rather they appear in pieces, triggered by one character's physical encounter with the other. The "touch of cloth" of Paul D's shirt on Sethe's skin reminds her of the "clean sheeting" she used to wrap the slaves' food (26, 27); when Sethe uncrosses her ankles, Paul D is reminded of watching her with Halle in the fields. For readers, it becomes increasingly difficult to differentiate one character's memory from the other's. The focalization changes from sentence to sentence—sometimes even within a sentence—and we can be confused as to whose view of the past we are reading. By the end of the scene, in fact, Sethe and Paul D are recalling the very same thing: the sensation of ripping open a young ear of corn at Sweet Home, on the night Sethe consummated her marriage to Halle. The final line of the chapter—"How loose the silk. How fine and loose and free" (33)—represents simultaneously their individual and shared experience of that meal. In this way they communicate, without ever speaking a word, the significance of being together again after all these years apart and their mutual longing for Halle.

Morrison stages a similar sort of unspoken communication between characters in *A Mercy*. The closing section of that novel comprises a response from Florens's mother to a memory her daughter has already shared with the reader—a correction or addendum to how Florens has previously recounted the moment of their separation in Maryland. "Hear a tua mãe," she pleads, explaining that she did not offer the girl to Jacob out of convenience, but rather "[b]ecause I saw the tall man see you as a human child, not pieces of eight. I knelt before him. Hoping for a miracle. He said yes" (167, 166). This section, like those narrated by Florens, is written in the second person, so its tone is immediate and conversational. Indeed, it implies that Florens's mother has somehow been exposed to her daughter's version of the story and wants now to affect her memory of the event. Given the distances of space and time that divide these two characters (not to mention the circumstances of their enslavement), this would be, of course, an impossible "conversation" to have. And yet, as in the scene described above from *Beloved*, Morrison again imagines a way they might share with one another their individual experiences of the past. Here it is another physical encounter—with the burning, flying fragments of Florens's narrative which "fall like ash over acres of primrose and mallow" (161)—that makes the communication possible, triggering an unspoken and unspeakable memory.

Quite significantly, this way of remembering slavery departs from how authors of the original slave narratives were compelled to describe their experience. According to James Olney, a fundamental premise of these antebellum works was that "there is nothing doubtful or mysterious about memory: on the contrary, it is assumed to be a clear, unfailing record of events sharp and distinct that need only be transformed into descriptive language to become the sequential narrative of a life in slavery" (151). The slave authors understood that in order to make their accounts appear credible to an audience who were not inclined to believe them, they had to represent the past as they actually experienced it. Based on the conventions of the time, this meant that their autobiographies adhered rigorously to a structure we now associate with literary realism: they were unvaryingly first-person, univocal, linear recollections of slavery, beginning with birth and ending with the author's escape and/or manumission.[27]

As a narratological strategy, then, Morrison's concept of rememory constitutionally opposes each of the "rules" to which the antebellum slave authors were beholden, for all of the reasons I have described. With their multiple narrators and points of view, and for the way they imaginatively link past and present on the same narrative plane, *Beloved* and *A Mercy* flout the realist structure of slave autobiography at just about every turn. And, if this seems too conspicuous to be anything other than strategic, Morrison would be the first to agree. In the same essay where she explains that her excessive style was cultivated—at least in part—to challenge the rationalist imperative of the original narratives of slavery, she makes a similar claim about her approach to memory. Specifically, she says that the situation she finds herself in as "a writer in the last quarter of the twentieth century" implores her to use her imagination to remember slavery in a way that was expressly forbidden the antebellum authors, given the milieu in which they wrote ("Site" 71). The comparative "freedom" this affords her makes it possible to "dispense with 'what really happened,' or where it really happened, or when it really happened" in favor of a less realistic, less factual account of the slave experience. This is, she grants, the reason why her work "frequently falls, in the minds of most people, into that realm of fiction called fantastic, or mythic, or magical, or unbelievable"—labels that she does not covet (72). But it is also what enables her to defy the limits imposed on the original narratives of slavery by an audience who demanded their credibility.

The tenor of defiance is so strong in Morrison's construction of rememory, in fact, that critics often link the concept to other modes of writing that similarly reject realism for a nonmimetic representation of the past. Most commonly they align it with one of two distinct traditions: either African spirituality or literary postmodernism. The type of expression associated with both of these traditions clearly resonates with Morrison's distinctive approach to the slave narrative form. This has led scholars to argue, on the one hand, that rememory "works in consonance" with African forms of belief that were suppressed by Western modernity (Zauditu-Selassie 145). Critics in this camp maintain that these alternative belief structures inform how Morrison uses rememory to put the present in conjunction with the past. They also demonstrate that an Africanist perspective on ancestral return can help to explain the more supernatural elements of Morrison's novels, including the resurrection of Beloved and the haunting of Jacob's house in *A Mercy*.[28] On the other hand, scholars such Rafael Pérez-Torres who relate the narratological disruptions in her work to a postmodern aesthetic underscore the fragmentary quality of rememory, pointing out that the concept—like other postmodernist tropes—challenges the idea of "history as a master narrative." Pérez-Torres and others like him contextualize Morrison's breaks with realism within the postmodern author's generalized distrust of verisimilitude.[29]

Both of these arguments are useful for the focus they bring to the relationship between memory and narrative in Morrison's fiction. Each in its own way emphasizes how dramatically the concept of rememory restructures the original narrative of slavery, stripping the classic form of its obligation to literary realism. This line of argument implies that the creative act itself, that is, Morrison's imaginative subversion of realist conventions, promotes a kind of redemption: a means of redressing the formulaic way that slave autobiographers were forced to remember their experience. But while I agree that the Africanist and postmodernist readings indeed have merit, what they do not—what they categorically *cannot*—do is account for the way Morrison imagines that redemption. In other words, they fail to acknowledge how thoroughly her concept of rememory is, like her excessive style, informed by Catholicism.[30] This oversight, I argue, jeopardizes our understanding of the redemptive quality of Morrison's concept, or what she means when she says, as she did in an interview with Marsha Darling about *Beloved*, that rememory "heals the individual—and the collective" from the legacy of enslavement (248).

To argue for a Catholic interpretation of rememory might appear incompatible with what I have been claiming thus far about the portrayal of Catholicism in *Beloved* and *A Mercy*. It is Catholic theology, after all, to which Morrison attributes by way of stylistic excess the debilitating psychological consequences of enslavement on African Americans. So how could the same religion be said to provide healing from that horror? The contention makes sense only when we consider how Morrison describes her "job" as a contemporary novelist of slavery: the reasons she gives, in "The Site of Memory" and elsewhere, for wanting to redeem the classic form of the slave narrative. For her, the "problem" comes down to the fact that all of the original narratives of slavery "were written to say principally two things. One: 'This is my historical life—my singular, special example that is personal, but that also represents the race.' Two: 'I write this text to persuade other people—you, the reader, who is probably not black—that we are human beings worthy of God's grace and the immediate abandonment of slavery'" (66). In her critique, Morrison correlates the prescribed structure of slave autobiography with the theological orientation of its antebellum readership and, specifically, with the way that readership imagined God's grace to be conferred. What this means is that Morrison understood as well as anyone that the religious sensibilities of their audience determined how the original narratives of slavery were written.

Those religious sensibilities were, of course, Protestant. Out of necessity, the authors of antebellum slave narratives appealed to the population most likely to sympathize with their abolitionist agenda. And, in the United States at least, Philip Gould has shown that that population was overwhelmingly white, northern, and evangelical—followers of the classic strain of Protestantism, who were inclined to disapprove of southern fundamentalists precisely because of the way they manipulated their theology to advance slavery (16).[31] The slave authors knew that they could (that they *had to*) capitalize on the evangelicals' disapproval in order to advance abolition, thus ensuring that their personal narratives reflected the theological principles that their readers held dear.[32] As a result, Gould demonstrates, evangelical Protestantism "provided many of the categories and tropes through which [the slaves]—whether they were speaking or writing—fashioned 'civilized' identities for public consumption" (16). Foremost among these "categories and tropes" was the spiritual autobiography, a literary form that emphasizes the author's morality and genuine religious faith in the face of ungodly circumstances.[33] Not surprisingly, then, as Morrison's critique of them indicates, the antebellum slave narratives turned on the question of grace: on whether, in the minds of an evangelical Protestant readership, their authors could be deemed "worthy" of Christian salvation.

It is by way of this conception of grace that we begin to see why Morrison would deploy Catholicism to remember slavery differently than the antebellum slave narrators were forced to by their evangelical readership. Grace has been called "the watershed that divides Roman Catholicism from Protestantism" (Ryrie 10). Disputes over its definition and revelation have raged since the time of the Reformation. Catholics always held that the world and its inhabitants exist in a permanent state of grace, meaning that they see all reality—every part of creation—as sanctified by the divine presence of God.[34] Protestants, in contrast, generally regard grace as a singular gift, bestowed by God only on the faith of the true believer. Therefore, for them, the salvific power of grace is radically removed from nature.[35] Sociologist Peter Berger explains that this distinction undergirds the Protestant worldview and, especially, how Protestants tend to think about reality:

> Protestantism may be described in terms of an immense shrinkage in the scope of the sacred in reality, as compared with its Catholic adversary. The sacramental apparatus is reduced to a minimum and, even there, divested of its more numinous qualities. The miracle of the mass disappears altogether. Less routine miracles, if not denied altogether, lose all significance for religious life. The immense network of intercession that unites the Catholic in this world with the saints and, indeed, with all departed souls disappears as well. Protestantism ceased praying for the dead. At the risk of some simplification, it can be said that Protestantism divested itself as much as possible from the three most ancient and most powerful concomitants of the sacred—mystery, miracle, and magic. (111)

Here, despite "some simplification," Berger convincingly relates Protestantism's divestment of "mystery, miracle, and magic" to doctrinal teachings about grace. He shows that the Protestant idea of grace actually depends on a realistic view of the universe.

Berger's explanation clarifies why the slave autobiographers who wrote for an evangelical Protestant audience needed to adhere so rigorously to the tenets of literary realism. They understood that, for their readers, God's grace was not universally granted; rather it was something they had to earn—or, as Morrison says, something they had to make themselves appear "worthy of"—through a prescribed set of literary conventions that emphasized their credibility and, thus, their capacity for being saved. Therefore, the way they remembered slavery, just like *what* they remembered about it, was determined by an Enlightenment-era ideology, which made liberty contingent on rationality. In order to justify their personal freedom as well as the freedom of their race, the antebellum slave narrators expunged all traces of irrationality from their accounts of slavery. As I argued in the previous section of this chapter, this resulted in a conspicuous "silence" about the true horrors of their experience, a silence that Morrison has tried to "fill" with her "excessive" style. But also—and perhaps even more important for her—the rationalist imperative divested these narratives of the very things that Catholicism aligns with redemption: "mystery, miracle, and magic." It is significant, then, that in describing how she imaginatively recovers those memories of slavery for which there is no record, Morrison has this to say: "If writing is thinking and discovery and selection and order and meaning, it is also awe and reverence and mystery and magic. I suppose I could dispense with the last four if I were not so deadly serious about fidelity to the milieu out of which I write and in which my ancestors actually lived" ("Site" 71). This statement suggests that Morrison associates the way she honors her ancestors with the supernatural and unrealistic elements of her narrative—elements that I will, in what follows, be relating directly to Catholicism.

According to the Catholic sociologist Andrew Greeley, Catholics "find our houses and our world haunted by a sense that the objects, events, and persons of daily life are revelations of grace" (1). This worldview, which is really just another way of describing what Berger calls the "sacramental apparatus," derives from a central doctrine of Catholicism: Aquinas's *analogia entis*. Aquinas argued that because God created all earthly matter, all earthly matter bears God's image and is therefore graced by his divine presence. Accordingly, humans can come to experience the "mystery, miracle, and magic" of God through the analogy of creation. *Analogia entis*, Greeley and others have claimed, determines how Catholics envision grace to reveal itself in the world and provides the foundation for what has been called their "analogical imagination."[36] As opposed to Protestantism, in which a more dialectical way of thinking about creation imagines a radical break of the supernatural from the natural, Catholicism accepts—indeed celebrates—substantive links between these two realms.[37] The seven sacraments of the church are the most obvious expression of those links. But, as Greeley puts it, the Catholic analogical imagination perceives the universe and all worldly phenomena "as a 'sacrament,' that is, a revelation of the presence of God" (1).

Ever since the term "analogical imagination" was first coined in the early 1980s, critics have been using it to illustrate the great variety of ways that works produced by Catholic artists depart from the mainstream Protestant tradition in the United States. No one has done this more thoroughly than or as well as Paul Giles, whose *American Catholic Arts and Fictions* endeavors to document the presence of "a competing antiromantic 'Catholic' tradition," which undermines the aesthetic trends conventionally associated with Protestantism (25). Giles's study makes the compelling case that artists raised in the Catholic faith demonstrate a strong tendency toward the analogical mode in their productions. Because they were indoctrinated into a belief system that portrays the world as a vast sacramental network of being, Catholics—even those who have since left the church or chosen not to believe its teachings, whom he calls "cultural Catholics"[38]—are much more likely than Protestants to stress "ontological similarity, expressed within the trope of materialized analogy" (392). To say it another way: where Protestantism emphasizes difference—between spirit and matter, God and man, heaven and earth—Catholicism deploys an analogical approach to emphasize an essential sameness in the chain of being. What this means for literary expression, in particular, is that the Catholic author places "more faith in the phenomenal world, whose ultimate validity it sees as guaranteed by the Incarnation" (202). It is along these lines that I am arguing Morrison develops her concept of rememory and the narratological strategy that the concept informs.

As an author who converted from Protestantism to Catholicism during her childhood, Morrison certainly conforms to Giles's (purposely nebulous) designation of a "cultural Catholic": she was raised in the church from a young age and considers it a primary influence in her development as a writer.[39] Moreover, her personal familiarity with both Protestant and Catholic theology indicates that she is well versed in what distinguishes the two, especially with regard to such a major point of departure as *analogia entis*. And yet, in his sweeping characterization of American Catholic writers, Giles fails to concede Morrison's place in this "oppositional" tradition.[40] The oversight is striking—and not only because she has said how important Catholicism is to her work (Schappel 87). More explicitly than perhaps any other contemporary author in his study, Morrison undertakes to disrupt the aesthetic sensibility that Giles associates with Protestantism: a sensibility that regards divine grace as "an uncertain phenomenon whose presence cannot be relied upon" (55). Indeed, this is the same idea of grace that Morrison problematizes in "The Site of Memory" and that her version of the slave narrative seeks to redress. Despite these facts—and despite the many critics who have highlighted Morrison's imaginative use of analogy—there has been some real resistance to addressing her engagement with Catholicism.

For example, in her well-known essay on *Beloved*, Valerie Smith goes so far as to suggest that the novel's "dominant mode of articulation is analogical" (350). She's referring here to rememory and how rememory facilitates the more supernatural moments in the text—including the resurrection of its title character. Still, even though she calls Beloved an "incarnation," Smith does not recognize the theological stakes of her claim nor that her reading aligns almost exactly with what Giles and others have argued about Catholic writers. To understand where their arguments converge, we need to look more closely at the way Smith defines rememory, and why she regards it as an analogue of the past. For Smith, the important point is that the concept embodies—in a physical sense—"something that is gone yet remains": the unspoken suffering of millions of slaves (349). This happens on the level of the text itself, accounting for the feeling of dislocation that Morrison says she wants readers to have when they encounter the novel for the first time. But it happens within the narrative as well, at those moments when, suddenly, because of some scent or sound or touch, a character will "bump into a rememory that belongs to somebody else" (*Beloved* 43). In both of these instances, as Smith points out, the phenomenological experience of the text permits a kind of knowledge about slavery that would be impossible otherwise—it opens up a means of sharing among individuals and across space and time that she says "is clearly prelinguistic" because of how it is embodied (350).

Thus, rememory materializes the inaccessible in a way similar to the Catholic analogical imagination, which regards all earthly phenomena as an analogue of divine grace—that is, as a sacrament. Rather than an encounter with God, however, rememory mediates an encounter with slave history, making tangible some lost experience from the unrecorded past. For that reason it is not, properly speaking, a sacrament in the theological sense. Nevertheless, Morrison does imagine its redemptive potential as sacramental. Regarding *Beloved*, she has said that it was necessary for her to write about slavery "in a manner in which it can be digested, in a manner in which the memory is not destructive" (Darling 247). This curious turn of phrase and the imagery it evokes—of a memory that one consumes and digests—is consistent with how Catholics perceive Holy Communion. According to theologian Richard P. McBrien, Catholicism regards the Eucharistic sacrament as, above all else, "an act of remembrance" that "not only recalls to mind what Jesus did but also effectively makes it present again" through the physical consumption of bread and wine. In this way McBrien explains that the Catholic faithful remember Christ by embodying him—by collectively "sharing in" his body and his blood (822).

If it appears that I am making too much of the sacramental overtones of rememory in *Beloved*, I would like to return to those passages we have already examined in which the Eucharist is directly invoked. First there is the image of the circled cross burned into the skin of Sethe's mother—an image that bears a remarkable resemblance to the Host. Then there is the scene where Denver performs the Communion rite. I have argued that these moments reflect the insidious role that Catholicism played historically in the slaveholding South. And they do reflect that. But they are simultaneously indicative of how Morrison imagines redeeming that history: the memories that she says must be confronted and shared in order to (begin to) heal from slavery. So at the same time that the Eucharistic resonances in *Beloved* evoke tremendous pain, they also point toward the possibility of redemption through fellowship and love—exactly what Catholics believe the sacrament of Holy Communion is capable of doing.[41]

For instance, just after Sethe recollects the scar on her mother's rib, she has a flash of understanding, which comes not linguistically but from the smell of burning hair "that had seeped into a slit in her mind right behind the slap on her face and the circled cross." Taken into her body in this way, Sethe's rememory summons "something she had forgotten she knew" about the woman who gave birth to her, pieces of a story about infanticide and survival she heard long ago in a language she no longer speaks. Tellingly, when it happens she cries, "Oh, my Jesus" (73), because—as Catholics do when they consume the Host—she is recalling a sacrifice that was as painful as it was salvific. In this case, though, the sacrifice was her mother's, and Sethe is forced to reckon with the knowledge that it is she, herself, who has been saved.

The point I want to make here is that the Eucharist determines not only *what* Sethe remembers (the image of the circled cross) but also *how* she remembers. In fact, Morrison structures the entire scene sacramentally, from the way that memory is materialized and consumed to the revelation of Sethe's salvation. Even the "forgotten" words that "Sethe understood then but could neither recall nor repeat now" have an equivalent in the Communion rite: they evoke the Latin that was traditionally recited during the Roman Mass—which required "picking meaning out of" another indecipherable, untranslatable "code" (74). For Morrison, Latin always represented "the unifying and universal language of the Church," and she has admitted to experiencing "a moment of crisis" following its abolition after Vatican II (Monda 118). This sentiment—which amounts to a kind of linguistic nostalgia—seems perfectly in tune with the displacement Sethe feels upon realizing that she will never again hear the dialect spoken to her as a little girl. Morrison writes that Sethe

> was angry, but not certain at what. A mighty wish for Baby Suggs broke over her like surf. In the quiet following its splash, Sethe looked at the two girls sitting by the stove: her sickly, shallow-minded boarder, her irritable, lonely daughter. They seemed little and far away. (74)

Clearly, the act of remembering what Nan once told her about her mother in the language that they used to speak is difficult for Sethe, and she responds in a way that emphasizes her separation from the two women who raised her—as well as from others with whom she previously felt close: Baby Suggs, Denver, and Beloved.

The passage I have just quoted indicates how the memory of a single loss, in this case a linguistic one, begets so many more, and this is precisely why Morrison says she objected to Latin being supplanted as the ceremonial language of the Mass. She feared that its elimination would undermine the communal spirit of the church, limiting the institution's ability to unify people separated by time, distance, and dialect. According to Catholic doctrine, the sacrament of the Eucharist is the moment in the Mass that most clearly celebrates the kind of fellowship that Morrison imagines as essential: "it should signify the unity of the Church; it should provide a sharing in the means of grace."[42] For her, though, in the immediate aftermath of Vatican II, that sacramental communion was threatened by the removal of its universal language. As I have been suggesting, we witness those concerns reflected in the "far away" feeling that emerges when Sethe confronts a similar loss. And yet, despite this keen sense of isolation, there lingers in Morrison's description some indication that Sethe is not as disconnected from her community as it might initially appear. The oceanic imagery, in particular, implies an affinity between her experience and the experience of the half-siblings she never met: those children fathered by white rapists whom her mother did not keep, including the infant she "threw away on the island" where she was enslaved for a time prior to being transported to the United States (74). For a moment, Sethe steps into the rememory of that lost child—sharing with her murdered brother or sister, who was presumably tossed from shore into the Caribbean Sea, the sensation of drowning. As it must have been for that thrown-away baby, a wave of filial longing breaks over Sethe "like surf," and in "the quiet following its splash," she shares with her absent brothers and sisters—if only for an instant—the physical sensation of being pulled under water, away from the living who remain.

Paradoxically, perhaps, it is Sethe's capacity for embodying the terrible final moments of the child murdered by its mother wherein Morrison locates the redemptive potential of this scene, and of rememory more generally. Because even as her narration underscores the impossibility of recovering that "which would never come back," it simultaneously offers a way to make it present again through the analogy of their shared experience. This is what forces Sethe to confront—all at once—both the horror of her siblings' death and the decision that ultimately saved her from that same fate. For, in rememorying what happened to her brothers and sisters, she is also rememorying that her mother chose to keep and to name her, in honor of the "black man" whom she "put her arms around" (74). Thus, Sethe encounters through fellowship with these unwanted, unnamed children the love that was her personal salvation. Whether or not this revelation actually ameliorates Sethe's pain or redeems the infanticidal act, the novel does not say. The scene ends abruptly, without resolution, and the memories dredged up are not explicitly referred to again. But I would argue that its sacramental structure—the way it rehearses and reframes the Liturgy of the Eucharist—suggests, at least, the possibility that Sethe can heal from her mother's story, since it foregrounds the kind of "collective sharing" that Morrison associates with redemption.[43]

The other Eucharistic scene I have highlighted, Denver's reenactment of the Communion rite, serves a similar function, albeit in a more protracted manner. Indeed, it takes us several pages following the ritualized meal of biscuits and jelly to understand that it, too, has facilitated a means of collectively sharing the experience of slavery. At first the solitary meal seems only to reinforce Denver's estrangement from the past, because it marks the departure of her closest connection to it: the ghost of her baby sister, whom Paul D has just banished from the house. The ghost's absence is the reason she eats so "miserably" in this moment—and it is also why, "[d]uring the first days after Paul D moved in, Denver stayed in her emerald closet," feeling as "lonely as a mountain" (123). There, in the circle of boxwood trees, she continues the sacramental act of feeding herself—"Denver's imagination produced its own hunger and its own food"—with hope of finding "salvation" (35). Of course, salvation from her loneliness does finally arrive in the form of a "fully dressed woman" who "walked out of the water . . . past a giant temple of boxwood to the field and then the yard of the slate-gray house" (60). By relating Beloved's emergence to Denver's temple in this way, Morrison implies what Denver later confirms: that the "miraculous resurrection" of her sister was what she had been wanting all along, so that "when she saw the black dress with two unlaced shoes beneath it she trembled with secret thanks" (123).

Figured in these terms—as an answer to Denver's "wish" for "salvation"—Beloved's materialization in the novel is appropriately Eucharistic. Not only does she embody the presence of a child who has suffered, died, and been buried, but Morrison also associates her with imagery reminiscent of the sacramental meal. For example, Beloved reveals a preoccupation with being chewed and swallowed.[44] Likewise, in one of the final passages of the novel, Morrison describes her character this way: "Thunder-black and glistening, she stood on long straight legs, her belly big and tight. Vines of hair twisted all over her head. Jesus. Her smile was dazzling" (308). The association of vines and Jesus recalls what Christ said to his disciples at the Last Supper, his promise to not "drink again from the fruit of the vine until the day when I drink it new in the kingdom of God" (Mark 14.25). It is the covenant of an eventual return, which Catholics celebrate during Holy Communion and which informs the sense of timelessness conferred by the sacrament. As Richard P. McBrien explains, Jesus's "presence in the Eucharist . . . is the presence not only of the crucified . . . one, but also the presence of one who is yet to come" (822). Similarly, just as Beloved re-presents the little girl killed in the woodshed two decades earlier—the girl whose sacrifice saved others from enslavement—her swollen, pregnant belly anticipates another coming as well.

Thus, like the Catholic Eucharist, Beloved marks the convergence of past, present, and future, signaling that she is (to borrow again from Valerie Smith) "someone who is at once in time and out of time" (351). Nowhere does this temporal convergence manifest more palpably than in the sections of the novel devoted to her monologue, where Beloved intones, about both her recollections and her desires, "All of it is now   it is always now" (248). The sense of eternal now-ness in these sections is also what makes them indecipherable, since Beloved speaks not only from her perspective but also from the perspective of slaves trapped in the belly of a ship during the Middle Passage. Moreover, to Stamp Paid, who stands outside the door of 124 Bluestone listening to her words, Beloved's voice cannot be distinguished even from the other women who speak alongside her. The monologues of Sethe and Denver eventually merge with Beloved's, to the extent that their individual identities are effaced. All three characters ultimately appear to share the same memories of the past, as well as the same need for unification—what Beloved calls "the join" (251).

In this way, then, these monologic sections near the end of the novel signify the fulfillment of Denver's sacramental wish, and they do so with language reminiscent of the Eucharistic ritual that occasioned it: "Beloved is my sister," Denver says at one point. "I swallowed her blood right along with my mother's milk" (242). It is what she has wanted from the beginning, the return of her banished companion and salvation from her loneliness. Now, many will argue (and I would agree, at least provisionally) that in spite of the collective sharing that she inspires, nothing about Beloved seems particularly redemptive. Rather than forgiving Sethe for the murder or Denver for surviving, she punishes her mother and sister by further estranging them from the community that could sustain them, Stamp Paid and Paul D most deleteriously. These fissures are clearly inconsistent with the fellowship that the Eucharist supposedly creates. And yet they are still informed by Catholic doctrine, which (following Paul's First Letter to Corinthians) states that when the sacrament is celebrated without fellowship or with "division . . . [and] insensitivity to those in need, there is no real community and [it] brings judgment, not grace" (McBrien 822).[45]

Beloved's tendency toward judgment is something that Morrison herself has underscored. She told Marsha Darling that while writing the novel, she "got to a point where in asking myself who could judge Sethe adequately, since I couldn't and nobody else that knew her could, really, I felt the only person who could judge her would be the daughter she killed. And from there Beloved inserted herself into the text" (248). For a while, the verdict appears more than anyone can bear. But it is also what motivates Denver to go out on her own and reestablish her family's connections with the neighborhood women who have learned to keep their distance. Denver's candid plea for help and her "soft 'Thank you'" are the reason these same women decide to come together to save Sethe from such dangerous isolation (294). And, significantly, when they do finally collect near her yard for the first time since the Misery—at "three in the afternoon on a Friday"—the gathering plays out like another sacramental act of remembrance (303). There are prayers and singing and a different sort of sound, which Beloved interprets as "the chewing laughter" that will "swallow her all away" (323). This time, though, instead of merely recalling her sacrifice, the Eucharistic resonances of the moment produce something else as well: an opportunity for Sethe to make up for the decision she made to kill her daughter two decades earlier.

Standing there on her porch steps, trembling "like the baptized" in the "deep water" of her neighbors' voices and "loving faces," Sethe imagines that she is reliving the instant when Schoolteacher drove up to her house to re-enslave her children (308). Now, however, she has what she did not have before—the strength and fellowship of her community. As a result, she chooses to turn her weapon on the white man who she believes would make them suffer, rather than on an innocent child. The impulse to raise her arm is the same, of course; she wants to save "her best thing" from enslavement (308). But here the flesh she sets out to destroy is not her own, and in that small way she finally heeds Baby Suggs's warning against the theologically conservative view of slavery. For that reason, it is a redemptive gesture, to be sure—yet one that also acknowledges the historical complicity of Catholicism in the suffering of slaves. Because at the same time that the sacramental structure of the scene creates an opportunity for Sethe to redeem herself and the infanticidal act, it also reminds readers that it was Catholic theology that inspired her to murder Beloved in the first place in a tragic attempt to set her free.

. . .

A Mercy reveals a similar ambivalence regarding the redemptive potential of the Catholic sacraments. In fact, Florens's entire narrative—the way she remembers her life in slavery—is itself a material analogue of her experience of suffering and abuse. The audience comes to understand that the words we are reading have been hand-carved, by nail, into the floor and walls of one of the rooms on the property where she was enslaved. As in *Beloved*, Morrison imagines the materiality of the text to have a sacramental function that aligns with how Catholics perceive the phenomenal world. (Each word stands for something gone that remains.) Moreover, the attention she gives to the way that Florens wrote her narrative emphasizes the context that enabled its production: her conversion to Catholicism and, specifically, her relationship with the priest who taught her how to read and write as a child. Florens became literate while living on the D'Ortega plantation where, in keeping with the Vatican's mandate for converting slaves, she was indoctrinated to her master's religion and required to practice it.

Richard S. Dunn has shown that, in comparison to those of Protestants, Catholic conversion practices among slaveholding societies in the New World depended to a higher degree on slave literacy (249). Whereas Protestant masters almost universally prohibited their slaves from learning to read, Catholics were much more likely not only to convert the Africans in their possession but also to view basic instruction in reading and writing as a necessary part of the conversion process. The lessons Florens received from the Reverend Father in Maryland—lessons the priest offered in defiance of "wicked Virginians and Protestants who want[ed] to catch him" for promoting literacy where they forbade it (6)—were integral to her religious education and inseparable from the way she practiced Catholicism. The first words she ever scrawled through sand or on "smooth flat rock" were those of "the Nicene Creed including all of the commas," which she memorized during her conversion (6). Florens's articulation of this most fundamental statement of Catholic belief ("We believe in one God, the Father Almighty, maker of heaven and earth . . . We believe in one holy and apostolic Church. We acknowledge one baptism for the forgiveness of sins . . .") constituted her primal experience of symbolic language and, as her narrative indicates, continues to influence how she regards the written word. For her, then, writing always feels like an expression of faith, a linguistic representation of the prayers and sacramental rites she was used to reciting aloud. That is why she instructs her reader, "You may think what I tell you a confession, if you like" (3). Although the Catholic act of Reconciliation requires the communicant to confess orally, Florens, because of the way she learned to associate literacy and religion, instinctively relates writing to sacrament.[46] In these terms, the terms she grants a reader may approach the text ("if you like"), the narration becomes a kind of penance, something that, according to Catholic doctrine, Florens must communicate in order to be redeemed of her sins.

By presenting Florens's narrative as a confession, or at least by allowing it to be received as one, Morrison once more deploys a major Catholic sacrament to structure how her novel remembers the experience of slavery. In keeping with the way that Reconciliation is performed in the church, Florens's narration involves a covenant between teller and audience. The Catholic rite requires the recitation of the Act of Contrition, a prayer to God expressing sorrow for wrongdoing, and a vow to confess all, as well as a resolution to make reparations and to sin no more. Likewise, Florens's story opens with a pledge: "Don't be afraid. My telling can't hurt you in spite of what I have done and I promise to lie quietly in the dark—weeping perhaps or occasionally seeing the blood once more—but I will never again unfold my limbs to rise up and bare teeth" (3). These lines fulfill the sacramental mandate for a Catholic confession of acknowledging culpability ("what I've done") and swearing atonement ("I promise to . . ."). Yet despite the resemblance to a sacred prayer for forgiveness, it is decidedly the reader here—not God—to whom Florens appeals and offers penance. And, as soon becomes clear, that intended reader is not some generalized presence who might stumble upon the story carved into the wood of Jacob's house, but rather a single, recognizable character: her estranged lover, the illiterate blacksmith, who cannot read the words written exclusively for him. "Maybe one day you will learn," she writes, and then vows, "If you never read this, no one will," because she plans to keep the room "closed up" or else burn it down before anyone else can access the writing (160–61).

In addressing her act of contrition to the smithy and making him the sole audience of her narrative, Florens ascribes to this free black man the authority of the Catholic godhead.[47] He alone possesses the ability to heed her words and to grant forgiveness. The degree of control she imaginatively assigns her lover entirely determines her fate; she places herself wholly at his mercy. Unsurprisingly, perhaps, this testament of spiritual surrender reverberates with the language she has always reserved for the blacksmith. From the moment they met when he came to work on Jacob's gate, Florens has been "crippled with worship of him" (63). She transfers all the reverence her Catholic education taught her to show God to a mortal man, telling him, "No holy spirits are my need. No communion or prayer. You are my protection. Only you" (69). Immediately the smithy becomes everything that God had been for her—her savior and her creator, her "shaper and [her] world" (71). While some of the novel's characters look upon Florens's devotion with amusement or even envy, Lina recognizes the danger that such total veneration portends for her young friend. Not only is the blacksmith noticeably less invested in the relationship than Florens, having "not troubled to tell her goodbye" after completing his work (61), but he also appears disturbed by the slave girl's absolute submission to him.

The theme of a lover's loss of selfhood is, of course, a common one for Morrison. By turns her novels celebrate and lament the impulse to give oneself completely to another person, as well as the risk that such excesses of emotion tend to carry with them. So, in a number of ways, the self-sacrificing passion Florens feels for the blacksmith could be understood as a thematic extension of the kind of love Hagar shows Milkman (*Song of Solomon*), Dorcas shows Joe (*Jazz*), or Jade and Son show one another (*Tar Baby*).[48] However, what makes this portrait different, what sets it apart from these other, earlier Morrisonian depictions of self-destructive love, is its theological resonances. Because Florens was born into slavery and stripped of her freedoms at birth, the single passion she had ever been permitted to exercise is a sacred devotion to God. Even the love she should have felt for her mother was tainted, disallowed by her status as a slave. Therefore, when confronted finally with the possibility of sharing her future with another human being, she chooses to love him the only way she knows how: as fully and completely as she had been taught to love the Lord. Her submissiveness, then, must be considered in light of the particular theology through which forcibly converted Catholic slaves interpreted their relationship with Christ. Specifically, it reflects the conservative pole of Saint Paul's interpretation of the Crucifixion and the idea that, in dying for their sins, Jesus effectively re-enslaved all sinners to God, who became their spiritual master.

As I discussed in the first part of this chapter, the Pauline epistles frequently deployed the metaphorical language of slavery to represent the appropriate way for followers to relate to the Lord. Unlike Protestantism, Catholicism retained this conservative formulation in its catechism. Accordingly, in transferring her worship from God to the blacksmith, Florens reveals a properly Catholic impulse to enslave herself to this new master—regardless of his aversion for the role. Consider the following exchange between the two lovers, which takes place just after she has injured Malaik and he banishes her from his home:

> I want you to go [the smithy says].
> Let me explain [Florens says].
> No. Now.
> Why? Why?
> Because you are a slave.
> . . . .
> What is your meaning? I am a slave because Sir trades for me.
> No. You have become one.
> How?
> Your head is empty and your body is wild.
> I am adoring you.
> And a slave to that too.
> You alone own me.
> Own yourself, woman, and leave us be. (141)

The blacksmith recognizes, even before Florens does, that she has given up possession of herself and become enslaved to him. Although Florens distinguishes between the type of real-world slavery practiced by her lawful owner, Jacob, and the type of spiritual slavery she willingly engages in with her lover, she believes she exercises no choice in either regard. These two men possess freedom, whereas she identifies—according to both legal status and religious affiliation—solely as a slave. Despite how far she has traveled from the D'Ortega plantation where the principles of real and divine slavery were first inculcated in her, Florens's relation to each "master" continues to be governed by the Catholicism she practiced as a child. For her, the condition of enslavement penetrates so far that it determines even her physical response to the blacksmith. While he pushes her away and out of his house, she finds herself offering one last sacred propitiation to him: "On my knees I reach for you. Crawl to you" (141). Facing ultimate rejection from her lover, Florens still assumes the posture of obedience and submission that signifies the Catholic follower's prescribed relationship to authority. In this case, however, her appeal goes unheeded. His banishment of her is final, and she remains unredeemed.

Florens's experience of love and unlove with the blacksmith in *A Mercy* is thus concomitant with—and indivisible from—the critique of Catholicism that Morrison presents in the novel. Like the Africans Jacob saw on the D'Ortega plantation whose "shockproof" eyes exposed their subjugation, Florens has fully absorbed the conservative Catholic interpretation of Paul's teaching that marks her first and foremost as a slave. Beyond the physical torments of enslavement, then, her narrative represents the devastating psychological consequences the institution holds for its victims: the way it has taught them to accept and to crave subjection in all areas of their lives. But, as we have seen, Florens's confession is not for the smithy alone. Written out as they are, her words are also capable of being shared with a wider readership, beyond the single audience for which she intended them. This is, of course, the conceit that makes it possible for contemporary readers to experience her story—and also what drives the final section of the novel: her mother's long-awaited explanation of why she offered Florens to Jacob in place of herself.

Once the narrative is written—materialized on the floor and walls—Florens cannot control who will encounter it next. She realizes this the moment she contemplates setting fire to what she has produced:

> These careful words, closed up and wide open, will talk to themselves. Round and round, side to side, bottom to top, top to bottom all across the room. Or. Or perhaps no. Perhaps these words need the air that is out in the world. Need to fly up then fall, fall like ash over acres of primrose and mallow. Over a turquoise lake, beyond the eternal hemlocks, through clouds cut by rainbow and flavor the soil of the earth. (161)

Like the rememories that Sethe describes in *Beloved*, Florens's story is imagined by her as part of the phenomenal world, something that can be perceived by touch, or taste, or sight, or sound. It is in this way that the novel anticipates her mother's response and ultimately permits her mother to explain that it was love, not a lack of it, that motivated the decision to give her daughter up. Although it remains unclear whether Florens ever acknowledges this revelation, its presence in the novel suggests the potential for forgiveness—which is, after all, precisely what a sacramental confession is meant to confer.

2

A Sacred Communion

The Catholic Side of Possession in *The Autobiography of Miss Jane Pittman* and *Two Wings to Veil My Face*

IN THE 1994 ESSAY "Elements of Style," which serves as a kind of manifesto of her nontraditional approach and as a guide for performers and directors, Suzan-Lori Parks makes clear that she has no interest in "bad-mouthing" more conventional modes of theatre, such as the "2-act plays with . . . linear narratives" that playwrights "are often encouraged to write." Realism can be "beautiful," Parks insists, citing Lorraine Hansberry as evidence, and so it is important for anyone studying her own writing to know that she doesn't "explode the form" simply because she finds "traditional plays 'boring.'" Rather, she says, "It's just that those structures never could accommodate the figures which take up residence inside me" (8). The "figures" Parks refers to here are, in a sense, the subject of this chapter. For what she is suggesting is that the formal quality of her work is dictated by "ghosts" who haunt the writing: by the spirits of people "from, say, time immemorial, from say, PastLand, from somewhere back there, say," (12) who inhabit her home—and even her body—while she puts words on the page, shaping how each line of text gets written. As she explains in another 1994 essay titled, appropriately enough, "Possession," Parks likes to think of herself as a medium for the living dead to communicate, and she imagines herself needing to "get out of the way" as these voices from the past speak their experience through her (3).

While Parks's take on the creative process might indeed seem unconventional, the phenomenon she describes—spirit possession—actually has a great deal of currency in contemporary African American literature and, specifically, in the neo-slave narrative genre. In fact, it bears a striking resemblance to the concept of "HooDoo writing" that Ishmael Reed first developed in the 1972 poetry collection *Conjure* and then later expanded in both his nonfiction and fiction.[1] The concept is based on the religious belief, fundamental to Haitian Vodou, that the *loa* or *lwa*, the souls of dead ancestors, play an active role in the affairs of the living and at times will temporarily occupy their bodies. In Reed's view, "Afro-American writers still summon" the *lwa* (*Shrovetide* 74), and his own work as a novelist involves giving those spirits voice, in a way that honors their history. To that end, the neo-slave narrative he produced in 1978, *Flight to Canada*, features multiple scenes of possession, in which characters—many of whom are writers—become occupied by subjects other than themselves, who speak through them and control their articulations. According to Ashraf Rushdy, the first-person narrator, Raven Quickskill, is possessed at various points throughout this novel—and this accounts for the "strange" quality of the narration: its polyvocality and anachronisms, as well as the way it switches between literary styles and modes of address. Rushdy argues that by making Raven a "possessed narrator, . . . Reed is attempting . . . in a literary text . . . to enact what Colin Dayan calls 'the *crise de loa*—that moment when the god inhabits the head of his or her servitor'" (128).[2]

The two novels examined in this chapter have similarly possessed narrators, as I will demonstrate. Indeed, I contend that Ernest Gaines's *The Autobiography of Miss Jane Pittman* and Leon Forrest's *Two Wings to Veil My Face* employ the trope of spirit possession in a manner comparable to how Suzan-Lori Parks and Ishmael Reed use it: to "explode" the realist conventions associated with narrating African American history in general and the slave experience in particular. This argument, as we shall see, has more significant consequences for the former text than the latter, since Gaines's novel has not been to this point interpreted as a possessed narrative, whereas it would be difficult to read Forrest's as anything but. In both cases, though, despite the markedly different ways they deploy the trope of spirit possession, it is striking that these novels each depict their radical breaks with realism through the discourse of Catholicism. In other words, the Catholic margin of the two texts serves to frame—and even to facilitate—the antirealist effect that the trope has on their narratives. Thus, I am suggesting, by considering where and how Catholicism informs both texts, we are better poised to understand the narratological disruptions that spirit possession makes possible.

I. Creoles, Catholics, and "Hoo-Doo" Culture

Ernest Gaines's *The Autobiography of Miss Jane Pittman* is widely regarded as realist historical fiction: as one of the initial wave of contemporary slave narratives that challenged traditional historiography by recovering—as accurately as possible—the voices of those who had been enslaved. Its first-person narration was so convincing, in fact, that countless readers and even a few journalists regarded the book as genuine testimony of a living source, similar to the Works Progress Administration interviews of former slaves conducted in the 1930s.[3] In some ways this generic confusion might have been predicted: not only does the title undermine the novel's status as a work of fiction, but the text is also framed as an oral history, recorded and transcribed by a black historian who asked the subject, Jane, "to tell me the story of her life" (vii). Indeed, Gaines has said that he drew heavily from the WPA interviews while writing *Miss Jane Pittman*, even calling them his Bible, and that he used these documents "to get the rhythm of speech and an idea of how ex-slaves would talk about themselves" (Rowell 94).

Critics often point to Gaines's investment in slave testimony when considering the formal properties of the novel, associating it with a wider trend in African American literature of the period toward a fuller, more accurate representation of lived history. For example, Madhu Dubey argues that realist narratives like *Miss Jane Pittman* were "kindled by" the political climate of the 1960s and, specifically, the push from civil rights activists to revise the historical record, which they viewed as entirely divested of the perspective of slaves ("Speculative" 781).[4] According to Dubey, the "revisionist historiographic enterprise" of this period accounts for Gaines's recourse to literary realism, since he was not attempting to discredit the "truth-telling claims characteristic of realist historical fiction" but rather to amend or correct what had already been written (782). This is the way she distinguishes a work such as *Miss Jane Pittman* from later, "antirealist" strains of the slave narrative genre (such as Leon Forrest's *Two Wings to Veil My Face*) that "overtly situate themselves against history, suggesting that we can best comprehend the truth of slavery by abandoning historical modes of knowing" (784). At the time he was writing his novel—in the late sixties, when the WPA interviews and antebellum slave autobiographies were first deemed legitimate evidence—Gaines was far too engaged himself in recovering a lost history, Dubey claims, to want to destabilize the historian's authority.⁵

The historian in *Miss Jane Pittman* is, of course, Jane herself: a century-old African American woman who was born into slavery and lived through the start of the civil rights movement. Her first-person narrative traces, in chronological order and with poignant verisimilitude, the major events that had an impact on Louisiana's black population during that time—the Civil War, Emancipation, Reconstruction, Jim Crow legislation—through her personal experience of that history. Thus, in structure and in content, the novel affirms its realist historiographical aims in a mode that Gaines himself liked to call "folk." As he told an interviewer in 1983, *Miss Jane Pittman* is "not a story told by an educated person, but an uneducated person, an illiterate person, but someone with a tremendous sense of being, of knowing" (Blake 139). And yet, despite how seriously Gaines takes his narrator and the historical analysis that her voice provides, he destabilizes her authority at key points in the novel to such an extent that Jane's ability to accurately record history is called into question. These moments, as I will demonstrate, confound the realist tenor of her narrative by introducing into the text elements of supernaturalism, which oppose the rational and objective historiography that she otherwise represents. In fact, one of my principal claims is that Gaines uses the supernatural trope of spirit possession to articulate alternative means of remembering slavery and to engage radically antirealist views of the past—views that, until this point, have been mistakenly overlooked in the novel.⁶

I argue that Jane's narration is haunted—*possessed*—by a community of unacknowledged co-narrators who give voice to an approach to history dramatically at odds with her own. Specifically, I show how the Creole characters in the novel, characters explicitly linked through the Catholic religion to the very supernatural and aberrant beliefs that Jane loudly disavows, force her to remember the past differently, in a way that challenges her rationalist impulse. When these characters take over the narrative from Jane, they articulate a distinctly "antihistoriographic" approach, which Dubey and like-minded critics associate only with later, post-1970s versions of the contemporary slave narrative that are plainly "speculative." In Gaines's text, I am suggesting, it is the Catholic orientation of the Creoles that makes them particularly well suited to this kind of narrative disruption, given that Jane—who joins the local black church in middle age—perceives Catholicism as inherently irrational. Gaines thus utilizes the theological distinctions between Catholicism and Protestantism (something about which he would have been highly informed, because of his theological training in both religions) to exceed the limits of realist historiography. I want to stress, however, that in discovering where Catholicism informs the novel's more radical moments, this analysis does not claim *Miss Jane Pittman* dispenses with historical realism altogether. Indeed, as I indicate in the first section, the portrait of Catholicism that first emerges in Jane's narrative—on the surface level, at least—is perfectly consistent with the predominant realist reading of the novel. It is only by examining the depictions of spirit possession in the text, as I do in the second section, that we understand how Catholicism affects the way Jane remembers slavery.

. . .

Although Jane practices a Protestant form of Christianity and spends the majority of her time with fellow congregants, she also lives among Creoles and Cajuns and is thus indirectly affected by the policies of their church. Therefore, Jane's perspective on church policy and her shifting attitudes toward Catholic culture encroach on the narrative in a conspicuous way, underscoring the religion's relevance for African Americans living in Louisiana over the years the novel spans. She betrays a particular fascination with the church's influence on "mulattoes" and its historical identification with that distinct racial caste.[7] Among her many meditations on the social and political gulf that divides one rung of black society from another is the implicit contention that Catholicism fostered—or, at the very least, sanctioned—the upward mobility of Creoles of color, often at the expense of those African Americans who could not claim Creole ancestry.

Jane's critique of Catholicism is not a new one, of course. As Thomas Haddox has shown in his study of southern literature, there exists a long tradition of criticizing the church for its "tacit approval" of the system that led to hierarchical divisions between African Americans of different ethnic heritage (26). Haddox dates the origins of this tradition to the 1840s, with the publication of an anthology of poetry called *Les Cenelles*, authored by members of the *gens de couleur libres*. According to Haddox, many of the *Les Cenelles* poems highlight the complicity of the Catholic clergy in the institution of *plaçage*, which he calls an antebellum form of concubinage that effectively permitted French and Spanish colonialists to enjoy common-law marriage with light-skinned black women, who were bred for that purpose (9). A hallmark of *plaçage* was the "octoroon balls" or "quadroon balls," where a European man would select a mistress from the choices paraded before him, typically installing his selection in a secondary property (to keep her away from his "legitimate" white family) and continuing to support her and the children they produced together for the duration of his life. These open-secret unions engendered a separate class of African Americans, who identified as Creole and Catholic and enjoyed financial security—yet were never fully embraced by white society. Haddox explains that the precariousness of their social position, as well as the sexual exploitation of their women, is behind the pointed criticism of the church that surfaces in *Les Cenelles* and in subsequent literary portrayals of *plaçage*.[8] For, even as the Catholic clergy provided refuge and spiritual support for Creoles of color, they turned "a blind eye" to the moral depravity of the system responsible for creating—and, in effect, isolating—this discrete group of people (9).

By implicating the Catholic Church in the unique situation of Creoles of color, Gaines's novel advances a position similar to the one Haddox documents in his study. Jane persistently links the mulatto characters in her narrative to Catholicism, implying that their religious affiliation exacerbates the isolation that defines them. For instance, in the short history she provides of the LeFabre family—a history that began with its light-skinned matriarch's conscription at one of those "great balls before the war"—she uses the church to emphasize their segregation from the rest of the community:

> After the war, the family moved from New Orleans to Creole Place. What brought them to Creole Place, I don't know; maybe they had people there already. You had always had some mulattoes there, since long before the war, and now it got to be a settlement for them.
>
> The people at Creole Place did everything for themself. Did their own farming, raised their own hogs, their own cattles, did their own butchering. Had their own church—Catholic; built their own school and got their own teacher. The teacher had to come from there just like the priest had to come from there. (156)

Clearly Jane is attuned to the way that Catholicism contributes to the ethnic identity of the mulatto class, which is precisely the argument Haddox makes about the poets of *Les Cenelles*. But as a "folk" historiographer who developed her own view of this society, having been in close proximity to them for most of her life, Jane also reveals the consequences of this segregation for the ethnic group with whom she personally identifies.

Specifically, Jane denounces the LeFabres and those they live among at Creole Place for profiting from the system of *plaçage* more than they ever suffered. She points out how, upon old man LeFabre's death, the family inherited "money and property—even slaves," thus solidifying their infidelity to the race. In Jane's telling, the LeFabres and other Creoles of color actively encouraged their separation from the African American community, and this division exceeded differences in skin color. "No matter how white you was if you didn't have Creole background they didn't want you" to associate with them, she says (156). As evidence she offers "a little story" about two non-Creole black men who were chased from a mulatto dance and nearly killed just for "messing round" with some of their girls (157). Since the characters involved in the episode do not appear elsewhere in her narrative and are ultimately extraneous to the novel as a whole, the purpose of this vignette is solely to emphasize the fierceness with which the population at Creole Place guarded their claims to European ancestry, to the extent that they would murder any African American who threatened to dilute the bloodline. It follows, then, that Jane portrays Catholicism as a source of ethnic pride for Creoles of color, a part of their cultural exclusivity—like their farming and educational methods—which they cling to primarily as a means of distinguishing themselves from other members of their race.

Besides the troubling bouts of violence that such exclusivity provokes, what is most significant to Jane about the way that Creoles of color have used the church to dissociate from the African American community is its bearing on the struggle for racial equality. Again and again, she suggests that their European heritage in general and their association with Catholicism in particular has inclined them to tolerate without complaint the systemic effects of racism, because they preferred not to identify as black. This theme becomes especially resonant in the final section of the novel, "The Quarters," where Jane considers the first stirrings of the civil rights movement in Louisiana. As she puts it, "Catholics and mulattoes don't generally get mixed up" in the protests and demonstrations, choosing instead to maintain their status quo (231). Her observation correlates with official Catholic policy of the period, which often restricted Catholics from joining organizations engaged in social protest.[9] Given how deeply involved other Christian congregations were with the movement, the decision by many U.S. bishops to caution their congregants against active participation in the struggle drew condemnation from many corners. Gaines was undoubtedly aware of this controversy while working on the novel, as Jane's assessment of Catholic indifference toward racial matters recalls the charges leveled against them by such prominent figures as Martin Luther King Jr.[10] But at the same time, *Miss Jane Pittman* also anticipates the way the church's public stance on civil rights would soon change, in the wake of Vatican II and increasing pressure from activists to support social justice campaigns.

Although it concludes at some point prior to the moment when the American Catholic Church finally endorsed the civil rights movement and publically committed to racial equality, Jane's narrative looks forward to these developments through its portrayal of two progressive Creoles of color: Mary Agnes LeFabre and the young Hebert girl from "up there in Bayonne," who volunteers to be "their Miss Rosa Parks" (230–31).[11] Together these characters defy the standard practice of their community by not only working closely with non-Creoles but also advocating for the advancement of African Americans—decisions that strain relations with their own families. For a novel that is otherwise quick to underscore the ethnic isolation of mulattoes, this shift appears noteworthy, particularly because Jane reminds the reader that despite the way they have deviated from traditional Creole values, both women remain Catholic. In other words, Gaines does not attribute their progressivism to leaving the church; by some means, though it is never clear how, Mary Agnes and the Hebert girl are able to reconcile social action with their Catholicism. This fact renders them outliers, for certain, in the period represented in the narrative; yet it might not have seemed quite as extraordinary just a few years later, when the work was actually written. Since Gaines published *Miss Jane Pittman* after Vatican II and during a time when the liberation theology movement was at the forefront of public consciousness, the idea of a radical Catholic response to racial inequality would have had precedent. One could even argue that his novel's portrait of these two

Catholic women reverberates with its broader outlook on the struggle for civil rights and the political agency of those who participated in the effort.

In the view of most critics, including Dubey, *Miss Jane Pittman* figures the struggle for civil rights as an outgrowth or "culmination" of the "fight for freedom" that began a century earlier with slaves who resisted the system that oppressed them. For these critics, this is what accounts for the novel's rigorous adherence to historical progress—the "straight line" it draws from "Emancipation to the 1960s" (Dubey 796). And, in the ways I have just described, the novel's treatment of Catholicism initially seems to adhere to a progressive trajectory: despite her early reservations about the role of the church in Creole culture, as the narrative moves forward in time, Jane cites two instances of Catholics who overcome the conservative social agenda of their religion, promoting new strategies of resistance that recall the heroic actions of their slave ancestors. This "straight line" approach to reading *Miss Jane Pittman* does appropriately highlight how Catholicism is involved in the work of historical recovery, which Dubey and others regard as a categorically realist endeavor. However, I would suggest that to read the Catholic margin of this novel solely in terms of realism is to neglect a critical feature of its composition—namely, the insidious and persistent way it destabilizes the identity of its narrator. For, as I will show, instead of contributing to the singularity of Jane's perspective and the accuracy of the folk history she recalls, her frequent references to Catholicism actually subvert the realist pretense of the narration by undermining its truth-telling claims.

. . .

Notwithstanding its obligations to literary realism—and its firm standing within that tradition—*Miss Jane Pittman* persistently upends the conventions of such writing, in ways that are coded Catholic. Indeed, beyond its associations with historical recovery, Catholicism in this novel also promotes a deep wariness about history that the criticism usually attributes to later, antirealist examples of neo-slave narratives. That wariness reveals itself most palpably in the moments where Jane's narration appears possessed by other voices—voices that, by virtue of their very presence in her "autobiography," call into question the authority of her claims. Witness, for example, the curious account she gives of Jimmy

Caya's response to the revelation from young Robert (Tee Bob) Samson that he plans to marry Mary Agnes LeFabre:

> "That woman is a nigger, Robert. A nigger. She just look white. But Africa is in her veins, and that make her nigger, Robert."
>
> But with all his shaking and screaming at him, he said Tee Bob acted like he wasn't hearing him.
>
> "Robert," he told him. "Don't you listen in class? Ain't you heard him" (I forget that teacher's name, but I think he said Gamby) "over and over and over? You think she changed since then? She's the same woman, Robert. She know her duty, and all she expect from you is ride the horse down there. But that's far as she expect you to go. The rest is her duty, Robert. She knows that. He" (I'm almost sure he called that teacher Gamby) "told you it was like that then, and it's the same way now." (171)

In recalling what Jimmy said to Tee Bob that day, Jane confronts the limits of her memory, as she admits to feeling uncertain about the name of the man who taught these two white boys the rules of interracial "courtship." On the face of it, this lapse would be expected—something included in the narrative, parenthetically, to remind the audience they are reading oral testimony, thus contributing to the verisimilitude of the novel's premise. Yet, by drawing attention to her inability to remember aspects of the conversation, the parenthetical remarks simultaneously emphasize Jane's distance from the event. In fact, it is revealed just a few pages later that she was not present when these words were originally spoken; nor was she there when Jimmy provided his account of the dialogue with Tee Bob to the sheriff investigating his death. So either this represents her best guess as to what was spoken between the two men based on a third person's recollection of the scene, or else it is one of those instances prefigured by her transcriber in the introduction to the text, where another teller—someone other than Jane—has stepped in and "carried the story for her" (ix). Both scenarios diminish the narrator's authority in key ways, the former by implicating her in hearsay and the latter by suggesting that the voice she speaks with is not her own. In each case Jane loses some control of the narrative as other perspectives intrude on her story, problematizing her identity as its sole author/speaker. Accordingly, the "I" that defines her no longer represents Jane alone, but rather an assortment of potential collaborators who haunt the telling.

My use of the term "haunt" here is purposeful, meant to convey the clandestine—and, yes, *ghostly*—quality of the narration.[12] Because even though Jane's transcriber freely admits that "someone else would . . . pick up the narration" when Jane "was tired, or when she just did not feel like talking any more, or when she had forgotten certain things," he never names these contributors, nor does he ever announce their intrusion, choosing instead to use "only Miss Jane's voice throughout" (ix). It is left entirely to the reader, then, to determine when Jane is speaking for herself and when another person is speaking for her—absent of all notification from the transcriber. Effectively, this places anyone reading the novel in a situation markedly similar to the way witnesses have described spirit possessions; without a clear signal designating a new arrival, they watch for variations in utterance or behavior to indicate that one of the participants has been taken over.[13] Likewise, the audience of *Miss Jane Pittman* must make its way through the narrative, perhaps even forgetting that alternate voices threaten to interrupt, until a moment such as the one highlighted above, where Jane's memories appear to contradict what is known about her actual experience, implying that another presence has possessed the narration.

These kinds of contradictions are, admittedly, rare and therefore do not bear heavily on the novel as a whole. (It would be possible to read most of the sections, I think, with little consideration of the additional narrators who take possession of Jane's story.) Regarding the portion of the text devoted to Mary Agnes, and the description of her relationship with Tee Bob, though, the narrative disruptions are so concentrated and so pronounced that the speaker's identity remains indeterminate throughout. Not only does Jane describe repeatedly in these pages events that she could not have witnessed herself—each time without explaining where she acquired the particulars of what was said or felt—but she also, quite uncharacteristically, includes details that resist rational explanation. Twice within this section, in fact, she suggests that people are capable of performing actions that they do not control—that their bodies can become occupied by other agents, who manipulate them and determine the way they move and speak. The first time this happens, Tee Bob has just attacked Jimmy Caya for what he said about Mary Agnes. Yet rather than accounting for the burst of violence in terms of Tee Bob's own feelings, she implies that the boy had no agency in the matter: "Tee Bob gazed at his hand like somebody or something else had raised it" (171). And she returns to the idea of bodily possession just a few pages later, when recounting the final meeting between the would-be lovers (another event for which she was not actually present). There her testimony indicates that the bodies of both Tee Bob and Mary Agnes were inhabited, in those desperate last minutes, by their ancestors, who transform a relatively innocent scene into one of sexual violence.

For a realist novel, with otherwise very limited discussion of the supernatural, these moments of possession stand out. They also stand in stark contrast to the claim Jane makes elsewhere in the narrative that she "didn't believe in hoo-doo" (91). Indeed, in every other section of the book, Jane takes pains to dissociate herself and her own beliefs from superstitions that do not conform to her Protestant faith. Although she admits to visiting Madame Gautier at one point and even purchasing from her some powder that was meant to keep her husband from riding a dangerous horse, she insists, "I didn't believe in her the way you suppose to. I went to her because nobody else would listen to me. But after I had gone I still didn't take her advice" (121). Likewise, she vehemently denies the rumor that she asked a hoo-doo to curse Albert Cluveau, the man who killed Ned—not because she did not want him to suffer, but because she says she did not think it would work. Jane thus makes a point of rationalizing her system of belief, expressing at every turn an unwillingness to accept alternative, non-Western explanations for even the most irrational experiences. In that way, her identity as a realist narrator remains largely unaffected by the occasional tales of root work and prophetic visions that populate the text; again and again, she discounts the credibility of any otherworldly event that falls outside the bounds of rational discourse. And yet, the story of Mary Agnes upsets the rationalizing impulse of Jane's voice, insinuating that her resistance to "hoo-doo" is not as absolute as she endeavors to suggest. The other speakers who haunt this section of the novel, wresting possession of it away from Jane, interject an element of supernaturalism for which her Protestantism cannot sufficiently account.

For example, although she is initially skeptical of the idea that Tee Bob and Mary Agnes were actually possessed by their ancestors—and even accuses Jules Raynard, the man who insists that they were, of "specalatin"—

Jane does nothing to oppose Jules's version of the scene, allowing his to be the final statement on the matter. After hearing him describe the way that "the past and the present got all mixed up" in a "flash" as Mary Agnes transformed into her grandmother and Tee Bob became "that Creole gentleman" (192), Jane appears to accept that these ancestral presences contributed to the horror of all that followed. Rather than refusing to believe that Tee Bob's suicide was determined by forces beyond his control, she takes Jules at his word, saying in reply, "He was bound to kill himself anyhow? . . . Poor Tee Bob" (193). The concession is significant, because it signals her acquiescence to an alternative way of remembering the history she is attempting to retell—a way that defies not just the existing written evidence (Tee Bob's suicide letter) but also the realist contract of her narrative. Jules's account of the Tee Bob/Mary Agnes affair therefore disrupts historiographic conventions in a manner that critics typically align with antirealist or postmodern fictions of slavery, not with a novel like *Miss Jane Pittman*. Just as Dubey argues about post-1970s "speculative" slave narratives, Jules takes an "incredulous approach to history," suggesting the impossibility of objectively representing the past (Dubey 784). He does not attempt to add to the historical record, or even to correct it; instead, he underscores that every iteration of the story will change with the teller and that the "gospel truth" depends on, among other things, the race of who is listening (192). It is for this reason that Jules advocates his own analysis of Tee Bob's final moments. "Nobody told" him, and he was not a witness himself, he says, "but it happened" (191).

The knowledge that Jules proffers is, then, subjective and corporeal in the sense that it comes not from anything written or spoken about the past, but rather from his affective experience of it. This way of accessing history conforms to the "deliberately antihistoriographic method" that Dubey correlates with "the postmodern turn" in neo-slave narratives, because it prioritizes a "structure of feeling" over "secular rationality" as the means by which to "learn the truth." Relying on his imagination rather than objective facts to convey what has occurred, Jules's testimony "violates the realist protocols of history by . . . narrating a type of event—belonging to the order of the sacred or miraculous—that is typically excluded from the purview of historical evidence" (Dubey 785). Furthermore, the supernatural tone of his narration, and especially the suggestion that Tee Bob and Mary Agnes were possessed by the spirits of their ancestors, prefigures some of the "paranormal devices" common to the antirealist slave narrative, devices that involve "a dramatic foreshortening of the temporal distance between slavery and the present" (Dubey 786). Indeed, the reason Jules can be so certain that a spirit possession took place is his commitment to the notion that "a set of rules our people gave us long ago" dictated the terms of the couple's relationship and ultimately caused Tee Bob to take his own life. As a member of the white Creole elite, Jules understands as well as anyone how the racial strictures of slave culture persist in his own time, "condemning" love between "men like Robert" and "women like Mary Agnes" (191). He even insinuates that those who adhere to the prohibitions against interracial unions without challenging them—including Miss Jane and himself—share responsibility, along with the antebellum arbiters of these "rules," for the damage they have caused. And his depiction of ancestral spirits who haunt the present, guarding against the threat of transgression, makes explicit this connection.

When Mary Agnes became possessed—first by her "mulatto" grandmother and then by Verda, the slavewoman with whom Robert, Tee Bob's father, produced an illegitimate child—Jules says that she "knowed how she looked to him, but she couldn't do nothing about it" (192). He means that, suddenly, both she and Tee Bob were forced to confront the terrible truth that she was just as powerless to resist the advances of a white man as these older black women had been; in that moment, despite the years that have passed between slavery and the present day, Mary Agnes remains bound by antebellum conventions that determined how her ancestors lived. Therefore, just as Dubey claims postmodern slave narratives use paranormal devices to "make possible an unmediated relation to the past as something that has not quite passed into the realm of history," the spirit possession that Jules describes promotes a way of experiencing slavery "other than [as] the characteristically remote object of historical knowledge" (787). According to Jules, in the last minutes they spend together, Mary Agnes and Tee Bob do not only come to *understand* the situation of their forebears; they involuntarily *re-create* it, thus exposing the inexorability of the racism they each, by different means, have tried to "make up for" (156). It is this prevailing tone of immutability that distinguishes Jules's testimony from the rest of the novel and dislocates the progressive trajectory that critics almost uniformly assign to Jane's narration. Instead of reinforcing a straight line of racial progress from the Civil War to the present, his possession narrative signals a dramatically different temporal mode—one that circles back on itself, revealing the timelessness of the racist attitudes that sustained slavery.

The "circular and vacillating sense of time associated with slavery" is, of course, common in fiction that pointedly defies realism, driven by a postmodern suspicion about historical progress (Dubey 791). But here, in an otherwise realist text written prior to the antihistoriographical turn in neo-slave narratives, the distinctiveness of the Mary Agnes/Tee Bob vignette cannot be ascribed entirely—if at all—to postmodernism, since it signifies such a departure from Jane's established voice. More accurately, the supernatural quality of this section of the novel must be related to the character of the man who takes over the narration from Jane, imposing his alternative view of history on her and her audience. It is significant, then, that Jules represents a perspective far removed from Jane's. In addition to being upper class, white, and Creole, he is Catholic—a fact underscored by his identification as Tee Bob's "parrain" or godfather (145)—and, as such, would have been more accustomed than Jane to the theological notion of timelessness. According to Paul Giles, Catholics are indoctrinated into a worldview, based upon Aquinas's theology of an atemporal God, that supports the possibility of existing *outside* or *beyond* time. As a consequence of its analogical orientation, Thomist theology holds that "every historical existence simultaneously participates in primary spiritual essence," which reflects the continuous presence of a divine being (Giles 186). This is what renders Catholicism especially attentive—at least, when compared to Protestantism—to the "limitations of linear history" (ibid.). While "the Protestant principle" (in Paul Tillich's estimation) maintains a rigid separation between the temporal world and the world of the spirit, Catholic doctrine stresses the interpenetration of these two worlds, signaled by a recurring interruption of chronological time.[14] To say it another way: in Catholicism, all time is potentially *sacred*, because of God's radical, immutable immanence in human experience.

The tendency to sacralize time has been linked, by Giles and others, to the way some Catholic writers defy a linearly progressive temporality, endowing their characters "with a 'spiritual' substance that epitomizes a higher, 'divine' grace" which is timeless and eternal (187).[15] For Giles, this trend reveals itself even in ostensibly secular works—including those produced by Catholic apostates, who he claims "transform and secularize the impulses of Catholicism" into an "implicit" framework that structures their imagination (186).[16] Although Jules is a fictional character—whose account of the Mary Agnes/Tee Bob affair is, like everything else in the novel, a product of Gaines's imagination, not his own—Giles's argument offers a useful means for understanding how Catholicism informs the portion of the narrative conceded to him, and particularly the distinctive way he imagines history. In other words, since Gaines portrays Jules as author of his own fictional "text," his character's religious identity has bearing on the form and content of the testimony he provides, just as Jane's Protestantism has on hers. Moreover, what distinguishes each narrator's approach to the past can be traced to the fundamental theological divergence in the way that Protestants and Catholics typically interpret historical time—a divergence in which Gaines himself was, notably, well versed.

As he explained in a 1973 interview, Gaines was raised Protestant—having been "indoctrinated into" the Baptist faith—but attended Catholic schools for a number of years (Ingram and Steinberg 51). Therefore, despite his abandoning organized religion in adulthood, his personal experience provided him with theological training in both branches of Christianity as well as an awareness of the differences between them. And, as I have been suggesting, Gaines's attention to these differences plays out in the disruption that Jules causes in the novel when he takes over the narrative from Jane. Not only does the nonlinearity of Jules's account point toward a Catholic conception of timelessness, but the spiritual possessions that he describes—and Jane struggles to rationalize—are also more consistent with Catholicism than Protestantism. Peter Berger has argued that "the Catholic lives in a world in which the sacred is mediated to him through a variety of channels—the sacraments of the church, the intercession of the saints, the recurring eruption of the 'supernatural' in miracles—a vast continuity of being between the seen and unseen. Protestantism abolished most of these mediations" (112). While the distinction may be less absolute than Berger suggests (especially when considering Lutheran strains of Protestantism), his analysis correctly reflects the frequency with which spirits and other "supernatural" forces intercede in Catholicism. Consistent with church doctrine on the communion of saints, for example, Catholics are taught that they maintain spiritual connections with one another—and, in fact, with "all departed souls"—through a "vast network of intercession" that transcends worldly notions of life and death (Berger 111).

A consequence of this theology, according to scholars of the African diaspora, is that Catholicism syncretized more readily with African religions during the period of New World slavery than did Protestantism. Albert Raboteau, for one, points out that the "nature . . . of Catholic piety . . . offered a supportive context for the continuity of African religious elements in recognizable form," in contrast with American evangelical Protestantism, which he claims "was not as conducive to syncretism" (88). This argument gained momentum and significant expansion in Leslie Desmangles's 1992 study of Haitian Vodou, a religion that though "West African in form" has "borrowed much from Roman Catholicism" (3). Specifically, Desmangles documents the "Voudisants' penchant for identifying" each of their pantheon of invisible spirits, or *lwa*, with a Catholic saint (123). Such an identification is possible because the *lwa*, like the saints in Catholicism, were real historical figures who, after death, continue to "direct the physical operation of the universe" (92). Therefore, at their ceremonies and in their homes, Voudisants use images of these saints—lithographs, statues, and other kinds of religious iconography—to signify their own ancestral spirits, who they believe are able to "manifest themselves in matter or in the possessed body of a devotee" (93).

Although the version of Vodou that developed in antebellum Louisiana does not correspond exactly to the form that arose in Haiti, it is also based on "similarities between African and Catholic myths and symbols," including the identification of ancestral spirits with saints (Desmangles 10). This syncretism, or "symbiosis" in Desmangles's terminology, is something Gaines highlights in his novel, when Jane describes the interior of Madame Gautier's house—the room where she takes those who come to her "for special business":

> She had candles burning in every corner of the room, and she had seven on the mantelpiece. She had another candle burning under a little statue on a little table by the window. She had Saint pictures hanging on the wall with crepe paper round each picture. (92)

As a hoo-doo and onetime rival of the famous Voodoo Queen, Marie Laveau, Madame Gautier signals the particular way that Catholic theology was assimilated into African traditions and rituals in Louisiana. Her appearance in the text thus establishes Jane's awareness of the relationship between Catholicism and hoo-doo culture. Moreover, the uneasiness Jane feels sitting in Madame Gautier's home, among the sacred icons and pictures of saints, implies that—in spite of her tendency toward rationalization—Jane cannot help being "a little scared" by what she sees. After all, like everyone in the community, she has heard the "talk" about hoo-doos whose religion enables them to communicate with the spirit world and defy the limits of physical death. So it is not until Madame Gautier puts a log on her fire—proving that "she can get cold just like anybody else" (92)—that Jane relaxes and remembers she does not believe in the power of the objects displayed in the room; she does not believe, as both the Catholics and hoo-doos would have it, that saints/ancestral spirits populate the material world, intervening in human affairs.

In this way, then, Jane's visit to Madame Gautier's house anticipates how Jules's account of supernatural possession will disrupt her narrative in the next section of the novel. Though there is no reason to consider Jules a practitioner of hoo-doo—or even someone who subscribes to its tenets—his Catholicism links him, by virtue of its textual association with African-derived traditions, to a similar conception of ancestral return. In other words, by the time Jules takes over the narration from Jane, Gaines has already affirmed a connection between Catholicism and hoo-doo which both explains and provides context for the alternative history that he articulates. The Catholic Church does not officially sanction the idea of spirit possession.[17] And yet, within the cultural matrix of the novel, the religion cannot be divorced from other spiritual systems that do, since characters who practice Catholicism—or are otherwise identified with its signs and symbols—reveal a simultaneous, and seemingly noncontradictory, affinity for hoo-doo as well. Remarkably, the same holds for black "Catholics," like Madame Gautier, as for white "Catholics," such as the family of Albert Cluveau. Both Cluveau and his daughter Adeline, who was raised in the church and strictly adheres to its doctrines, exhibit a fear of "curses" that Jane calls "simple-minded" (121). This suggests that, despite being even less familiar with hoo-doo culture than Jane, their Catholicism inclines them to believe more readily in the power of spirits to possess and control humans.

Clearly, Jules shares the same inclination, a *supernatural* inclination that I am arguing Gaines associates exclusively with his Catholic characters. The association is significant because it creates a space in the narrative to challenge Jane's rationalizing impulse—but to do so without abandoning a formal commitment to realism. By displacing belief in spirit possession onto Catholics in this way, Gaines effectively maintains the realist properties of the novel (including its progressive temporality) while at the same time giving voice to a decidedly *anti*realist view of history characteristic of postmodernism. Even though Jane expresses skepticism and doubt about the potential for spiritual intercession which the text links to Catholicism, these perspectives still intrude on her narration, calling into question her ability to rationalize them. Therefore, when Jules takes over the narrative and contends that Mary Agnes and Tee Bob were possessed by the spirits of their ancestors, he is not only articulating a distinct theological position but also offering another means to approach the past that Jane is attempting to recover—one not determined by the conventions of literary realism. The intrusion of his voice thus exposes the possibility of remembering differently, according to a set of principles that resist the prevailing tenor of her story.

The fact that the novel can entertain both approaches simultaneously, counterbalancing the linearity of Jane's historiography with a sense of timelessness indicative of Catholicism, is an effect of Gaines's framing device and the way he imagines "folk" history to translate in writing. In his essay "Miss Jane and I," Gaines indicates that he originally planned for the book to have multiple narrators, who would trade memories about the title character on the day of her death, based upon their individual experiences with her and from their unique viewpoints. Presumably this technique of narrating Jane's life would have created even more opportunities to explore alternative modes of telling that, like Jules's account, incorporate a variety of temporal perspectives, since the different narrators all spoke "in their own way." After a year of writing, however, Gaines discarded the polyvocal structure, opting "to tell the story from a single voice—Miss Jane's own" because the "others were making her life too complicated in that they had too many opinions, bringing in too many anecdotes"; he "thought a single voice, Miss Jane's, would keep the story in a straight line" (618). Gaines's choice of the words "a straight line" here is noteworthy because it implies that the transition from multiple narrators to one (and from a fictional work tentatively titled *A Short Biography of Miss Jane* to *The Autobiography*) contributed to the progressive trajectory that critics have identified with the novel. Dispensing with others' opinions and anecdotes, he suggests, helped move the narrative forward chronologically, as Jane—alone—took control of the telling. And yet, Claudine Raynaud importantly points out, the process of "giving up the 'authorship'" that had been originally "bestowed upon" multiple characters is not as seamless as Gaines would have it, for the introduction makes clear that the diverse perspectives of would-be conarrators are still present in the novel, even when they have been completely effaced by the voice of the "'I' narrator" (447). Thus, as Gaines himself has written, "Miss Jane . . . is not any one person"; at any point, her narration represents a community of people, each of whom remembers history from a different point of view ("Miss Jane" 618).

Owing to this logic, and despite the "straight line" temporality its primary narrator favors, the novel is capable of accommodating various historiographical approaches—including what I (following Dubey) have called Jules's *anti*historiographical approach—whenever a new character takes possession of the narrative. By acknowledging that "there were times when others carried the story for her" (ix), Gaines's introduction efficiently accounts for the disruption that such distinct ways of remembering cause, all the while foregrounding Jane's historical memory as the principal mode of the text. The framing device therefore provides a convenient, formal explanation for internal inconsistencies in how the novel describes the past: any deviations from its realist orientation can be blamed on characters, such as Jules, who speak from a subject position far removed from Jane's own—in his case, a subject position determined by Catholicism. It is worth noting, though, that however much this narrative structure supports the novel's claims of realism, it also, somewhat paradoxically, corroborates the decidedly *anti*realist claims that Jules's account puts forth. In other words, the very idea that other voices haunt Jane's narration, determining what she says, resonates with how Jules remembers Mary Agnes and Tee Bob as well as his description of their final moments together.

As I have already suggested, the speakers who intrude on Jane's story do so in a clandestine and mystifying way that evokes spirit possession. Because her transcriber withholds both the names of these additional narrators and their precise contributions to the narrative, the authorship of her words is always in question. At any point, another character—be it the "old man called Pap" who "was her main source" or any of the "other people at the house every day" during the interviews (viii)—could be speaking through Jane, in the voice identified as her own. This renders her subjectivity as unstable as Mary Agnes's or Tee Bob's in the scene that Jules describes, since throughout the text she is not just herself but also always potentially someone else. Even though the figures that take over the testimony are not spirits in the traditional sense (they are portrayed by the transcriber as living people, friends of Jane's, who gladly helped her remember what she had forgotten), their effect on the narration is similarly haunting. Indeed, like the ancestral spirits who possess Mary Agnes and Tee Bob, the ghostly presence of these conarrators problematizes Jane's narrative authority to the extent that her "individual experience intersects with collective experience," so that it becomes impossible to distinguish one from the other. The "intersubjectivity" that this formal structure promotes is, as Ashraf Rushdy has shown, a feature of texts that use the trope of spirit possession to emphasize the "mutuality" of storytelling—the sense that speaking about one's past is a "community enterprise," rather than an individual endeavor (126).

For the antirealist neo-slave narratives Rushdy refers to, then, spirit possession serves to disrupt the idea, implicit in historical realism, that there is a single, primary and objective account of *what actually happened*. This is what constitutes "the HooDoo aesthetic," as Ishmael Reed first defined it: a prevailing sense that the subject speaking about the past is "intimately at one with others in his or her community" (127).[18] Given her reluctance to associate, on any level, with the principles of hoo-doo, Jane's character would undeniably reject the suggestion that her testimony has anything supernatural about it. And yet, by creating space in her narrative to voice Jules's (Catholic) version of history, Gaines manages to incorporate these alternative viewpoints into an otherwise realist novel.

II. Inscrutability and Catholicism

Published thirteen years after *The Autobiography of Miss Jane Pittman* and well into the period Madhu Dubey correlates to the postmodernist turn in fiction about slavery, the novel I consider next has all but abandoned the realist pretense of historical recovery that features so prominently in Gaines's writing. Leon Forrest's *Two Wings to Veil My Face* is famously (perhaps *in*famously)[19] complex: a work, like all of his fiction, that resolutely undermines the possibility of accurately representing the past. For that reason, critics often cite it as an example of the later wave of contemporary narratives of slavery that involve alternative ways of remembering history and challenge modern historiographical methods by means of supernatural devices, such as the trope of spirit possession. Indeed, Forrest appears to embrace the trope much more thoroughly than Gaines ever did, effectively using it to suggest that no single voice has the authority to state unequivocally the truth of what occurred. Within a postmodern context, in which truth claims are relentlessly and purposefully called into question, the indeterminacy occasioned by spirit possession is entirely acceptable: the sort of feature readers might even expect from a novel that seems intent on disrupting historical realism at every turn.

And so, because of its overtly postmodernist structure, *Two Wings* does not couch its narratological investment in the trope of spirit possession within the framework of Catholicism as Gaines does in his novel. In fact, it does not couch it at all. Rather, Forrest's novel takes as its starting point what Rushdy calls a "Hoo-Doo aesthetic," and reveals no obligation to explain or to justify in any way the supernatural content of its narration. Yet, as I will show, *Two Wings* still persistently links spirit possession to Catholicism, implying a fundamental connection between the two. That connection gets expressed in terms of a desire for coherence, as the novel's protagonist, Nathaniel Witherspoon, seeks to make sense of his family's inscrutable history. To Nathaniel, who struggles for most of the narrative *against* the very indeterminancy that the trope of spirit possession enacts, accepting his own lack of historical authority amounts to having faith in the "mystery and miracle" of the Catholic Mass. Therefore, I argue, for him and for the novel as a whole, Catholicism comes to stand for the inability ever to know the truth about the past and—more important, even—his ultimate acceptance of that inability.

. . .

Like *Miss Jane Pittman*, and so many other contemporary slave narratives, *Two Wings* frames its historiography as oral testimony: a story told by an elderly African American character to a member of the younger generation, who has been tasked (for one reason or another) with preserving those memories in written form. In this case the listener/transcriber is Nathaniel Witherspoon and it is his ninety-one-year-old grandmother, Sweetie Reed, to whom he appeals in 1958 for knowledge of the past. Specifically, Nathaniel wants to know why Sweetie chose not to attend the funeral of her husband Jericho fourteen years earlier, a question she promised to address when Nathaniel came of age. The answer, though, which takes the entire novel to unfold, involves more than just Sweetie's experience alone; among others, it includes that of her father, I. V. Reed, whose story she also relates, in the voice that I. V. himself used when making his deathbed confession. I. V.'s first-person account of slavery and emancipation, in fact, takes up nearly half of the book's total pages, threatening to eclipse the main purpose of Sweetie's narrative.

Just as in *Miss Jane Pittman*, the narrator's testimony gets interrupted and displaced by alternate speakers who take over the telling, preventing her—temporarily, at least—from achieving the kind of straightforward, *straight line* resolution that the audience expects. What Nathaniel seeks from his grandmother is "some order over my disorder," a means of addressing that part of his family history that has always been left out, so that he might look upon his own life with more clarity and understanding (250). As a child, he noticed that the stories he heard at home were different from the lessons he was taught at school. Unlike learning the ABCs, when "you went from A to B to C" according to a prescribed formula and in sequence, he was frustrated to find that when his family talked about the past, they "often went from A to C to E" instead (11). Nathaniel's expectations, then, for the narrative Sweetie tells him once he has finally reached "his majority," point toward the closing of those gaps of knowledge. He desires a full and sequential accounting of everything that was previously withheld. This is the promise of the novel and—by extension—the promise of realist historiography more generally, especially with regard to the theme of historical recovery. The other voices that take possession of Sweetie's narration, therefore, like those that take possession of Jane's, disrupt the history that Nathaniel wants to recover, calling into question her authority to represent accurately what has occurred.

But whereas in *Miss Jane Pittman* the narrator regains at least some control over these disruptions, ultimately taking back her story from any speaker with whom she does not agree, the same cannot be said for Sweetie. Indeed, no single voice or way of remembering the past predominates in *Two Wings* as it does in Gaines's novel. Sweetie's perspective is relentlessly undermined by I. V. and others who dispute the accuracy of her memory, casting doubt upon every detail she recounts, even the most seemingly objective ones, such as the identity of an individual in a photograph. By the time the testimony concludes, Nathaniel feels uncertain what—or whom—to believe, saying to his grandmother, "I never said you were a liar. But you do have a fabulous imagination" (271). His tendency to question the truthfulness of Sweetie's narrative reflects what Keith Byerman has called its "multivoiced character" and underscores the inherent difficulty of the novel. Because every voice that takes over the telling "is self-critical and also challenged by other voices about its veracity and interests in the narrating process," it becomes impossible to know *what really happened* with any degree of confidence. Instead, like Nathaniel, readers must confront a past that "is not a finished product of agreed-upon data but a struggle for coherence in a field of competing . . . desires that constantly shape and reshape the story" (Byerman 139).

On account of the intrusion of so many contending perspectives, the view of history offered in *Two Wings* is far more consistent with the antihistoriographical tenor of postmodernism than with the realist historiography that Nathaniel looks to his grandmother to provide. Of course, this would be expected, given its overtly postmodernist orientation. The disjointed, hybrid quality of its narrative—the way it shifts between not only discordant voices but also a variety of conflicting genres (diary entries and newspaper articles, for example) as means of accessing the past—emphasizes the radical contingency of all knowledge. This places *Two Wings* among a host of post-1970s slave narratives, and postmodernist literature in general, which resolutely deny the possibility of objectively representing historical truth. According to A. Timothy Spaulding, the discourse of postmodernism and the critique of realism that it supported were "potentially useful" for African American writers who sought to deconstruct essentialized, univocal notions of "*the*" black experience (13). In the wake of the important strides made by the first wave of neo-slave narratives to recover a lost history of slavery, authors such as Forrest turned their attention to destabilizing historiographical methods more generally— particularly the idea, implicit in Enlightenment thinking, that there can be just one "absolute and objective" record of what happened (Spaulding 13). Thus, as Byerman points out, the complex method of storytelling that Forrest developed in *Two Wings* implies that the past is most accurately represented not by a single authority but rather "a profusion of speakers, each with his/her own master narrative" (138). The fact that these master narratives pointedly contradict one another only contributes to the sense, foregrounded in the novel, that history itself is multidirectional and multivoiced.

Having abandoned the straight-line historiography that Gaines used in favor of a postmodernist approach, Forrest refrains from explaining or smoothing out its many contradictions. Indeed, those contradictions and inconsistencies are an integral part of the narrative—something that he purposefully incorporates to convey the complexity of the story Sweetie is attempting to tell. The trope of possession, therefore, serves a noticeably different function for *Two Wings* than it does for *Miss Jane Pittman*. In the introduction to the earlier novel, Gaines's transcriber laments that he "could not tie all the ends together in one neat direction," as he had hoped, because of the various characters who take over the telling from Jane (x). The haunting presence of a community of conarrators, as I have argued, provides justification for those—rare—moments of transgression, when the narration deviates from the tenets of literary realism. Despite the pronounced supernatural associations of the possession trope, it nevertheless works within the realist framework of the novel to bolster Jane's credibility and to account for the other less realistic (and often recognizably Catholic) voices that intrude on her "autobiography." In *Two Wings*, however, being possessed does not render Sweetie's narrative more believable; nor does it promote her way of remembering the past over conflicting interpretations from alternate narrators. Rather, as Forrest deploys it, the trope of possession plainly defies realism at every turn, "amplifying" the "antihistoriographic impulse" of his text, in terms consistent with its postmodernist orientation (Dubey, "Speculative" 789).

The primary reason that possession affects the narrative structure of *Two Wings* so differently than it does *Miss Jane Pittman* is that the ghostly presences haunting Sweetie's story are *actually* ghosts, as opposed to living characters. They are the "spirits of those lost souls and the dead brought to life" through her words (286). As Nathaniel explains, when Sweetie tells her personal experience, her memories are possessed by ancestral figures who "emerge from the steam in the room out of the power of . . . storytelling" (7). This way of understanding possession—as a supernatural phenomenon by which long-dead people communicate freely with those still alive—is responsible for much of the novel's complexity, including its deliberate obfuscation of historical truth. For the spirits that haunt Sweetie do not "speak with one voice" (7) about the past; they argue among themselves and with Sweetie to the point that no single one inspires trust above the others. What Nathaniel contends with, then, in the face of all Sweetie's spiritual interlopers is a polyphonic, revisionist family history that recalls how Brian McHale has defined postmodernist historical fiction—especially its propensity to "juxtapose the officially-accepted version of what happened and the way things were, with another, often radically dissimilar version of the world" (90). Moreover, the fantastic nature of the voices possessing Sweetie further "exacerbates the ontological hesitation" between "the supernatural and the historically *real*" that McHale also aligns with postmodernism (95).

In fact, as a number of critics have been quick to point out: when deployed narratologically as a strategy for blurring the line that distinguishes historical truth from fiction, the trope of possession is a quintessentially postmodernist device,[20] not only "integrating history and the fantastic" but also dramatically revising the standard means—chronological and progressive—by which that history is traditionally conveyed (McHale 90). These are the literary features that we come to expect from postmodernist texts; accordingly, in *Two Wings*, these features do not involve the same degree of contextualization and rationalization that a realist historiography such as *Miss Jane Pittman* obliges. Thus when Sweetie intones that "*then* is always *now* in my heart" (270), she is calling attention to the way her narrative vacillates between the past and the present, as she herself—and the voices emerging from her story—remain suspended in a timeless space, where history has not yet been relegated to the *already passed*. Unlike Gaines's narrator, then, Sweetie takes for granted both the presence of ancestral spirits and their ability to affect how her testimony translates to its audience. There is no attempt on her part to deny or otherwise distance herself from the supernatural content of her narration—this despite being Protestant, just as Jane Pittman is, and therefore theologically predisposed against the idea of communication between the living and the dead.

In the fictional world of *Two Wings*, and really in all of Forrest's fiction, though, one's denominational affiliation does not determine the extent of one's supernatural beliefs. Most of the characters—Protestants, Catholics, and non-Christians alike—accept without question that they live among the spirits of their dead ancestors and that "lost souls" are capable of interceding in their affairs. According to Danille Taylor-Guthrie, this is due to "the cultural context from which the ideas and aesthetics of the novel are derived" and, specifically, the multidimensionality of the "African-American spiritual culture" depicted therein. She demonstrates that, given how many different religions and religious denominations Forrest incorporates into his work, the characters have an expansive range of "rituals and theology" from which to choose (or not choose) and that even the Christian faiths they subscribe to "are not monolithic" (219). For example, Nathaniel was baptized and confirmed in Catholicism, yet his personal beliefs as well as the prayer he makes at the end of the novel reflect the impact of Protestantism. (The prayer is, as Taylor-Guthrie suggests, modeled on the style of testifying that he used to hear in the Protestant church that he attended as a child with his father's side of the family.) Likewise, Auntie Foisty, a roots worker and spiritual healer who learned her craft in Africa before being captured and enslaved in the United States, converts to Christianity—but successfully interweaves components of her adopted theology with traditional practice.[21] Stories of religious boundary-crossings such as these proliferate in *Two Wings*, implying that for all of the attention Forrest devotes to precise theological imagery and expression, religion itself is in a constant state of flux, as characters adapt a prescribed set of beliefs to their own immediate needs.

Nowhere is the fluidity of religious belief more apparent—or more humorously conveyed—than in the argument between Sweetie and her father regarding how to interpret Auntie Foisty's "resurrection" of Master Rollins from death. Contending that Foisty "had only healed up enough of Rollins Reed so as his soul would not come unraveling out of his crawling condition" (148), Sweetie asserts that the old roots worker used the resurrected body of their master to curse I. V. for the "balance of [his] days." I. V. clearly objects to the suggestion that he has been cursed, telling his daughter:

> Commandment says out plain as salt through a widow woman, honor thy father and thy mother; and you suspose to be a Christian, 'bout as much one as old persecuting Saul. If only I had a rod, I would reel your spoilt body in till spilt blood racked your hide as drops of rain-salt cross a bee-bit back; sure would be sweetmeat to my good eyes to learn you some humility. (149)

The "leaps of faith" that make it possible for I. V. to defend his view of Reed's rebirth while reprimanding Sweetie according to an Old Testament conception of moral law are mind-boggling indeed—particularly because it is all in the service of proving that his master really was brought back to life by an Africanist healer. To a perverse and utterly absurd degree, I. V.'s tirade highlights the way that Forrest's characters negotiate different belief systems, seemingly without acknowledging any conflict between them. And although Sweetie later criticizes her father for using "the Good Book to hide behind" (159), when he in fact has never adhered to other tenets of Christianity, she reveals an equivalent tendency to make religion her own. After all, in spite of a deep personal faith and historical commitment to ministering at "camp meetings and revivals" (45), Sweetie long ago abandoned organized worship within the Protestant church, when it started to conflict with her social justice agenda. Instead, as Nathaniel says, she developed a unique kind of "mission" that does not correspond to any established doctrine, but rather honors her private "covenant . . . with Almighty God" to "re-create a miracle" for the world's poor (46).

Because of their individualized and highly adaptable approaches to religion, Sweetie and I. V. might be said to fit Philippa Berry's definition of a "post-religious" *flâneuse* or *flâneur*: someone who, on account of "extremely fragile" and "porous" cultural boundaries, moves "intelligently amid . . . contrasting systems of meaning" to foster an "uncanny *coexistence*" among them (177). Admittedly, Berry's definition depends on an ethical imperative that neither Sweetie nor—clearly—I. V. is motivated by. (Berry believes the post-religious *flâneuse* or *flâneur* represents our best chance to unravel the "potent aporias within western thought" responsible for sectarian conflict [177].) And yet her analysis confirms how acceptable it has become, given "the extreme commodification of the religious impulse" which characterizes postmodernism, for individuals to customize a spiritual identity, if not an entire religion, according to their own (changeable) interests (172). As a journalist quoted by Berry observes, within a postmodern cultural context, many people

> have moved away from "religion" as something anchored in organized worship and systematic beliefs within an institution, to a self-made "spirituality," outside formal structures, which is based on experience, has no doctrine and makes no claim to philosophical coherence.[22]

Thus Forrest's characters exhibit a religious indeterminancy that is symptomatic of the postmodern spiritual condition—what Berry has termed "post-religion."[23] The novel in fact reads as a pastiche of holy texts: along with the prayer Nathaniel makes at its end, there are entire chapters devoted to meandering church sermons, as well as fragments of hymns and devotional poetry scattered throughout. But rather than reinforcing the specific religious content of each individual fragment, the effect of this proliferation—as with all postmodernist pastiche, according to Fredric Jameson—is to create "a field of stylistic and discursive heterogeneity without a norm" (17). To say it another way, the sheer number of religions alluded to in the narrative threatens to strip every belief system of its unique value, reducing it to something Jameson refers to as "blank parody" or a random act of semantic play. We see this especially in the sermons that comprise two chapters of the novel. These ostensibly Protestant expressions of faith are imbricated with so many religious discourses and modes of allusion—both sacred and secular—that they supplant the very tenets of the religion they were intended to uphold, rendering the sermonic form itself little more than a repository of other styles. The first, Reverend Browne's, transforms into a political call-to-action that celebrates how a declared nonbeliever (Jericho Witherspoon) imagined God. The second, Sweetie's, contains a sweeping and intimate description of an encounter with the spirit of her deceased husband which recalls, at turns, the Catholic sacrament of confession, a baptism in the Baptist tradition, and the way an "African ontological system" understands the "proximity of the dead to the living" (Taylor-Guthrie 231).

Within the novel's cultural system, then, just as religion is something that can be molded to fit an individual's personal desires, so too are its formal discourses. This is, of course, not an aesthetic technique confined to postmodernism. As Sacvan Bercovitch has persuasively demonstrated, American authors from the colonial period through the Civil War manipulated a sermonic form, the jeremiad, for a wide range of purposes, many of them secular in nature. But what is striking—as well as particularly postmodern—about how Forrest deploys the religious discourses that appear in *Two Wings* is the diversity of belief systems they represent. It is a diversity that corresponds, perhaps not surprisingly, to Forrest's own experience of religion and to the feeling he had as a child of being "divided between" faith traditions (Cawelti 24). For although he was raised Catholic by his mother and trained in the catechism of the church, he denies ever becoming "sufficiently indoctrinated" as some of his family members were, because of all the other, often competing, influences in his life (Warren 45). Most palpably, there were the "regular weekends" he spent "with the Protestant side" of his family, when he read the Old Testament to his great-grandmother and "became very interested . . . in the thrust of negro spirituals and gospel music and the great sermons" that he witnessed at Chicago's Pilgrim Baptist Church (Cawelti 24). As he told an interviewer in 1992, his religious heritage was "so splintered" by the divisions among the denominations of Christianity—and "all kinds of other divisions within divisions"—that he never developed a coherent spirituality (Warren 44–45).

Initially, when he started writing fiction centered on the African American family, Forrest admits this lack of coherence stymied him, and he that worried about how to draw from a personal background that seemed, given all its spiritual and cultural dissonance, "rather chaotic" (Cawelti 24). Of particular difficulty, Forrest has explained, was the fact that "the Catholic church at that time seemed to be so far from the ethos of African Americans," who, prior to Vatican II, were still officially subject to racial segregation and other sanctioned forms of discrimination by clergy.[24] It was not until "reading Joyce and also later reading the Latin American writers," he says, that he found a "certain confidence in using the Catholic experience" in his work, a way to write "out of it with a certain strength and robustness" (Warren 44–45). The significance of this statement, with regard to how Forrest crafted his approach to Catholicism, is that it foregrounds the *literary*, rather than the theological or doctrinal. Thus he came to perceive the religion he was born into as a set of aesthetic practices and formal techniques that could be incorporated, discursively, into his fiction—a point that he elaborates in the following passage discussing what he gained from his family's "two heritages":

> From the Catholic side, I was always attracted to the ritual . . . and to the grandness of the tradition, the concept of original sin and the secret self of confession. Maybe that's where my interior monologues come from. . . . It was the Baptists, on the Protestant side, that made me aware of eloquence as a form, not only a protest, but as it evoked the anguish and the celebration of black life on a larger stage. It wasn't writers, because after all, when I was coming along, there weren't that many well-known African American writers. . . . It was the eloquence of these great public speakers, mainly preachers, . . .

that shaped me. It made me want to try to do something in a grand manner, in the grand style. (Cawelti 24)

Forrest indicates, then, that just like any other literary device, the Catholic confession or the Baptist sermon provides form for the aspects of black life he wants to articulate. And the literariness of these religious structures is only compounded by their fluid juxtaposition in the text with elements from diverse cultural sources: other religions, as we have seen, but also canonical works of literature, such as *Macbeth* and Blake's "The Lamb," in addition to contemporary music and art.[25]

What emerges from the "discursive *bricolage*" of *Two Wings* is the sense that all religious experience—indeed, experience of any sort—can be appropriated linguistically, without a cohesive "spiritual agenda" (Berry 172). The trope of spirit possession, which structures Sweetie's narrative and accounts for much of its supernaturalism, does not necessarily signal the beliefs of a distinct cultural group (like the Creoles and the Cajuns in *Miss Jane Pittman*), nor is it relegated to the novel's periphery. Assorted characters, regardless of denominational affiliation, regularly refer to the way their "souls" are "possessed" by ghosts of the dead. In some cases, these possessions are acrimonious: a kind of retaliatory gesture meant to avenge a grievous injustice. This is how both I. V. and the wife of his master, Mistress Sylvia, describe their relationship with the spirit world. They regard the ghosts who haunt them as recompense for the advantages taken during slavery. Claiming that "I am possessed by niggers . . . solely by niggers my soul is owned," Sylvia blames the countless Africans on whose bodies her fortune was made for eventually bringing her to the brink of poverty and powerlessness on the eve of the Civil War (66). Likewise, I. V. believes that he suffers all sorts of indignities because the spirit of Reece Haywood visits nightly to punish him for turning his back on a fellow slave and for indirectly causing his death. (Not only did I. V. instigate the confrontation between Reece and Master Rollins, but he also threw a rock at Reece to prevent him from killing their master, thus ensuring his capture.) The idea that a formerly *dis*possessed person—a slave—would return, after dying, to impose his will on a living body can be interpreted as an act of resistance against the deplorable conditions of slavery. It is in these terms that scholars such as Colin Dayan and Michel Saturnin Laguerre have described the "political" thrust of spirit possession, pointing out how for many cultures being possessed is as much "a symbolic reaction against a dependent societal status" as it is a religious event (Laguerre 232).

Along similar lines, although Nathaniel himself is far removed from the material conditions of enslavement, his experience of possession reflects less his particular theological orientation than his need to reckon with an unsettled past. Ever since he was a boy, Nathaniel "knew that he would always be haunted by the memory and presence" of his grandfather (28), both because of the stories about his daring escape from slavery and because of the mystery surrounding his relationship with Sweetie. He regards Jericho as a force who, like so many of his dead ancestors, will forever "be with the family in spirit, power and voice" as they struggle to make sense of their history (6). When these ancestral spirits come to possess Nathaniel, though, it is not the result of some sacred ceremony with a prescribed set of ritualistic practices, but rather through the art of Sweetie's storytelling: a fundamentally secular undertaking, occasioned by Nathaniel's desire to learn about his past. For all of these reasons, then, spirit possession as Forrest depicts it in *Two Wings* transcends both its religious and cultural associations, suggesting a means of remembering and accounting for history that is not defined by any single theology or set of beliefs. And yet, despite being theologically unmoored, the trope is still—quite remarkably—linked to Catholicism in ways that have profound implications for the meaning Nathaniel draws from the stories Sweetie tells him.

The link between Catholicism and spirit possession first appears in the opening passage of the novel, as Nathaniel recalls listening to his grandmother's stories when he was a child eating in her kitchen. Back then, the steam from the food she had prepared days earlier and then wrapped in warming sleeves

> opened him up to Great-Momma Sweetie Reed's storytelling powers and recollecting of leftovers to be remade once again by the boy when Great-Momma Sweetie unveiled the last of the sleeves and his imagination produced a vision of preserved mummies sliding forth (perhaps because of the thinning, see-through condition of the warm-up jackets) as if to play a joke on himself, but instead (as always) a bevy of life-giving celebrants of bread emerged almost bursting with life, not crumbling (4)

The "vision" of dead bodies (mummies) baked into bread and then transforming into "life-giving celebrants" under the "powers" of Sweetie's voice is one distinctly reminiscent of the Catholic Mass—an event that Nathaniel had witnessed countless times during his service as an acolyte. In fact, in his imagination, his grandmother and the priests he served at church were performing equivalent acts: both using their words and their memory to call forth figures from a past that was otherwise inaccessible to him. Therefore, he thought of "the mystery of the water and the wine, and the bread and the wine that mysteriously took the place of Jesus Christ's body and blood" whenever Sweetie spoke about their family history (9). And he imagined the leftover food she gave him as a kind of Eucharist, which he chewed and absorbed faithfully in spite of its "decaying smell," hoping to satiate his desire for knowledge (10).

For young Nathaniel, a boy trying desperately to decode the adult world, there was little to distinguish the "wonders and mysteries" of his grandmother's storytelling from "what they said at Mass" (10, 9). Sweetie's words were often just as inscrutable to him as the Latin the priests spoke while pouring wine into the chalice in preparation for Holy Communion. Even with the English translations that his Aunt DuDora would whisper into his ear during the consecration ritual, Nathaniel believed those prayers were "beyond his powers of understanding," because they purported to accomplish something "so bedeviling" and "overpowering" that it defied rational explanation. Indeed, to him, the mystery of the Mass—and the miracle of Jesus being made present again—was a direct result of this verbal dissonance, a direct result of the impenetrable language he heard recited over the gifts. Because it was in the midst of the estranging yet "beautiful prayer the priest prayed, at the Epistle side of the altar," that DuDora said the divine spirit of Christ "deigned to become partaker of our humanity" through the Eucharistic sacrament (9). Thus, from an early age, Nathaniel learned to associate his experience of linguistic incomprehension with the promise of a "wondrous" possession. And so Catholicism provided him with a mechanism to explain what he tasted and felt in Sweetie's kitchen, as he gulped down her leftovers "along with what she said about the strange, nourishing beginning times" (10). He came to regard his struggle to understand his grandmother in sacramental terms, since—like the priests whom he served at church—the inscrutability of her voice indicated the presence of "the dead brought back to life" (286).

It was at the times Sweetie's stories were most confusing and difficult to follow that Nathaniel took to imagining them as "Catholic mysteries." For in those moments, when her words became incomprehensible to him, he witnessed the emergence of ghostly spirits: lost souls from slave times, who suddenly appeared where they had not been before—in "all of the parts of her stories that Great-Momma Sweetie Reed always left out, even as she added to her stories inside of stories" (10). Just as Jesus was said to reveal himself at Mass through the priests' mysterious mediation, so too did Nathaniel relate the halting and mystifying way his grandmother spoke to the appearance of all these forms of "dead life" that surrounded him in her kitchen. In his mind, then, there developed an indelible connection between "the mystery of history" revealed through the spirits that possessed Sweetie's storytelling and the mystery of Christ's sacramental revelation (9).

When he was a child, this connection brought him comfort, because it was premised on the existence of a supernatural truth that was both absolute and eternal. In other words, Nathaniel *had faith* that out of the obscurity of his grandmother's language he would ultimately be granted full knowledge of his past. This was, for him, akin to believing in the miracle of the Eucharistic sacrament—that when he was old enough to receive his First Holy Communion, his body would "feel new and wondrous" as the meaning of the sacrament finally became clear. Significantly, though, by the time the novel begins, Nathaniel has rejected this childish association, agreeing with his Uncle Hampton that "Colored Catholic mysteries of the Mass only add to the mystery of our History" (10). Hampton had always been skeptical of Nathaniel's tendency to apply what he learned from the catechism and from Aunt DuDora to his own family's experience, warning that Catholicism would make the boy "more mucked up than . . . those Creoles" (10). He was implying, of course, that given the historic racism of the Catholic Church, Nathaniel should avoid using its doctrines as a means of understanding a past that was already hopelessly out of reach. Better, Hampton cautioned his nephew, to study Frederick Douglass and the verifiable "wonders" of his story than to seek truth from an institution that had systematically threatened and abused its black congregants. The warning has obviously stayed with Nathaniel, since in adulthood his reverence for Catholic mysteries has diminished. Now, in the novel's present, when he listens to his grandmother's storytelling, he thinks "yes, give me Frederick Douglass," instead of the sacraments of his youth (10). If his conscious thoughts turn to Catholicism at all, it is to recall the "guilt and fear" priests made him feel about his burgeoning sexuality (82), or that time white Catholics burned down their own cathedral "rather than see it be turned over to the coloreds" (65).

Thus the young man we meet at the start of *Two Wings* is highly attuned to the social and theological inconsistencies encountered in his boyhood experience with Catholicism. He laughs, from both shame and bemusement, at the way he for many years "stubbornly held to this idea," inspired by the Catholic Mass, that Sweetie's "special gift of entering another world of hearing and seeing" was bestowed on her by God (6). Given how his grandmother has broken from organized religion, imagining her stories as sacraments now seems ridiculous to him—made all the more so when she reminds him, "I'm not Catholic" (250). Accordingly, in preparing to receive her answer to the question about his grandfather that occasions the novel, Nathaniel takes a classically rationalist approach, which establishes his ambivalence toward Catholicism and the doctrine of theological mysteries that undergirds it. Rather than faithfully accepting as he did as a child that supernatural truths are beyond human reason, he vows to record everything Sweetie tells him in longhand on a pad of yellow legal paper, in order "to bring all of the recollections together" in a way that will finally unlock their meaning (7). His quest for historical knowledge is therefore coextensive with his turn *away* from Catholicism, since Catholic theology, for him, signifies an inscrutability that, having reached "his majority," he is no longer willing to abide.

Nathaniel's determination to capture his grandmother's words in writing arises from a desire to make sense of what seemed insensible to him as a child. As he remarks to her near the end of the novel, just before she reveals to him why exactly she became estranged from Jericho: "it's not for the story alone that I need to . . . get the story right. But to get right what is missing from you and me. Between us, too." Nathaniel says he wants "to know what is hidden from me and what you have hidden maybe from yourself, as unspeakable in the long ago" (250). And so the act of transcribing Sweetie's testimony becomes, for him and for her both, the best way to account for all that has been lost over the years when memories were too painful to speak out loud. In fact, it is Sweetie who first advises him to "bring along a pen and pad, not a pencil, either," to establish for all time a permanent and indelible documentation of their family's history (7). This would suggest that even she believes in the power of the written word to meaningfully convey something she found impossible to understand as it unfolded before her. Yet the novel itself seems determined to refute this suggestion, indicating again and again how "indecipherable" Nathaniel's longhand is—a fact that the transcriber blames on his penmanship's being "culled from a thousand influences, going back to the beginning time." In other words, when Nathaniel looks at the five legal pads he has filled up with Sweetie's story, he does not see just his own handwriting but also the handwriting of countless additional scribes, mixed together in "a labyrinth of calligraphy" that appears to him "as whirled cobwebs spun back to dancing ghosts" (218).

Although Nathaniel has been the only one transcribing what his grandmother tells him, the polyvocality of her narrative translates onto the page, changing how he shapes each word when different speakers take over the story from her. His very hand seems possessed, then, by the "dancing ghosts" that possess Sweetie herself as she talks about her past. Nathaniel, in fact, imagines a direct correlation between his grandmother's physical form—which trembles with the presence of ancestral spirits—and the letters he has inscribed on the legal pad: "Ah, the characters within her cedar-colored clay, the richest kind and kin of calligraphy in its broadness, he thought" (220). To him, both "texts" are haunted with the voices of many different authors, whose distinct perspectives challenge and confound the possibility of finding a single explanation for the history being recalled. Even when Nathaniel endeavors to write that history himself, he finds there is no way to manage the competing discourses intruding "from the boundaries" of the document (218). Thus he discovers that his own writing reflects precisely what he always found so frustrating about the family stories he used to listen to as a child. It is replete with the same gaps and inconsistencies and circumventions that mystified him in his youth. Confronting his failure to achieve coherence in this regard proves almost as difficult for Nathaniel as contending with the startling revelation Sweetie makes at the conclusion of her testimony: that the baby she raised as her son—Nathaniel's father, Arthur—was actually the bastard child of Jericho and a teenage girl named Lucasta Jones.

For a young man hoping to achieve mastery over his past by sorting out all the divergent strands of his grandmother's memories, the revelation amounts to a devastating blow, because it all but confirms the impossibility of constructing a coherent meaning out of the information Sweetie gives him. Indeed, what she reveals upsets the balance of every other historical "certainty" on which Nathaniel has come to stake his identity: his grandfather's integrity, his father's legitimacy, his own blood ties to his grandmother. If all that Sweetie says is true, no part of his personal history can be thought of in the same definitive terms again. In response, then, he asks her something that exposes just how lost he feels by the close of the novel: "Is nothing as it seems but the visions we have in nightmares that demand that we question the easy sleeve of sleep?" (282). After listening to his grandmother talk for hours upon hours on subjects he has long been wanting to learn about—to bring "order" to his existence—he ends up even more disordered than he was previously, unable finally to distinguish between the imaginary and the real. Notably, the disorientation and utter lack of resolution he experiences at the conclusion of his grandmother's narrative mirrors the way Sweetie herself felt following I. V.'s deathbed confession. Like Nathaniel, she had at one time sought answers for the aspects of her life that were inexplicable to her. In particular, she wanted to know why her father sent her away in the aftermath of the Civil War, choosing to remain loyal to his former master rather than building a home together with the only family he had left. The reason behind I. V.'s decision had always been a mystery to Sweetie—as nonsensical to her as portions of Nathaniel's past were to him. And so, upon receiving news of her father's imminent death in 1904, she traveled to see him, hoping to understand what motivated him to ship her north at the age of fifteen for an arranged marriage with a man forty years her senior. But, as she recounts to Nathaniel by way of the story that takes up half the novel, I. V.'s explanation does not resolve the uncertainties in her biography; it only compounds them, since, as she said to her father, "I. V. Reed, truth never had a pumping bloodline to your heart," even while he lay dying (143).

The tale of Sweetie's visit to I. V. thus doubles the sense of irresolvability that Nathaniel confronts as his grandmother's narrative concludes. Although the former slave's deathbed confession ostensibly sheds some light on the secrets that have plagued the Witherspoon family from the beginning—explaining, among other things, why Sweetie and Jericho were married in the first place, as well as the resentment that ruined their relationship—it ultimately opens up more questions than it answers. For the history that I. V. provides is, like his daughter's, multidirectional and multivoiced: a composite of many conflicting perspectives, which shift and contradict each other as he talks. I. V. was famous for being able to impersonate anyone he heard, and Sweetie remembers "he was known to have a thousand voices by the old slaves, in the old days! From old Master Rollins Reed—to birdcalls" (56). In the view of Nathaniel's grandmother, this renders every word of his testimony untrustworthy, given the way he could turn, in a flash, into someone other than himself, his very soul "going off in seven different directions" at once, as alternative narrators speak through him (148). Therefore, it appears that Sweetie also understands what it is like to try to wrest meaning out of a story possessed by numerous speakers—that she, too, has struggled to make sense of "the multilayered collectivity" of voices that give radically divergent interpretations of the past. For that reason, Nathaniel comes to regard her experience with I. V. as a model for how he might approach the "indecipherable" words transcribed by his aching, burning hand over five pads of yellow paper. Specifically, he thinks about how "in her retelling" of I. V.'s confession his grandmother added yet another layer to the narrative, transforming it with the sound of her own unique articulation:

> shape-changing, now-you-see-him, now-you-don't, laminated onion of soul; beyond all peeling, but flavorful in the soup of any stewing story; and the others as well—pruning and culling, superimposing (editing?) even as the word was given to her, *charged* and *changed*. (246)

It is significant, I would suggest, that near the end of the novel, as Nathaniel comes to terms with the disordered and intrinsically unmanageable nature of the saga he has transcribed, his thoughts turn to what Sweetie did with the troubling story her father told her, half a century earlier. As he sees it, his grandmother was not merely a passive vessel through which I. V.'s voice—and the myriad other voices possessing his narrative—could communicate. Rather, Nathaniel acknowledges that Sweetie plays an active role in the retelling, charging and changing "the word" that "was given to her" and transforming it into something that he calls "miraculous" (245). The image he envisions is of a cook, whose particular talent involves bringing together many assorted, and potentially changeable, ingredients into one "stewing," "flavorful" concoction. Since Nathaniel has always celebrated Great-Momma Sweetie's ability to create memorable meals from the leftovers in her kitchen—to "make caviar out of short rations" (246)—this imagery recalls the times he spent with her during his childhood, when he would gulp down her stories along with the food she prepared for him, the "wonders and mysteries" of both churning deep "in his gut" like the Host he consumed at church (10). Indeed, the persistent inscrutability of what she tells him in the present moment reminds him of how he used to feel as a young boy who had neither the knowledge nor the perspective to decipher the strange and halting way she spoke. Back then, as I have argued, he embraced the mystery of Sweetie's language, out of faith—premised on the Catholic sacrament of Communion—that the truth would at some point be revealed. And now, even though Nathaniel has long since stopped believing in Catholicism, the way his grandmother calls forth the spirits of her ancestors still evokes in his mind the Eucharistic sacrament, because it resonates with the transformative power ascribed to the priests he served as a child. He goes so far as to say, "If I can be part of that transformation, magician-like, I'll be happy to be quiet, if not still, serving as acolyte at her High Mass" (245).

In spite of his obvious aversion to Catholicism and his desire for historical accuracy, Nathaniel thus seems to be reverting toward the conclusion of the novel to the very same sense of mysticism that he consciously turned away from upon attaining adulthood. I am arguing that this happens as a result of his increasing awareness of how mysterious and unsettled his family's past will continue to be to him—even once he has heard everything that his grandmother has to say. To put it another way: accepting the irresolvability of Sweetie's story is commensurate in his imagination with believing in the sacramental rite of Communion, for it requires faith in "a higher stage of consecration," which exceeds all rational explanations (244). After listening to her testimony and contending with the competing voices from their collective past, Nathaniel no longer feels capable of distilling a univocal meaning from all that he has heard. By the time his grandmother stops speaking, he knows that his inheritance—the history she has bequeathed to him on pads of yellow paper, plus the assorted documents she used in the telling—comes not from a single source, but instead from a complex web of progenitors, whose individual experiences are hopelessly entangled with his own. Every word of this family saga, he realizes, is imprinted by countless hands, each one of which has some claim over how it gets told. In his very penmanship, he witnesses the presence of ancestors whom he calls the "black and unknown bards of Calvary, Auntie Foisty, Shank Haywood, Wayland Woods, Angelina [Sweetie's mother], Grandfather Witherspoon, . . . even I. V. Reed" (295). And because he cannot wrest possession of the narrative away from the ghosts who haunt his writing, the only option available to him—as he see it—is to share the story with them, in all its harrowing complexity.

Embracing the complexity of the past is a fundamentally postmodern gesture, consistent with the antihistoriographical impulse of the novel as a whole. Thus it seems perfectly appropriate that, at the end of Sweetie's testimony, Nathaniel would be unable to resolve the tension and conflict to which her historical account gives voice. According to Byerman, "tension and conflict" are essential components of the "deeply ambiguous history" that Forrest sought to represent; his text therefore concludes without a conclusion, implying that "truth" lies "not in resolution but in the multiplicity of voices" that the act of remembering brings forth (145–46). For many critics, the implicit value of a polyvocal narrative is that it resists closure, making it impossible to reduce our collective understanding to one person's idea of *what happened*. That is why Ashraf Rushdy argues the trope of spirit possession has proved so useful to contemporary novels of slavery: because it promotes a communal ("intersubjective" is the term he prefers) rather than an individual view of the past (126–27).

Forrest uses the trope to similar effect in *Two Wings*, as suggested by the way Nathaniel comes to regard all his ancestors—including those he is not particularly proud to claim—as coauthors of the story he has just transcribed. At the close of the novel, then, readers witness a young man who has finally acceded to the dissonance and ambiguity that these many divergent perspectives bring to light, effectively giving himself over to the antihistoriographical approach that characterizes postmodernism. The text's final pages find him in a state of utter incredulity, incapable of trusting even the most objective evidence about his past as a straightforward path to truth. Much to his grandmother's dismay, for example, he swears that a tintype of Lucasta (which is labeled with her name) is actually a photograph of Sweetie's mother, Angelina; then a few seconds later, he sees in her the image of his own deceased mother, Madeline. All three women appear to haunt the face in picture. This kind of uncertainty signals how difficult it has become for Nathaniel (and for readers too) to settle on a single, definitive account of his family's history, when it is possessed by multiple personalities, each with his or her unique story. Forrest's text accomplishes what Madhu Dubey argues is at the heart of paranormal literary devices like spirit possession: the drive to fuel "a strong reaction against the rational and realist principles" of modern historiography ("Speculative" 794). But what is so striking about how *Two Wings* ends is that Nathaniel's reaction *against* rationality and realism constitutes a move *toward* Catholicism. For among the very last words he speaks in the novel is a Eucharistic prayer, in which he asks God to help him discover a meaning amid the overwhelming disorder of his grandmother's narrative:

> Oh dear God, grant that through the mystery and the miracle of water and the bitter grapes of Golgotha's wrath and the broken bread of His flesh (all suffering together), we may know the meaning of our furnace-refined chalice cup of suffering and affliction, forever, Great-Momma Sweetie, and ever, world without end . . . Oh, to live in luminous light ever rekindled is to live forever in doubt, as pure as faith is . . . (295, original ellipses)

This prayer suggests that, to Nathaniel's mind at least, "communion" with the spirits of his ancestors—and "the mystery and the miracle" that such communion entails—is still resolutely linked to Catholicism and his (childlike) faith in a truth beyond all reason.

. . .

In these novels by Gaines and Forrest, then—two works usually taken to represent vastly divergent approaches to the contemporary slave narrative form—we discover that Catholicism informs the breaks from realism in both, accounting for the disruption that alternative views of history bring to the text. Thus the voices that intrude on the narration, wresting control away from the primary storytellers, do so in a manner consistent with how Suzan-Lori Parks and Ishmael Reed describe the trope of spirit possession in their work. But whereas Parks and Reed foreground the non-Western resonances of their possessed narratives,

Gaines and Forrest filter their deployment of the trope through a Catholic sacramentality that explains the way it "explodes" realism. It is worth noting, however, that although I have focused on *The Autobiography of Miss Jane Pittman* and *Two Wings to Veil My Face* in this chapter, works by Parks and Reed also use Catholicism in ways that warrant further study—though not necessarily with respect to spirit possession. For example, Parks has said that she structures her plays as Catholic rituals, while Reed often equates excessiveness in his characters (excessive violence or sexual desire) with their Catholicism.

3

Catholicism and Narrative Time

Transcending the Past and the Present in *Stigmata* and *Oxherding Tale*

TEMPORAL DISJUNCTURES—or the abrupt and often inexplicable ways that texts destabilize conventions of linear time—will, by now, be recognized as a common feature of contemporary narratives of slavery. To various degrees, all of the works examined in my earlier chapters feature the alternative temporalities that I consider in this one and in the next. As we have seen, the tropes of rememory and spirit possession compel representations of narratological time radically different from the straight-line progressive chronology of realist historiography. For instance, in *Beloved*, which uses rememory to suggest that a slave's traumatic history lives on in material form even after her death, the distinction between past and present is relentlessly undermined as characters encounter (literally "bump into") the experience of their ancestors. Likewise, Gaines's *Autobiography of Miss Jane Pittman* interrupts the otherwise conventional linearity of its narrative with descriptions of spirit possession that emphasize the sense of immutability associated with slavery. These examples reflect what A. Timothy Spaulding indicates is a fundamental concern of contemporary slave narratives: to "challenge our impulse to bury the past with willful ignorance or abstraction." According to Spaulding, African American authors tend to "conflate time" when writing about slavery because doing so forces readers to acknowledge that the history of racial oppression persists long after Emancipation, by "expanding the critique of . . . slavery to include a critique of its legacy in contemporary America" (25).

There can be no question that an abiding consequence of temporal disjuncture in contemporary slave narratives is, as Spaulding and other critics claim, the "conviction that slavery is not yet a matter of history" (Dubey, "Neo-Slave" 344). This largely cynical view of race relations in the United States sustains a considerable number of works in the genre—particularly those that deploy assorted time-bending devices to draw explicit, unsettling parallels between antebellum slave society and post-civil-rights America. Indeed, the entire subgenre of speculative or postmodernist fiction about slavery is typically defined by its resistance to an Enlightenment concept of historical progress. On this point, scholars have found widespread consensus: they consistently read the flash-forwards, anachronisms, and time-travel ubiquitous in these texts as indications of a broader skepticism toward historiographical methods that stress the continual forward movement of time.[1] Ashraf Rushdy, for one, relates the disorienting temporal landscape of Ishmael Reed's *Flight to Canada* to its author's outspoken campaign against modern historiography.[2] Rushdy's analysis suggests that the anachronistic images of a fugitive slave narrator who watches television and travels by plane to such places as the White House contribute to the sense, pervasive in the novel, that the "cultural production" of contemporary society is still driven, more than a century since slavery's official conclusion, by "the machinery of the racialized state" (120, 121).

Along similar lines, the alternative temporalities of the two novels I analyze in this chapter do, undoubtedly, underscore the persistence of racial oppression in contemporary culture. Through their manipulations of past and present modalities, respectively, Phyllis Alesia Perry's *Stigmata* and Charles Johnson's *Oxherding Tale* implicitly contradict the principle that history moves forward progressively and linearly. So in that way they each might be said to confirm Frank Yerby's oft-quoted assertion from the preface to *A Darkness at Ingraham's Crest*: "American slavery lasted from 1619 to 1865, two hundred forty-six years. It was further extended under various shabby subterfuges until well into the 1960's, that is if one concedes that it has even ended yet" (9). But however much these novels participate in the historiographical critique that Yerby articulates—by using temporal disjuncture to imply that aspects of the slave system endure well into the present and even the future—their representations of time are not as "pessimistic" as some scholars have argued.[3] What sets them apart from other contemporary narratives of slavery, in fact, is that the alternative temporalities they imagine do more than just confront "the concrete and material connections" between the antebellum period and their own moment in history (Spaulding 29). The novels I discuss here actually manipulate time as a means of transcending those connections, of imagining a way *out of* the cycle of racial suffering they depict. That is, as opposed to the branch of speculative or postmodernist slave fiction that expresses its suspicion about the idea of historical progress by implying the interminable persistence of slavery over time, these two texts refuse to foreclose the possibility of moving beyond it.[4] This, I hasten to note, does not make them any less critical of the "historical narrative of racial emancipation" on which modern historiography is founded, nor does it suggest they regard the future of race relations in the United States with any more optimism than do comparable works in the genre (Dubey, "Speculative" 793). Rather, I will be arguing that, for the two novels considered in this chapter, temporal disjuncture is itself the means by which they contend with the persistent trauma of the slave experience, because it creates an imaginative space outside the limits of Western temporality.

In other words, the novels by Perry and Johnson (as well as Edward P. Jones's *The Known World*, which I examine in chapter 4) privilege temporal disjuncture—and the kind of aesthetic that foregrounds disorienting shifts in chronological order—in a way that distinguishes them from other contemporary slave narratives employing similar techniques. As these texts demonstrate, art that self-consciously interrupts standard chronologies of time has the advantage not only of upsetting the traditional historiography of slavery but also of promoting non-Western approaches to time, which have been delegitimized in the West since the Age of Enlightenment. *Stigmata*, for example, makes a clear attempt to recover in its narrative (and in the artwork its narrative celebrates) an Africanist perspective of human temporality, while *Oxherding Tale* quite baldly proclaims the influence of Eastern religions (Buddhism primarily, but also Hinduism and Taoism) on its narratological structure and on how it orders events. Ultimately, it is as a result of these non-Western conceptions of time that both these novels imagine the potential for a future liberated from the legacy of slavery—a future in which it might be possible to transcend, or at least to transform, that legacy through art.

Yet what strikes me most about the non-Western temporal modes that each of the novels privileges is how dramatically they are informed by Catholicism. Specifically, as I will demonstrate, their alternative temporalities reveal a strange and often disconcerting *faithfulness* to the theology of time that Augustine of Hippo laid out in the *Confessions*. Since Augustinian theology has had such formative, lasting consequences for Western Christianity, and for Catholicism in particular, it might appear contradictory to insist upon its relevance here in the novels under consideration, which very plainly reject Western conceptions of chronological progress. However, I endeavor to show that theological contradictions of this sort actually sustain the way these texts distort the accepted historiography of slavery.

I. Embodying the Past: Phyllis Alesia Perry's *Stigmata*

I turn first to *Stigmata*, which engages more overtly with Catholicism than perhaps any of the texts in this study. The novel's title refers to wounds resembling those endured by Jesus during the Crucifixion that are believed to mysteriously appear on the bodies of saints and other devout persons. Since the thirteenth century, when Saint Francis of Assisi had the first recorded case of stigmata, stigmatics have been celebrated throughout Roman Catholic Church history for the supposedly supernatural cause of their suffering. And unlike other branches of Christianity, whose credence in the phenomenon has receded over time, Roman Catholicism persists even today in its veneration of "confirmed" stigmatics. As Phyllis Alesia Perry has explained in interviews about her fiction, it was the church's veneration of contemporary cases of stigmata that drew her imagination to the subject. Though she was raised Baptist and does not identify with any religion currently, Perry attended Catholic schools, where she says certain aspects of the faith had a tendency to "seep in" more than others. In particular, the stories of modern-day stigmatics stayed with her "in the back of my conscience [sic], for many years" (Duboin 642). These stories eventually provided inspiration for her first novel, in ways I will describe, and helped her articulate the struggle of its narrator, a young African American woman whose mysterious wounds correlate not to Christ's crucifixion but instead to the historical trauma of her enslaved ancestors. In fact, Perry quite explicitly foregrounds Catholicism in the text, using a Catholic explanation of stigmata (voiced by a priest) to account for her narrator's experience.

So it would seem that Catholicism is inextricably bound up in how

Stigmata depicts slavery's persistence over time, and thus in how it challenges conventional narratives of racial progress. Yet, to this point, there has been no attempt to locate the theological basis of this connection, nor to understand the stakes of Perry's appeal to Catholicism. Most critics regard the stigmata themselves as a convenient, yet otherwise immaterial, vessel—an empty signifier—that Perry deploys for the sole purpose of expressing the supernatural phenomenon of time travel at the novel's center. Indeed, Perry herself has described stigmata in similar terms. But, as I will demonstrate, readings like these neglect the very palpable ways that Catholic theology informs the novel, specifically with regard to the temporal disruptions that define its narratological structure. I argue that the narratological structure of *Stigmata* and the temporal disruptions that distinguish it actually depend on a fundamentally Catholic conception of time, which Augustine developed originally in the *Confessions*. Acknowledging the novel's recourse to an Augustinian logic of temporal unknowability is vital, I argue further, if we seek to understand the reconciliatory power it assigns to art. For despite Perry's intentions to excise the religious symbolism of her narrator's stigmata, the text repeatedly—and somewhat problematically—reinscribes the theological significance of the wounds by associating them with aesthetic production.

. . .

Stigmata recounts the story of Lizzie DuBose,[5] a thirty-four-year-old woman who, in the opening scene of the novel, is preparing to be released from the psychiatric hospital where she has been confined for more than a decade. At present the year is 1994, a fact indicated by the chapter heading. But the narrative soon shifts abruptly in time—first backwards to 1898, by way of a journal entry that contains the first-person testimony of a former slave, then ahead to 1974, when Lizzie started to experience the early symptoms of the mental disorder with which she would eventually be diagnosed. Each subsequent chapter follows a similar pattern of temporal disjuncture, as the text moves back and forth between distinct moments in history without a clear sense of what compels these narratological turns. It is in fact the central conceit of the novel that its alternative temporality mirrors the pathology of Lizzie's psychotic episodes. Ever since exploring the contents of a trunk belonging to her deceased grandmother when she was fourteen, Lizzie has been subject to disorienting breaks from reality, during which she either travels to a historical period far removed from her own or speaks with the voice of a long-dead ancestor. In roughly equivalent fashion, then, Perry's narrative re-creates for readers the sensation that Lizzie feels herself every time she is thrust unwittingly and usually without warning into another temporal realm.

If this all sounds a bit like *Beloved* and the concept of embodied memory developed in that novel, I will affirm that the resemblances are palpable. As an early reviewer was quick to note, *Stigmata* was written "in the great tradition of . . . Toni Morrison."[6] Perry's nonlinear plot structure and often confusing lapses in narrative chronology recall Morrison's attempts to engender a "shared experience" between her audience and "the novel's population," by snatching them "just as the slaves were [snatched] from one place to another, from any place to another" with no warning of where they were headed (Morrison, "Unspeakable" 32). Similarly, in *Stigmata*, the act of reading enacts not only the displacement Lizzie suffers as a result of her psychiatric condition but also the displacement her African ancestors felt when they were kidnapped and sold into slavery. Lizzie's "illness" and the trauma associated with it are, indeed, intimately connected throughout the text to the memories of her great-great-grandmother, Ayo: a woman who was taken as a girl from Africa and forced to endure the horrors of the Middle Passage before being dragged *"like a sack of meal"* from one New World slave market to the next (155). For most of her life, Lizzie has been remembering Ayo's past as if it were her own—despite never meeting her great-great-grandmother and knowing almost nothing about what she experienced during slavery. Initially, these recollections came in the form of terrible "visions," which were likely triggered by the journal Lizzie found among her family's possessions when she was still a child, but as she got older, Lizzie started to feel Ayo's pain, along with the slave girl's "fear" and "blood," coursing through her own body (175). Her physical identification with Ayo grew to such an extent that she would bleed from the very places where her great-great-grandmother was scarred by the slavemaster's whips and shackles.

Clearly, then, it is not just in terms of narratological structure that *Stigmata* supports comparisons to Morrison's writing. The novel's content, too, is deeply indebted to the idea—rooted in rememory—that traumatic experiences do not die with the person to whom they belonged; they "stay . . . out there, in the world," as Sethe explains in *Beloved*, "waiting for" future generations to experience them again (43–44). Like Sethe, Lizzie insists that the phenomenological effects of Ayo's memories exceed anything she could think up on her own. She believes her maternal ancestor has actually passed on to her, the way one might hand down any other kind of material possession, "the terror" she lived through as slave. Now, she says, "every . . . part" of that ugly history "belongs to me" (*Stigmata* 175). In language strikingly reminiscent of the famous scene from *Beloved* where Sethe invokes the word "rememory" for the first time, Lizzie describes the sensation this way:

> What I'm trying to tell you is that these are memories, that's what they feel like. And when the . . . conditions, I guess . . . are right, they're more than memory, they're events. They're replays of things that have already happened. Do you understand? I'm there, I see things, I hear things, I feel everything that's going on. . . . Truthfully? No. I don't think they're dreams. (139)

The point Lizzie tries to make here is precisely the one Sethe makes to her daughter Denver in Morrison's novel: that these encounters with the dead conjure up *more than* a mental image of the past in dreams (or what Sethe dismisses as "a thought picture"). Both characters emphasize the tangibility of the memories they experience by detailing their sensory responses to them. For these women, the body itself—the way it sees, hears, and feels—establishes the *truthfulness* of their claims. At one point, when discussing how she "remembers" Ayo, Lizzie simply holds out her arm, as though the "faint, reddish mark" on each wrist proves beyond any possibility of doubt that she is the living embodiment of her great-great-grandmother's suffering (138).

But of course, whereas the concept of embodied memory is legitimized within the context of Morrison's narrative, *Stigmata* refrains from making an equivalent gesture. Indeed, one noteworthy difference between Perry's novel and *Beloved* is the way the larger African American community responds to the supernatural experience that each woman describes. As opposed to Sethe, whose family and neighbors eventually accept the truth of what she says (given the materialization of her murdered daughter, whose physical presence they cannot deny), Lizzie struggles to convince nearly everyone in her life of her relationship with her ancestors. The community's resistance to Lizzie's version of the past is underscored in the first pages of the novel when Dr. Harper, a young clinician with "Pretty brown skin," quizzes her on the day she is scheduled to be released from the hospital (2). More than any of the other psychiatrists who cared for her during her long confinement, Harper was the one "who really got to" Lizzie and made her want to reenter the world—a fact she attributes to his race and his "familiarity" (4). Harper reminds Lizzie of everything she misses at home, and so she decides to give him what he and the rest of her community want from her: a persuasive account of "redemption and restored mental health" (5). This means she must disown the "fantasy" of embodying Ayo and concede that the episodes of time travel she experienced were only elaborate delusions resulting from a pathological condition.

Because freedom for Lizzie depends on her explicit renunciation of irrational beliefs, the situation she finds herself in at the start of the novel is not unlike that of the fugitive slave autobiographer, who for reasons of personal and communal survival had to demonstrate a capacity for rationalist discourse.[7] Thus we might relate the way Lizzie "dazzle[s] Harper and everyone else" with her story of psychological recovery (5) to, for example, Frederick Douglass's attempts to distance himself from the "heathen" he was as a child.[8] As Eric Sundquist has argued, Douglass felt compelled to construct a "traceable metamorphosis" of his life in order to show how completely he had absorbed the Enlightenment tenets of self-possession and objective reflection by the time he reached adulthood.[9] Likewise, Lizzie takes pains to assure Harper that she has abandoned the "Confusion" of her teenage years, to which she ascribes the erratic, self-destructive behavior that landed her in psychiatric confinement: "I lost myself there, for a long time," she confesses. "But . . . I'm all right now. I just want to go home" (5–6). And, as evidence for her transformation into a competent adult with a rational mind—someone who can distinguish between the fantastic and the real—Lizzie grants, when prompted, that the wounds on her body were caused by her own hand instead of by Ayo's slavemaster, as she previously asserted. This pointed reversal of earlier testimony once again calls to mind Douglass and, specifically, his notorious footnote in the *Narrative* denigrating Sandy's root as mere "superstition."[10] Just as Douglass seemed to understand that his audience would not tolerate any suggestion of the power of African root work, Lizzie knows her psychiatrist will refuse to sign her release forms if she continues to insist that she can feel her dead ancestor's pain. Therefore, she refers to what happened to her as a suicide attempt, rather than risk further accusations of irrationality.

Her performance succeeds. Soon after hearing Lizzie admit that her scars came from a paring knife—and not chains and manacles—Harper pronounces her free from confinement, releasing her to her parents' care. As confirmation that she has provided him with the answers he was hoping for, he tells her, "You done good. It's finally over" (6). But even when she arrives home in Tuskegee, Lizzie feels obligated to maintain the narrative that she "polished... to such a high shine" at the hospital (5). For most of the novel, in fact, it is solely the reader who knows that Lizzie faked her recovery and that she still believes she can travel through time to distinct moments in her family's past. To everyone else in her hometown, including her mother and father, she toes the line of reason, recognizing that she will be "rewarded" by them with increasing amounts of freedom only if she proves to be "on the right side of normal" (26). This discrepancy—between what Lizzie reveals in the journalistic portions of the text and what she reveals to members of her community—makes the reader complicit in a so-called irrational experience that other characters tend to pathologize. Not only is anyone reading the novel privy to the knowledge that Lizzie deliberately "fooled" her entire medical team with some "well-acted moments of sanity," but we also learn quite quickly by way of the abrupt shifts in narrative time that the "madness" persists (6). She continues to suffer disorienting episodes of temporal disjuncture, with the reader as witness to (and participant in) her experience.

Sharing in the experience of disorientation forces readers to acknowledge how real the episodes of time travel are for Lizzie. Although this cannot necessarily protect her against charges of unreliability—Perry reports that she is often asked whether her narrator was actually insane (Duboin 645)—the novel's structure implies that Lizzie's clinicians and, by extension, her family and her friends have failed her in some profound way. Instead of providing a "cure," their treatment plan only encouraged Lizzie to conceal her symptoms from them—a choice, it becomes clear, that proves as inadequate for her as it does for those who love her. None of her relationships will prosper, nor will her ancestors leave her at peace, if she maintains the story of recovery that she delivered at the hospital. The stakes of *Stigmata* are unequivocal in this regard: to heal herself and her community, Lizzie must discover a means of communicating to them the truth about how she relates to the past. Most significant of all, she needs to help her mother understand that denying the memories embodied in Lizzie is preventing them from moving beyond the hold those memories have on them both. Thus Lizzie comes to view it as her responsibility, as well as her singular mission upon returning to Tuskegee, to discover "the best way, the gentlest way" of articulating her experience "without freaking people out" (222).

The desire to make "the subject of my past" accessible to those around her is what drives Lizzie toward a new narrative form (222). Having determined that she cannot talk openly about traveling through time, she turns instead to the medium of quilting, clandestinely stitching scenes from her unspeakable episodes into a project of which her family can approve. Her mother and her father even contribute to the effort, not realizing they are enabling Lizzie to express something they have otherwise forbidden her to discuss for fear of triggering a relapse. The "story quilt" therefore promotes an alternative means of narrating what happened to her, one with decidedly transformative consequences for everyone involved. As they work on the project together, Lizzie and her parents confront both the traumatic history that their ancestors lived through and the way that history materially affects the present—but they do so through a nonlinguistic aesthetic that is inherently less threatening than speech or writing would be. To Sarah and John DuBose, who, for reasons not limited to the concerns they have about their daughter's mental health, remain unwilling to hear "all of that . . . goddamn reincarnation stuff" (226) from Lizzie, the quilt does not necessitate a complete upending of their core set of rationalist beliefs. They can appreciate its beauty and the skill involved in designing such an intricate piece of art without acknowledging the memories stitched into it. And yet the quilt's imagery and the strange, disjointed pattern of its fabric test the limits of the DuBoses' rationalism, exposing them to a worldview that implicitly challenges their own. For example, Lizzie detects a feeling overtaking her father as he gazes upon the near-finished design. "My father the doctor, wistful?!" she notes in obvious amazement (195). This nostalgic turn—as well as the burst of sentimental dialogue it spurs—stands in sharp contrast to the objective, dispassionate tone John usually takes with his daughter, which she has always associated with his medical training. In the terms dictated by the novel, and certainly to Lizzie, Dr. DuBose's reaction to the quilt is thus potentially enabling for their relationship, because it gestures toward a different kind of understanding, one that is not informed by scientific reason alone.

While Lizzie feels bolstered by her father's uncharacteristic display of emotion, her primary audience for the quilt is, first and foremost, Sarah. Indeed, as Lizzie explains to her cousin, she will not be able to leave Tuskegee or start making a life for herself outside her parents' home until she can convince her mother of the material link between past and present. The success of the entire project for Lizzie hinges on Sarah's willingness to believe something that she has been conditioned on multiple fronts to perceive as irrational. Not only has her long marriage inculcated Dr. DuBose's empirical sensibility in Sarah, but it is also implied that her religious faith and her status in the community are at odds with what Lizzie is trying to accomplish. The always "completely composed Mrs. Dr. DuBose" has striven to make her life as orderly as possible: she attends (Protestant) church services regularly, maintains a pristine house as well as a pristine appearance, and seems in every way to model an upper-middle-class American lifestyle (19). That this value system predisposes Sarah against the disorder represented by Lizzie's quilt is something Perry underscores rather heavy-handedly in the novel, such as in the following scene:

> We've taken the quilt project out of the dining room—Mother cannot abide the scraps of thread and fabric falling and becoming part of the carpet—and to the attic, where we sit under the crazy whirl of the fan. . . .
> "You could tell better what was going on if the pictures were in a row," Mother grumbles, wiping the film of sweat from her forehead before continuing her task: tracing an outline from one of my drawings. "This is hopelessly jumbled."
> Mother made it clear early in the quilt project that she finds the design unsettling. I look at the outline under her fingers, which draw tailor's chalk across midnight blue background fabric—the moments of a life moving in a semicircle. . . .
> "Life," I say, "is nonlinear, Mother."
> "Depends on how you look at it. You may see it as a circle. But it always seems like a line to me." She puts the chalk down and wipes her fingers daintily on a paper towel. "The past is past." (93)

With her preference for narrative linearity and commitment to the continual forward movement of time, Sarah gives voice here to a view of history that is classically Western in orientation. She appears to have assimilated, without irony, the totalizing rhetoric of historical progress that (as I discuss in chapter 2) suggests modern societies are moving ever away from the "darkness" of the past and thus toward freedom, knowledge, and prosperity. The last line of the above passage makes clear that, as someone whose personal trajectory reflects a steady rise in both affluence and social prestige, Sarah does not want to dwell on the struggles of her African American ancestors; to regard time "as a circle" would be, for her, to risk backsliding into a way of life she deliberately left behind.

None too subtly, then, in this passage and elsewhere, Perry correlates Sarah's wariness about the quilt—and the "unsettling" nature of its design—to her desire for class mobility. Among the society in which the DuBoses have established themselves in Tuskegee, there is no place for anything that falls outside the bounds of the linear, progressive temporality to which they subscribe. That is why they were quick to send Lizzie off for psychiatric treatment when she first showed symptoms of an "obsession" with the past. And, significantly, it is also what renders her daughter's suggestion that the "world . . . move[s] in cycles" (93) so problematic for Sarah. A cyclical notion of time cannot be reconciled with the Western model she unabashedly privileges. Its vaguely African resonances recall a belief structure that she associates with ignorance and superstition. Sarah's own mother, after all, as well other relatives on her maternal side were—in her estimation—inhibited by similar ideas. In fact, as the text hints, part of the reason Sarah fears the memories stitched into the quilt is that they lay bare a connection she has taken pains to avoid: between the women in her family and a spiritual tradition inherited from their slave ancestors from Africa. Although *Stigmata* never explicitly connects Lizzie's time-traveling episodes or her view of the past to African spirituality (leaving ambiguous the source of her visions in a manner consistent with speculative fiction), it implies at various points that she comes from a long line of female seers, who share her supernatural experience and abilities.[11] Moreover, the novel's prequel, *A Sunday in June*, which Perry published six years after *Stigmata* in 2004, explores the roots of this matrilineal heritage, ultimately tracing it back to Ayo—the very same slavewoman who haunts Lizzie. There, Ayo is figured as a "strong spirit, in life and in death" (260), whose conjuring powers are unmistakably African in origin.

A Sunday in June, therefore, makes plain something Perry intimates in *Stigmata*: that the tendency to pathologize Lizzie's visions and to discount her cyclical worldview are symptomatic of a larger cultural resistance to non-Western—and particularly African—modes of knowledge. In interviews, Perry has said she uses fiction to promote greater "openness about religion and spiritual experiences, meaning I would like for our culture to not have so many rules about it, or only so many avenues that are considered to be 'normal.'" Both novels highlight what she called in 2007 an increasing "tension" in upwardly mobile communities of color surrounding alternative approaches to spirituality. Because, while Perry acknowledges that African Americans have been historically syncretistic in their religious beliefs, she claims the drive for wealth and social acceptance in the United States often negatively affects this historical sense of "inclusiveness." To her, the wholesale rejection of traditional practices like root work, spirit possession, and mystical visions comes down to a "class issue," because "one of the ways to 'move on up' is not to have these associations with Africa and African religion, or even Native American religion." Thus she conceives of her fiction as a vehicle for reclaiming a lost or threatened syncretism in the contemporary world, where the dominance of a monolithic Western value system has made it harder for divergent spiritualities to "exist side by side" (Duboin 643). In *Stigmata* the reclamation happens by means of Lizzie's quilt, which is, as I have been suggesting, a double for the novel itself. The circular and disjointed, yet not completely inaccessible, narrative structure of the "story" stitched into it compels the DuBoses to share in, if just for a moment, their daughter's supernatural relationship to the past. And although they willfully reject the irrationality represented there (as evidenced by Sarah's attempts to straighten out its "jumbled" pattern), *Stigmata* concludes on a note consistent with the religious inclusivity that Perry espouses.

Indeed, the penultimate scene of the novel depicts Sarah's response to the quilt as a kind of conversion experience. Witnessing the design for the first time in its finished form, she finally recognizes the memories stitched into it, and thus can no longer deny the devastating story her daughter has been trying to tell. The effect on her is one of immediate alterity: Lizzie notes, "Her face is wet and wild. I've never seen her look so lost, my always so-correct mother" (225). Yet in the midst of this confusion—which is, of course, a consequence of having shaken her faith in the Western discourses of rationalism and historical progress—Sarah grants that what appears "crazy" to her is *also true*. All at once, the distinction between past and present that has defined her perception of sanity does not hold. She even communicates with the spirit of her dead mother, whom Lizzie channels, effectively participating in an African-derived possession ritual that she would have previously deemed "insane." This radical, transformative act not only affirms Lizzie's cyclical worldview and the temporal disorientation of the narrative depicted in her quilt, but it also—quite significantly—confronts the intergenerational legacy of slavery. As one critic argues, by engaging the voices of her maternal ancestors through her daughter's body, Sarah is, at once, "ensuring the survival" of their traumatic memories and discovering how "to heal the rupture" those memories have inflicted on her own life (June 70). Thus the scene ends with the image of the quilt sliding to the floor as Sarah puts her head in Lizzie's lap and allows her daughter to "stroke the hair out of her eyes" (230). Ultimately, it seems, the two women have discovered together a way out of the tragic cycle of loss and misunderstanding represented in the design. Sarah's now-clear vision suggests the possibility of a future that transcends the immutable pain of their ancestors. By first acknowledging and then "putting . . . aside when we're through" the material link between past and present, the novel indicates she is free to move beyond it (228). And so the quilt, like Perry's text, has served the function its creator intended, underscoring the redemptive potential of artwork that disrupts the dominant Western mode and challenges its audience to see the world differently.

The hopeful, reconciliatory tone of spiritual inclusiveness on which *Stigmata* ends, however, is complicated by the fact that the non-Western worldview that inspired it is validated throughout by Catholicism. In other words, Perry presents Catholicism as the authorizing force of Lizzie's narrative and, by extension, of the transformative aesthetic vision her quilt—and thus the novel—confers more generally. The authorization comes by way of Father Tom Jay, a Catholic priest whom Lizzie meets while living in the psychiatric hospital, at the depths of her emotional and physical despair. Through a series of short flashbacks, in which Lizzie describes her initial impressions of this "charity visitor" (208) as well as the conversations they had during her confinement, Father Tom's significance is swiftly established. First, he is the only person to perceive, and to state explicitly, that she does not belong in a mental health facility, stating within minutes of knowing her, "You're not like the others. You're not babbling, no rambling, no talking to unseen people. Completely rational as far as I can tell" (211). Although these claims of rationality are ironic on multiple levels (and not just because, as she is quick to confess, Lizzie does in fact have an active relationship with the "unseen"), they provoke her to speak openly with him about her episodes and the scars on her skin. Second, in listening to the "fantastic" account of "walking, talking memories and the lifetimes layered one on top of the other" in her body, Father Tom gives Lizzie something that manifestly changes how she interprets the experience: a name for the suffering she has endured. Simply hearing the term "stigmata" invoked for the first time brings her a degree of comfort, since the word's very existence denotes a precedent for the mysterious wounds. Moreover, from the priest, Lizzie learns of at least one institution where her story could be accepted as "authentic" (213). Within the Roman Catholic Church, he tells her, stigmatics have been insulated against charges of insanity and, in some cases, considered healers—even saints. The fact someone like Father Tom would want to honor Lizzie's "tortured flesh" instead of being repulsed by it is a "new feeling" for Lizzie (214), and it impels her in turn to doubt the legitimacy of the system that has pathologized her from the start.

According to Camille Passalacqua, whose analysis is representative of how other critics tend to read Father Tom's role in the novel, the priest helps "Lizzie begin to connect with the outside world" by "relinquishing the fear of what happened to her body and mind and discovering her identity in light of whom and what she carries." Articulated in these terms, his character performs a valuable service, to be sure, but one not necessarily unique to him. Indeed, Passalacqua brackets together the scenes involving Father Tom with a number of such "encounters"—Lizzie's conversations with Mrs. Corday, for example, or her relationship with Anthony Paul—all of which also, she argues, constitute "an essential part of her psychological and physical healing (154). Yet while the acceptance of a fellow patient and her lover is undoubtedly beneficial for Lizzie, I would submit that neither of these characters, nor even the transformation her mother undergoes at the end of *Stigmata*, affects her as profoundly as does this Catholic priest. It is Father Tom, after all, who endows her with language to articulate the sacredness of her experience (the importance of which is substantiated by the novel's title) and convinces her to try to communicate that sacredness to others with conflicting points of view. In that sense, both the text on page and the quilt which doubles its narratological structure are the direct result of Father Tom's intervention, for the final chapter of the novel confirms that Lizzie's aesthetic will—her drive to produce artwork that "overflow[s] with past-life episodes"—was cultivated by the priest's insistence that she take a *monastic* approach to writing and creating. He encouraged her to devote her art to resisting the "unrelenting pressure" of "the world at large," suggesting that doing so is effectually "clearing a path to your place among the saints" (232).

That Lizzie's journals and sketchbooks are linked so unambiguously at *Stigmata*'s conclusion to Father Tom is suggestive, I am arguing, of how Catholicism shapes its larger narrative. This is a point necessary to make, given the gap in critical attention to even the most overtly Catholic elements of the novel and of, as my project argues, African American literature in general. Among critics who do consider the "religious connotations" of Father Tom's influence on Lizzie, there remains little attention to the specific nature of the theology he represents; their focus is limited to the way his character highlights Lizzie's "Christlike" capacity for "deliverance and recovery" (Passalacqua 160n7)[12]—an argument that, while sound with respect to Christianity broadly conceived, cannot speak to the priest's particular denomination, nor to the theological justification he gives for her artwork. This oversight wrongly marginalizes the Catholic overtones of *Stigmata*, foreclosing questions that demand scholarly attention. Furthermore, it prevents us from contending with an inconsistency at the heart of Perry's notion of spiritual inclusivenesss. Because if Catholicism, a sine qua non of Western religious orthodoxy, is really what instigates Lizzie's artistic expression and what defines the reconciliatory effect of her art, then does this not further compromise the threatened (non-Western) belief systems that Perry aims to recover? Why, of all the religions she might have drawn from, would Perry choose to depict Lizzie's redeemer as a Catholic priest, when she might just as easily have imagined another type of spiritual guide, maybe a conjure woman or roots worker, in his stead?[13] What could Father Tom possibly teach Lizzie about telling her family's story or how to represent—to transcend—the traumatic history of slavery?

To answer these questions we need to attend carefully to the depiction of the stigmata themselves, as both a theological and an aesthetic concept, for it is from a stigmatic's perspective that Father Tom spurs Lizzie to produce art. In particular, he feeds her information about "a devoted monk" whose name he can't remember but whose case of inexplicable bleeding "is well documented with photographs" (213–14). The referent here is almost certainly Padre Pio, one of the most prominent stigmatics of the twentieth century and the subject of a protracted campaign for canonization during the time Perry was writing the novel.[14] Perry has said that ever since attending Catholic school as a child and learning about religious devotees "like Padre Pio," she "was just endlessly fascinated . . . with the idea that someone would carry someone else's pain on their body." In fact, she had been actively researching his biography (there was a file on her computer with notes about him and other "famous stigmatics") when the plan for her first work of fiction started to take shape. Yet she describes the sudden realization that its main character would suffer the stigmata too as something she never could have predicted, given the discrete and seemingly disconnected manner in which she approaches her craft:

> I have bits and pieces of things that occur to me, vignettes that I get down, but sometimes I don't know that they belong together for some time. So I had the word "stigmata" in a computer file all by itself and I had [the notes about] Padre Pio. I also had the names [of the novel's characters] in another file. . . . I don't remember the moment when I realized that Lizzie was going to be stigmatic. I had the story and I had the character of Lizzie. I knew that I wanted connection between her and her slave ancestors. But until I put these two elements together, I didn't know what was going to happen. (Duboin 642)

It is striking how closely Perry's depiction of the text's inception mirrors Lizzie's own drive to write and to create. In other words, Perry suggests here that the plot and structure of the novel ("what was going to happen" in it) came into being only after she had a name for the connection between past and present that she had been trying to articulate—only after she was made to realize, by the chance proximity of files on her desktop, that there exists a language and a precedent for "the bits and pieces of things that occur" to her. As we have seen, Lizzie experiences a comparable rush of aesthetic output following Father Tom's revelation, his naming, of her wounds as stigmata.

Thus stigmata, as Perry imagines them both for herself and for Lizzie, constitute a fortunate wound—a *felix culpa* in the original Augustinian sense of the term—which permits the articulation of new forms of representation. Hélène Cixous has argued that this meaning of "stigmata" sustains a great number of literary descendants of Augustine, all of whom cite the bodily mark, the injury as a creative stimulus for memory:

> It all begins with a *Felix Culpa*. A happy fault, a blessed wound. Blessèd. This is what St. Augustine tells us in his *Confessions*. The remarkable fortunes of this thematics of the wound are well known in the work of the other Augustine, James Joyce, but maybe less perceptible or explicit in other notable texts. In Proust it is buried, one must exhume it. For Genet the wound is the founding secret of all major creation. (243)

Cixous's analysis, as well as the neologism "stigmatext" that she uses to classify such works of literature and art, underscores both the sacred and prolific nature of suffering—something that always struck her, she says, "as very 'Catholic'" (244). She is referring to the theological compulsion in Catholicism to use the body as a way of remembering Christ's sacrifice—manifest in the ritualistic performance of the Stations of the Cross at Lent, for example, and in the church's doctrine of transubstantiation, as well as in its persistent celebration and canonization of stigmatics.[15] Augustine's *Confessions* and the stigmatexts that descended from it signify, for her, the textual equivalent of this compulsion, because of the way they circle back, again and again, to the memory of the primal wound, maintaining and reanimating its traces. In Cixous's view, by making something out of his suffering and his being marked, Augustine in effect justified a type of narrative testimony that has since been exceedingly attractive to artists (herself included) seeking to mediate their "own relation to the inscription on the body of psychomythical events" (245). What Augustinian theology brings to bear on the "thematics of the wound," then, as she sees it, is "the promise of a text" in which "resurrection is hatched" out of the aesthetic impulse to remember and to share one's pain (xiv).

I want to claim that Father Tom performs a similar function in *Stigmata*—that his role in the novel and the theological validation he gives to Lizzie's art are Augustinian in the way that Cixous means. To understand why this matters and how a fundamentally Catholic aesthetics could inform a text so clearly opposed to Western narratives of progress will require a brief explanation of Augustine's theology of the *felix culpa*, as well as the complex temporal theory that undergirds it. As Cixous indicates, the *Confessions* both endorses and gives rise to a memorializing compulsion in literature that posits "traumatism"—the continual revisiting of historical injuries in the form of a stigmatext—"as an opening to the future of the wound" (xiv). The premise that narrating the past involves the simultaneous actions of looking back and looking forward is founded on Augustine's construct of the threefold present, developed in book XI. Because, unlike God, human beings are intrinsically incapable of measuring time with any precision (given the nonbeing of time itself), he writes that our only option for contending with this ontological aporia is by rethinking the past and the future as temporal qualifications of our experience of the present. Hence, for Augustine, the present insofar as we are "permitted to speak" of it comprises three separate modalities at once: "a present of things past, a present of things present, and a present of things to come" (11.20. 26). The tripartite structure of time comes into play whenever we attempt to narrate suffering, he asserts, because it remains the sole means available for expressing the trauma of human existence (and thus the stigma of our essential difference from God). That is to say: by meditating on—and giving language to—the impossibility of distinguishing between a past, present, and future time, we acknowledge "just how distended and scattered our temporal lives are" in contrast to the forever stillness of the eternal Word (Kearney 149). Yet, far from succumbing to hopelessness in the face of eternity, these meditations on the nonbeing of temporality, according to the logic of the *Confessions*, represent an eschatological desire for reconciliation which confirms one's faith in the transcendent power of God.

While Cixous is not especially interested in confirming the power of God per se, her theoretical investment in stigmata (and the stigmatext) alights on the relationship Augustine draws between the way we narrate temporal experience and an abiding faith in transcendence. For it was in the *Confessions*, she implies, that narrative accounts of the wound were first associated, through the figure of *felix culpa*, with acts of self-renewal—and thus with the hope for some "blessèd" future time that transcends the here and now. In Perry's novel, Lizzie ultimately comes to a similar conclusion about her own pain, and I am arguing that Father Tom is the one who delivers her there by way of Augustinian theology. Although he does not refer to Augustine directly, he invokes the construct of the threefold present when he tells her, "Maybe you're marked so you won't forget this time, so you will remember and move on" (213). His point, which she immediately heeds, is that instead of rotting away in the psychiatric hospital where she has been confined, Lizzie should devote her stay, like a monk in a monastery, to "quiet contemplation" of the source of her suffering (232). On its surface, the priest's suggestion might not seem so different from what the psychiatrists and other clinicians were imploring her to do all along; Lizzie's treatment, from the beginning, has involved thinking and talking about the painful episodes she experienced. But in Father Tom's phrasing we hear the echoes of something far more radical than a therapist's invitation to discuss one's feelings. We hear the echoes of Augustine's famous—and disarming—thesis that the present ("this time") exists only to the extent that we conceive it in our minds, through the fluctuating acts of memory, attention, and expectation (*memoria*, *contuitus*, and *expectatio*). By proposing that Lizzie's marks, her stigmata, compel her to envision the past, present, and future not as separate things in themselves but rather as modifications of her own experience of temporality, Father Tom effectively asks her to concede how unknowable and immeasurable time really is—the very foundation of book XI of the *Confessions*.

Augustine believed that accepting the unknowability of time constitutes a necessary step toward genuine faith. Therefore, he stressed that even the construct of the threefold present, which represents the human soul's best attempt to make sense of "a present of past things, a present of present things and a present of things to come," cannot hold up to scrutiny from without: "In the soul there are these three aspects of time, and [I do] not see them anywhere else" (11.20.26). As Augustine made clear, any means we use to measure time or to speak of what has passed and what is coming will always be implicated in the "tumults" of the mind's "impressions" (11.27.36). And that is why Father Tom does not contradict Lizzie when she responds rather despondently to how he explains her stigmata, murmuring, "So, it *is* all in my mind," as though he has just confirmed her insanity. Instead of insisting that she is not just imagining the ancestral memories she describes, he says: "Nothing is that simple. I think it's all in your mind in the sense that this person, this ancestor, is with you in some way, just as Christ was with the monk. The merging of spirits and all that." (213). Notice that, in trying to comfort Lizzie and convince her that he trusts her story, Father Tom applies almost exactly the same logic that her psychiatrists used to justify her hospitalization, telling her that the way she remembers the past is entirely psychological—a product of her mind. But, to him, acknowledging this fact does not discredit her sanity or render what she has told him any less true; quite to the contrary, he maintains it actually bolsters her chances of being "considered a saint, a healer" (213).

The theological motivation for such a claim, I would suggest, comes also from the *Confessions*, and the skeptical attitude toward time revealed therein. In other words, it is precisely because Father Tom—following Augustine—locates the measure of all time within the human psyche that he does not appear particularly disturbed by Lizzie's nontraditional view of the past or her so-called irrational visions. Her experience, as he perceives it, is simply one among many possibilities for the way the mind conceives the "intricate enigma" of temporal existence (11.22.28). Yet what sets her apart, and places her on the path to sainthood, is how radically her standard of measurement diverges from the standard that has been normalized by a rationalist society. This divergence—this "separation from the world at large" that Lizzie's unique memories afford—well poises her, in Father Tom's estimation, to seek after something that does, in fact, transcend the limits of time: a promise of reconciliation and purpose to her life (232). For, as opposed to the clinicians treating her and the family members who hold so rigorously to their rational explanations of the world, Lizzie understands the feeling that Augustine described as being "severed amid times, whose order I know not" (11.29.39). She has come face to face with the disordered and intrinsically unknowable aspect of time. Father Tom encourages her to trust—to give herself over to—that sense of temporal disjuncture, which, in Augustinian terms, opens one up to the possibility of transcendence. Like Augustine, he believes that attending to the great schism at the center of the human temporality will lead to an intensification of faith in that which lies outside time, that is, the "Father everlasting" of the *Confessions*.[16] And it is with this belief in mind that Father Tom directs Lizzie to submit to the strange, confounding, painful memories afflicting her, rather than to try to rationalize her experience.

Of course, Lizzie is not seeking spiritual transcendence or a closer relationship with God. Her concerns are much more material than that: she wants to know what "to do" with the lifetimes of suffering that plague her, the seemingly inescapable and immutable trauma of slavery that her ancestors have passed along to her (214). The theological motivation behind Father Tom's encouragement seems irrelevant to her, and she dismisses out of hand his suggestion that she is anything close to a saint. The frequent references to faith and holiness in the letters he sends her only annoy her, since she does not "feel very holy"—nor does she consider herself religious in any way (232). So the result of their conversation and ensuing correspondence is obviously quite different from what Father Tom might have hoped, if (as Lizzie's father sardonically offers) the priest's intention was, in fact, "recruiting" her "for the church" (217). But I stipulate that Lizzie's reservations about the theology he espouses cannot discount the impact Father Tom has on her or the radical changes he provokes. For, as the final pages of the text reveal, she discovers in talking with him a new desire to represent her memories in writing and in art. This will to create, which she describes as "a need . . . that wasn't there before" (218), manifests itself in the journals and sketchbooks that she fills up with uncommon vigor, in the weeks and months following her initial meeting with the priest. As I indicated earlier, Lizzie's aesthetic production—like Perry's—is thus figured as a response to, and unintended consequence of, the stories of the stigmatics to which she was exposed by her Catholic "education."[17] And, because the novel itself is composed entirely of those journal fragments that Lizzie wrote after receiving Father Tom's encouragement, the priest has an undeniable and abiding effect on the work as a whole.

We should not ignore this effect, I argue, or otherwise bracket off its significance, since doing so would be equivalent to denying the value that the novel assigns to artistic creation. For, Lizzie's art—her writing, her sketches, her painting—is what ultimately enables her to recover from the devastating toll of psychiatric confinement. As she puts it in one revealing journal entry, the act of creating something out of her memories "eases my mental pain and illuminates it, makes everything swimming through my head touchable" (219). Furthermore, it is another artistic creation—her quilt—that accounts for the redemptive and hopeful tone on which the narrative concludes, as well as for Lizzie's reconciliation with her mother. The transformative power of art thus constitutes a primary theme of *Stigmata*, one that defines how the novel imagines *getting past* the persistent trauma of slavery. In no uncertain terms, Lizzie's personal transformation (from hopeless mental patient to thriving artist) and the transformation of her parents (especially her mother) are mediated through an aesthetic experience that challenges the limits of rational discourse by incorporating past-life episodes. However, as I have been contending, the stimulus for this "irrational" aesthetic experience comes from an unlikely source: not from someone familiar with the particular worldview represented in Lizzie's art, but instead from a Catholic priest. The way to make sense of the rather paradoxical function of Father Tom in the novel is by means of the Augustinian theology to which, I have argued, he appeals. Not only does Augustine's skeptical attitude toward time provide theological justification for alternative temporal experiences such as Lizzie's, but the emphasis he puts in the *Confessions* on narrating one's suffering also validates the art that Father Tom spurs Lizzie to create. For a text committed to religious inclusivity and the reclamation of non-Western belief systems, it seems contradictory—troubling, even—to discover Western theology at its center. Perhaps that is why critics have tended to ignore or marginalize its Catholic elements. Likewise, it could explain why in the novel she wrote after *Stigmata*, *A Sunday in June*, Perry resists making any reference at all to Catholicism and depends exclusively on an Africanist conception of time as explanation for its temporal disruptions.

II. The Timeless Present: Charles Johnson's *Oxherding Tale*

The novel I turn to next, Charles Johnson's *Oxherding Tale*, privileges temporal disjuncture in a manner similar to *Stigmata*. As in Perry's text, the narrator's transformation—and potential for redemption—hinges on the alternative temporalities that define his memories of slavery. Except, of course, that Johnson's narrator, Andrew Hawkins, is not remembering someone else's suffering; his first-person account of the trauma of enslavement is distinctly his own: a tale told, as Johnson explained in the introduction to later editions, from the imagined perspective of a more-than-hundred-year-old freeman, who decides "at some time in the twentieth century" to write about the experience of being enslaved, escaping, and, eventually, achieving emancipation (xvi). So, on the face of it, *Oxherding Tale* adheres much more faithfully to the classic form of a slave narrative than other speculative or postmodernist fiction about slavery. Its trajectory follows a fairly straight-line progression from bondage to liberty. And yet, Johnson quite jarringly interrupts that chronological progress at various points to suggest the unfeasibility of depicting Andrew's "journey to freedom" in any traditional configuration (xiv). These interruptions to the temporal continuity of the narration, along with a host of other metafictional and parodic digressions, are responsible for the transformative vision the novel promotes. According to Johnson, it is "technical virtuosity" and the drive to exceed the "galaxy" of "forms that are our inheritance as writers" that push literature "toward new possibilities," thereby liberating a text from the limits of tradition (*Being* 52–53).

For African American artists in particular, Johnson regards formal experimentation as a necessary feature of the creative process that, in his view, is too often neglected in favor of ideology. He has been famously critical of fiction born of the Negritude and Black Arts movements, which for the "noble" purpose of "counteracting cultural lies" and combating racism, "easily slips toward dogma that ends the process of literary discovery" (*Being* 29). In his doctoral dissertation, *Being and Race: Black Writing Since 1970*, he called for an innovative type of African American literature that would surpass the "depressing sameness" of contemporary publications in two ways: first, by drawing upon a larger variety of genres and styles than what is currently in circulation and, second, by relentlessly—but "lovingly"—transfiguring those forms of expression through original interpretations (51, 53). *Oxherding Tale* represents Johnson's attempt to make good on both of these demands. Thus, interwoven into the basic structure of a slave narrative are allusions to various fictional and philosophical works not commonly aligned with representations of American slavery, from Fielding and Sterne to Schopenhauer and Marx, as well as Eastern parables. Indeed, the novel's title refers to a twelfth-century Chinese illustration series that depicts a young man searching for his lost ox, a Buddhist symbol for the self. The goal of combining—and then adulterating—so many diverse intertexts, Johnson claims, is patently different from that of postmodernist pastiche (which, as Fredric Jameson has said, constitutes a value-*less* imitation of past forms). *Oxherding Tale* endeavors "to move beyond the pastiche" and to "project a new vision" of African American life that is not beholden to any single, circumscribed way of writing (*Being* 53).

Specifically, Johnson says that he envisioned his narrator as "the first protagonist in black American fiction to achieve classically defined *moksha* (enlightenment)." By this, he goes on to explain, the narrative is intended to trace Andrew's path toward "liberation from numerous kinds of 'bondage' (physical, psychological, sexual, metaphysical) right down to the aesthetic preferences of one-celled chlamydosauria" (*Oxherding* xvi). At the conclusion of *Oxherding Tale*, then, Johnson sought to reveal a narrator who is not only free of the *actual* chains of chattel slavery, but also of the *figurative* chains that persisted for more than a century after Emancipation—in the guise of "aesthetic preferences" which determine how he can tell his story. That latter set of chains, the result of proscriptions placed on African American writing by white and black audiences alike, finally gets thrown off toward the end of the novel in a tongue-in-cheek chapter called "The Manumission of First-Person Viewpoint," wherein Andrew is liberated formally from the conventions of slave narratives. Notably, his literary manumission from "the *limitations* imposed upon the narrator-perceiver" precedes his physical manumission and, the novel indicates, might even make it possible (152). The final sentence of the section implies that Andrew's ultimate freedom in fact depends on his ability to write without restriction and without containment about the world as he has experienced it: "Having liberated first-person, it is now only fitting that in the following chapters we do as much for Andrew Hawkins" (153).

As a number of critics have argued, it is because of Johnson's desire to transcend the (aesthetic) legacy of slavery that he portrays time in multiple dimensions. James W. Coleman, for example, discovers in the temporal disjuncture of *Oxherding Tale* a "deep faith" in the idea that at some future point "there will be a free world for black people collectively; or, if this is not true, black people will make a better world along the way, as they devote themselves to spiritual interaction with others and with the universe." In Coleman's analysis, the novel's alternative temporalities reflect Johnson's attempt to move "in a moral direction" toward that final goal by undermining how slave narratives typically unfold. He therefore reads Andrew's path to *moksha* as a corrective for African American texts whose emphasis on "oppression and struggle" suggests that "blacks will always be slaves, no matter what the laws and institutions of society say, and no matter what time it is" (633–44). Likewise, William Gleason demonstrates that Johnson appeals in *Oxherding Tale* to the tenets of Zen Buddhism—and particularly the principle of opening the "third eye"—in order to "rebuild the Afro-American literary tradition, in relation to which Johnson stands, paradoxically, as both father and son, looking optimistically ahead to the day" when its productions will not be circumscribed by identity politics and will have no particular history delimiting it (723). Both of these readings, as well as many others that followed, have highlighted the way that various Eastern religions (Taoism, Hinduism, and different strains of Buddhism) shape Johnson's transformative approach to the historiography of slavery.[18]

At the time he was writing *Oxherding Tale*, during a seven-year period that preceded the book's publication in 1982, Johnson immersed himself in Eastern philosophy, with special attention to Buddhist scholarship. That study, he says, and the novel that grew out of it, being structurally and thematically inspired by the quest for *moksha*, was supposed to quench his lifelong interest in Zen meditation. Ever since he first tried meditating as a teenager, Johnson had been avoiding a sustained commitment to the practice because he worried that it would restrict him from pursuing more worldly goals. Meditation, as he describes it in the introduction to *Oxherding*,

> radically slowed down my sense of time, cleared away the background noise always on the edge of consciousness, and divested me of desires. My vision was clearer; I felt capable of infinite patience with my parents, teachers, and friends. Within me, I detected not the slightest trace of fear or anger or anxiety about anything, [sic] Nor was I conscious of myself, only of what was immediately in front of me, and *that*, I assure you, was indeed an unusual experience for a fourteen-year-old boy in 1962. . . . It came to me that if I kept this up, I might well become too detached and dispassionate and lack the fire—the internal agitation—to venture out into the world and explore all the things, high and low, that I, as a teenager, was burning to see, know, taste, and experience. (x)

Thus, rather than committing to regular practice, Johnson implies that he sought to "deal with" these early meditative insights at first academically, by consuming "the major and minor texts" in the Eastern spiritual traditions (xi), and then creatively, by incorporating into his fiction both his personal knowledge of Zen and what he gleaned about it from those texts. It is perhaps no great surprise, then, that in *Oxherding Tale* Andrew's transformation at the end of the novel is expressed in terms quite similar to the way Johnson depicts his own primal experience of meditation. For the narrator, liberation—from slavery as well as from the formal conventions of the slave narrative—happens in a revelatory instant, when time gets suspended and a "mystical feeling of transport" takes over (140).

That moment of temporal suspension, in which time moves neither forward nor back but appears locked in an all-encompassing present, structures Andrew's journey to freedom and determines how the novel represents his final revelation. It is the textual equivalent of the feeling of immediacy that Johnson associates with Zen meditation: a disjuncture in the endless succession of "nows" that defines Western temporality and, thus, narratives of progress.[19] But as I show here, the narrator's transformation is not determined by Eastern religious practices alone. In what follows, I argue that the Catholic theology of salvation informs, to a considerable degree, the liberation Andrew experiences at the end of *Oxherding Tale*, and that this theology creates an irresolvable tension in the way he becomes free. Arguing that Johnson's fiction—and his fictional representation of liberation—is informed by Catholicism will understandably surprise some readers, especially those who are acquainted with his biography. For, unlike the other authors in this study, Johnson was never a practicing Catholic, nor did he attend Catholic schools, nor were any members of his family Catholic. In fact, he was raised in the African Methodist Episcopalian Church, to which he belonged until he "fell away in college from a belief in institutional religion" and began to study Buddhism (O'Connell 24). Since that time, Johnson has referred to himself as "always" a "sincere Christian *and* a Buddhist," whose personal religious identity incorporates diverse theological traditions, even though his "roots" are in the AME (McWilliams, "Interview" 296). The inclusivity of Johnson's approach to religion led him to study the theology of the Catholic Church, and he counts works by Saint Francis and Augustine of Hippo among those that influenced his interest in the "life of the spirit" (Boccia 205). And so I argue here that his intellectual engagement with Augustinian texts, and the *Confessions* in particular, bears itself out in *Oxherding Tale*.

. . .

Johnson's engagement with Augustine reveals itself in the opening pages of *Oxherding Tale*. A quote from the *Soliloquies* is the first of four epigraphs introducing the novel, the sum of which quickly establishes a wide swath of Western and non-Western influences. (Alongside the citation from Augustine are references to the *Rig Veda*, *Ten Oxherding Pictures*, and a short story by Kafka.) Later in the text, in one of the two metafictional chapters that interrupt the progress of Andrew's journey from slavery, Augustine is referred to a second time—and, once again, his name is listed among a variety of literary and nonfictional sources from which the narrative draws. Chapter VIII, called "On the Nature of Slave Narratives," attempts to sketch out the history of the form that the novel ostensibly adheres to. According to the voice of the "essayist interlude"—which is suspiciously close to Johnson's own voice[20]—*Oxherding Tale* follows the classic style of the fugitive slave narrative, an autobiographical genre whose formal components derive from a number of other types of autobiographies, all of which "are the offspring of that hoary confession by the first philosophical black writer: Saint Augustine" (119). By referencing the *Confessions* in this way, the narratological "intermission" endeavors to show that underneath even the most content-specific and original texts, such as "authentic" experiences put into writing by fugitive slaves, there lies "a long pedigree that makes philosophical play with the form less outrageous than you might think." Case in point? Frederick Douglass's *Narrative of the Life*, now considered one of the foundations of African American literature, is modeled with "only slight variation," according to the author of this interlude, on the Augustinian movement from sin to salvation—a movement that was itself inspired by Plato and then, in turn, went on to inspire the Puritan version of spiritual autobiography (118).

The notion that Augustine's *Confessions* provided the formal logic both for Puritan and slave narratives is not unique to Johnson, of course. Variations of this argument had been made by scholars of literature and religion for decades.[21] But what is suggestive about its appearance here, in *Oxherding Tale*, involves the ambivalence with which the text approaches its literary forebear. On one hand, the author of the chapter insists upon acknowledging the influence of Augustine: "No form, I should note, *loses* its ancestry; rather these meanings accumulate in layers of tissue as the form evolves." Evoking a palimpsest, an image used to comparable effect in *Being and Race*, Johnson contends that divesting any narrative of slavery of its Augustinian intertext would be impossible. So instead of trying to silence or deny this ancestral history, he (via the persona of the intruding essayist) implores the "modern" slave narrator to "dig, dig, dig—call it spadework—until the form surrenders its diverse secrets" (119). The grim connotations of the racially charged term "spadework" bespeak Johnson's awareness of how controversial it is to suggest that contemporary African American writers owe *anything* to the canon of Western literature. And yet, given his scholarly investment in broadening the number and scope of sources to which "black writing" appeals, he deems it necessary to grapple with the layers of accumulated meaning that works such as the *Confessions* impose on *Oxherding Tale*.

On the other hand, there arises in this chapter and throughout the novel a competing sense that Augustine's inscription on the narrative has been overwritten—or, at least, over*whelmed*—by the sheer volume of intertextual references accompanying it. In other words, implicit in Johnson's acknowledgment of the *Confessions*'s influence on his writing is an acknowledgment of every text, before or after, that has likewise affected the conventions of representing slavery (as the allusions to Plato and Douglass imply). And, as we might expect from an author with his academic training and wide-ranging reading interests, those intertexts proliferate in *Oxherding Tale*, making it futile to try to excavate a single, fundamental archaeology of its formal structure. The "hole" of influence "is very deep" and the "archeological work" so necessarily "slow," the chapter seems to be saying, that it would diminish the reading experience in some significant way to focus too rigorously on all this excavated material. Speaking directly to the reader, he says by way of drawing these metafictional musings to a close, "already you are frowning impatiently, and with good reason, about this essayist interlude. (Only one more intermission follows; I promise.) We will, therefore, rejoin the action in Spartanburg, where Horace Bannon is unloading the human cargo from his wagon" (119). The abruptness of this transition back to the chronological progress of Andrew's journey forecloses, rather strangely, the chapter's stated purpose, which is to come to terms with how the form of the slave narrative has evolved over time. So despite the light Johnson wants to shine on the origins of the form, it is clear that he also views his own novel as unbeholden to its Augustinian—or any other line of—ancestry.

This two-part gesture of acknowledging and moving beyond a text's formal predecessors, of course, constitutes Johnson's optimistic view of the future of African American literature. What I have interpreted as *ambivalence* in his approach to Augustine, then, he would likely ascribe to "mastery" over the literary styles and structures implicated in his adaptation of the slave narrative form. For, as we have already seen, he promotes in

Being and Race a type of writer "who slides from genre to genre, style to style, leaving his or her distinctive signature on each form lovingly transfigured and pushed toward new possibilities. No creator, black or white, can be exempt from this standard. No genuine artist would wish to be." The standard of genuine artistry that Johnson delineates both here and in *Oxherding Tale* pivots on the way a writer controls and manipulates the various sources alluded to in the work. According to his analysis, in the hand of a masterful creator, strands of influence are always in the service of something greater than their original function; thus they should bend and be molded at will to whatever "new possibilities" the author endeavors to push them toward. Following this logic, all the intertexts of *Oxherding Tale*, including those that naturally "contradict each other," would articulate Andrew's path to *moksha*, the direction in which Johnson says the novel unambiguously moves (*Being* 53).

But, as I am going to argue, the intertextual engagement with Augustine in *Oxherding Tale* exceeds the meaning Johnson assigns to it. Indeed, the *Confessions* informs the novel on multiple levels and is altogether less manageable than the text self-consciously allows—to the extent that even Andrew's transformation at the conclusion of the narrative can be interpreted in Augustinian terms, in accordance with how the theologian defined forgiveness. By this, I do not intend to suggest that Augustine's confessional theology replaces the Eastern concept of *moksha* Johnson foregrounds, but rather that it supplements the novel's totalizing vision of Zen-inspired liberation in ways that are worth considering. In particular, I want to claim that the "freedom" Andrew ultimately achieves depends—rather problematically, it turns out—on the timeless and eternal logic of salvation espoused in the *Confessions* and reified for centuries by the Catholic church. As numerous critics have noted, the affirmative ending of *Oxherding Tale* is compromised significantly by the manner in which Andrew actually becomes free: he marries an Anglo woman and passes for white. Andrew's passing has posed an insurmountable hurdle for scholars such as Spaulding, who point out that this act of racial denial diminishes the novel's liberating potential, effectively proving that race, and the social systems that govern it, cannot really be transcended—neither by the principles of Zen Buddhism to which Johnson appeals, nor by any other textually constructed "solution" (91). Along similar lines, Gleason suggests that, to some readers, it will appear at the end of *Oxherding*

Tale that Johnson "authenticates the very power structures he seeks to undermine (or, perhaps more indicting, that he never sought to undermine them at all)" (724).

Arguments such as these, which cast doubt on the terms of Andrew's liberation from slavery and its legacy, highlight a tension the text leaves unresolved: that, in spite of his personal experience of freedom, the world the narrator inhabits remains "mired in Eurocentric racial ideology" (Spaulding 91). This is true with regard to both the historical moment depicted at the narrative's conclusion (in the early part of the Civil War) and the historical moment from which Andrew supposedly writes his memoir (roughly eighty years after Emancipation). *Oxherding Tale* never goes so far as to deny the persistence of debilitating racist structures in the United States, either during the slave period or a century later. Yet, in keeping with Johnson's own views about the transcendent possibility of art, the novel does imply that "great writers" possess the ability to imaginatively bypass those structures—because, as he put it in *Being and Race*, "language is transcendence and so is fiction" (39). Critics opposed to the idea that ideologies of race could ever be transcended, imaginatively or otherwise, are thus wary of how Johnson applies the Buddhist philosophy of *moksha* to the "dilemma" facing African American literature; they are wary of what Gleason calls "the liberation of Zen as enacted by *Oxherding Tale*" (725). One result of all this wariness has been a long and lively debate about the spiritual principles informing the final moments of the novel. Is Andrew's freedom as consistent with "classically defined" *moksha* as Johnson claims? If so, would Zen Buddhism offer comparable freedoms to a character who could not pass for white? Does Johnson's Eastern aesthetic have any real-world significance for African Americans still contending with racism and the legacy of slavery?

Instead of directly tackling these questions—which are handled much more ably by scholars, such as Jonathan Little and Linda Furgerson Selzer, who have written convincing analyses of various Eastern religions present in *Oxherding Tale*—I aim to shift their focus a bit by bringing Augustinian theology into the conversation. It is my contention that Johnson's ambivalence toward the *Confessions* betrays an abiding attraction to Augustine's timeless vision of salvation that he has, consciously or unconsciously, integrated into the classically Buddhist framework of the narrative. Furthermore, in considering how Augustinian salvation supplements the liberation Andrew achieves at the conclusion of *Oxherding Tale*, I believe we are better poised to address its problematic implications for the future of race relations in the United States. Those familiar with Jacques Derrida's "logic of the supplement" from *Of Grammatology* will recognize the gesture I am making: my argument turns on the idea that supplemental material can have unintentional—indeed "dangerous"—consequences for text being supplemented. In this case, the "danger" of the Augustinian supplement to *Oxherding Tale* is revealed in the unresolved racial tension at the novel's end. Bringing Derridean theory to bear in this way on *Oxherding Tale* might appear counterintuitive, especially since Johnson is by training a phenomenologist, and even his investment in Zen Buddhism amounts to, as he has described it, his "own quirky variations on phenomenology" (*Being* ix). Derrida's work relentlessly critiques the phenomenological approaches central to Johnson's thinking about identity and race, and so I grant that evoking it here does a sort of interpretive violence to the ostensibly affirmative view of racial identity with which his novel concludes. Yet, as I hope to demonstrate, that violence is already written into the text of *Oxherding Tale*, by way of the (supplemental) presence of the *Confessions*.

For example, let us look more closely at the language Johnson uses in chapter VIII to convey his novel's formal relationship to Augustine:

> In point of fact, the movements in the Slave Narrative from slavery (sin) to freedom (salvation) are identical to those of the Puritan Narrative, and *both* these genuinely American forms are the offspring of . . . Saint Augustine. In *The Confessions* we notice (and perceive also in the Slave and Puritan Narratives) a nearly Platonic movement from ignorance to wisdom, nonbeing to being. (118–19)

I have indicated that the goal of this metafictional interlude is to establish—for the purpose of getting beyond—the literary ancestry of *Oxherding Tale*. The chapter highlights how radically the contents of the form have shifted over time, while their "movements" remain "identical" to those of the source texts. Aware that some readers might object to his unconventional adaptation of the slave narrative, Johnson's "essayist" self-consciously deflects the critique by pointing out that a precedent for this kind of formal variation can be found in earlier narratives of slavery, in Puritan narratives, and even in the *Confessions* itself. Thus the bracketed nouns "sin" and "salvation" in the quoted passage are meant to show that authors like Douglass simply swapped out the Christological implications of confessional autobiography for a secular objective when they adapted the form to suit their abolitionist politics.[22] But, as we know from reading Douglass's *Narrative of the Life* as well as countless other autobiographies by fugitive slaves, the religious content of the confessional did not ever really fall away as Johnson implies. Quite to the contrary, in fact: scholars of African American literature have long recognized the spiritual imperative of these antebellum texts; fugitive slave narrators, just like their Puritan predecessors, were expected to testify that they too had been saved by Christ (as a way of justifying their own worthiness vis-à-vis the abolitionist cause).[23]

The religious contours of Augustine's *Confessions* are still, then, of great significance to the narratives of fugitive slave authors. I would submit that Johnson's parenthetical references to "sin" and "salvation" suggest that those foundational Christian principles are inscribed in his narrative as well, and that they provide a necessary supplement to the way *Oxherding Tale* defines the terms with which they are linked. In other words, a full understanding of the meaning of Andrew's "slavery" and his "freedom" requires understanding the Augustinian concepts that are bracketed to them here, in this passage. What is more, the two other pairs of opposing terms mentioned above ("ignorance" and "wisdom"; "nonbeing" and "being") supplement the narrator's personal transformation in ways that must be considered as well, if we endeavor to make sense of the irresolvability at the novel's end. Indeed, Andrew's journey to freedom is figured as the inversion of *all four* of the pairs of binary oppositions Johnson lists in this chapter, each of which is implicated in the revelatory moment of temporal suspension that irrupts in the final pages of the text. Therefore, that instant of timeless presence, in which Andrew becomes free from slavery and its legacy, is also commensurate in the narrative with his coming into wisdom, into being, and into spiritual salvation.

To perceive how these other sets of inversions inform the narrator's Zen-inspired liberation, we will need to examine in more detail the transformation he undergoes from the start of the novel to its conclusion. Andrew's journey begins, as most fugitive slave narratives do, with his birth into slavery. As in a large number of those antebellum texts as well, there remains some uncertainty regarding the precise circumstances of the narrator's parentage, though it is clear he resulted from a transgressive liaison between a white slaveholder and a black slave. Andrew rather humorously writes that since his white mistress/mother refuses to acknowledge him, he has only his father's "version of the story" to go on, and that this may or may not be an accurate account of his origins (7). While the obscurity surrounding the event of his conception might appear to substantiate the narrator's resemblance to other well known slave autobiographers (Douglass among them), who also knew very little about their progress into the world, it turns out to have an altogether different effect. In fact, the first chapter of *Oxherding Tale* amounts to a comical reimagining of the typically traumatic origin story of the biracial slave, meant to convey the exceptionalness of Andrew's situation. It is a vehicle to explain the entirely unconventional education he received while enslaved on Cripplegate plantation—his extensive instruction in "a program modeled on that of James Mill for his son John Stuart" (12). For, in the context of American slavery, only an episode as outlandish as the one Andrew tells at the beginning of the narrative would account for his master's decision to pay for the private instruction of his wife's illegitimate black son. And, as Johnson makes clear in the book's introduction, it was essential to the structure of the novel that its narrator "start his journey to freedom already knowing everything western intellectual history could offer . . . so that as he quests for a deeper knowledge of the self, he is poised for whatever eastern philosophy might offer" (xiv).

Put in these terms, the Western texts that Andrew studies until the eve of his twentieth birthday constitute the "ignorance" from which his journey will ultimately deliver him; Eastern philosophy signifies the deeper and more profound "wisdom" he acquires when his transformation is complete and he finally becomes free. Thus the novel's trajectory, from slavery to freedom, involves a playfully ironic take on the standard of intellectual enlightenment celebrated in the West. Rather than achieving self-knowledge by "learning everything" in the Western scholarly tradition, he must learn to embrace what that tradition cannot provide—what, in Johnson's view, it is fundamentally incapable of giving him: the radical self-*less*-ness or no-self intrinsic to Zen liberation. And so, after briefly explaining and then summarizing the education Andrew received at Cripplegate, *Oxherding Tale* immediately proceeds to chronicle its narrator's progress toward a new (to him) Eastern way of conceiving the self that resists any attempt at categorization and containment. Andrew's narratological progress traces, in broad strokes, the path illustrated in the twelfth-century Chinese pictorial series from which the novel takes its name.[24] Like the oxherder depicted in *Ten Oxherding Pictures*, whose seeking after a lost ox (self) leads him through a succession of experiences that culminate in his liberation from the very idea of self, Johnson's narrator embarks on a quest for legal emancipation (that is, self-determination under law), which also finds him moving progressively closer to Zen's no-self ideal. Every step of Andrew's journey, then, from the moment he leaves Master Polkinghorne's plantation in search of money to buy his manumission, contributes to his final realization that selfhood cannot ever actually be possessed since it is "interwoven with everything—literally everything—that can be thought or felt" (152). Thus the "wisdom" he arrives at when the novel concludes confirms the Buddha's no-self doctrine, which teaches that "Grasping after self is clinging to illusory ignorance" and that ignorance must be abandoned before real freedom is achieved (Burns 94).

In this way, Andrew's transformation encapsulates and absorbs the "the nearly Platonic movement from ignorance to wisdom" that Johnson associates with Augustine's confessional form (even though the "wisdom" he achieves is, at its base, antithetical to Plato's own philosophy of the self). And, by pressing a bit further, we can see too how it involves that other pair of oppositions, "nonbeing" and "being," which the novel likewise correlates in chapter VIII to narratives of confession. At the end of *Oxherding Tale*, as condition of his liberation, Andrew radically shifts his view of what it means *to be* in this world. The shift is sudden; according to the "classically defined" experience of *moksha*, it happens in a revelatory instant— during his last conversation with the slavecatcher Horace Bannon, at the moment he believes Bannon will kill him. But, also in accordance with the framework of Zen enlightenment to which the novel adheres, the seeds of the narrator's liberating revelation were sown much earlier in his journey, when he met Reb on the Leviathan plantation.[25] In fact, the way of being that Andrew assumes in this moment clearly reflects Reb's influence and the phenomenological approach his character stands for in the text.

Reb is "Leviathan's Coffinmaker," the man responsible for building the boxes that carry all of Flo Hatfield's slaves to their final resting spots. A slave himself, Reb is the first person Andrew encounters after leaving Cripplegate under an agreement with Master Polkinghorne to work toward his freedom in service to Flo. The ominous connotations of being welcomed into his new role by a coffin maker increase measurably as Reb refers to the narrator as "fresh meat" and then laughs "the laugh of a hangman" while showing him into the mistress's house. "Had you entered with us that day," Andrew writes,

> you'd have passed through outside odors arranged in a strata so that we moved, slowly like a funeral procession, from room to room through curtains of smells that included cabbage, hominy made from Indian corn, and fresh fish. You'd have seen a white-pillard doorway leaded with sidelights, then, as Reb stepped aside, an oak-paneled, high-ceilinged boudoir of whorehouse luxury. (36)

Reb later tells Andrew that, in his opinion, Flo Hatfield died in her sleep from heart failure fifteen years earlier despite having ostensibly recovered from the episode. So in one regard the funerary images and "curtains of smells" redolent of rotting flesh in this passage point to her death—or at least to what Reb perceives as dead inside her. Additionally, though, there is a palpable sense here that the Coffinmaker is simultaneously leading Andrew to *his* grave, by means of a luxurious "oak-paneled" box that smacks of uncontrollable desire. And, as we come to find out, that is precisely how Reb interprets the scene. Not only have years of experience at Leviathan taught him that handsome young men who find themselves "in the services of the senses" to Flo do not live long, but he also recognizes in the narrator a worldview that fundamentally contradicts everything he believes about the nature of being. To his mind, Andrew has already died, condemned to a state of nonbeing the moment he set out from his master's house in search of his selfhood.

Reb's beliefs about nonbeing and being are determined by the (fictional) African tribe into which he was born. As he explains to Andrew, Allmuseri tribespeople hold fast to the principle that there is no singular identity. All life, as they see it, is interconnected—part of a vast expanse of absolute being that resists individualization. Thus Reb rejects personal pronouns. In his native language there are "no words for *I, you, mine, yours,*" and Andrew learns the Allmuseri "had, consequently, no experience of these things, either, only proper names that were variations on the Absolute" (97). This linguistic system makes it impossible for the individual to position him/herself in the world, promoting a set of communal values that recall the Buddha's teachings on radical no-self-ness. Of all the characters in the novel, in fact, Reb comes closest to the Zen ideas that Johnson was studying at the time and later committed himself to practicing.²⁶ According to Reb, rugged individualism—or the desire to distance oneself from life's diverse interconnectedness—remains a failing proposition. That is why he perceives both Flo Hatfield, a woman consumed by her need to satisfy personal desires, and Andrew, who wants to establish his place in society, as dead inside. His early spiritual training in Africa, combined with what he learned about the slave system in the United States, taught Reb to embrace "self-obliteration" and, therefore, to neither expect nor hope for anything beyond what is immediately available to him; he grasps after nothing, saying yes to "suffering" and "misfortune." While this way of living might appear to readers a sad and destructive consequence of Reb's enslavement, the result of having his "food, property, and loved ones . . . snatched away" (76) for more than forty years by an unjust institution, the novel ultimately validates its liberating potential through the narrative of Andrew's Zen-like transformation.

Indeed, as Ashraf Rushdy has argued, the "Allmuseri phenomenology" that Reb advocates provides Andrew with the education necessary for his eventual liberation (190).²⁷

Although the narrator is initially skeptical of Reb's resignation to slavery and does his best for most of the novel to disavow the Coffinmaker's embrace of suffering, there can be no doubt that in the final moments of *Oxherding Tale* he comes to see the world as an Allmuseri. The last scene, which I would now like to consider in some detail, signifies what Rushdy calls Andrew's "surrender to Being" (190), meaning that his character finally accepts Reb's belief in the interconnectedness of all life forms—past, present, and future—effectively completing his movement from nonbeing. Here is how it unfolds: after a complicated series of events that depicts Andrew and Reb's narrow escape from death at the Leviathan plantation by fleeing to a small town where they are unknown and the narrator can pass for white, they are eventually tracked down by Flo Hatfield's slave catcher, Horace Bannon, who plans to murder them both at his convenience. By the time Bannon catches up with Andrew, Reb has already left Spartanburg with plans to move further north, but the narrator presumes his fellow fugitive was killed before even leaving the town limits. With Reb's murder a near certainty—and his own only a matter of time—Andrew allows the "Soulcatcher" to take him without much resistance from the home he shares with his pregnant white wife, so as to avoid a violent confrontation in front of the family he has come, to his own surprise, to love. It is, therefore, in a vacant field a short distance from his house that the narrator finds himself at the end of the novel with Bannon, preparing himself for what he hopes will be a "clean, quick kill" (170).

Instead of being killed, however, Andrew engages in a life-altering conversation with Bannon, during which he experiences the revelation that confirms—as Johnson's introduction promises—his "liberation from numerous kinds of bondage." (The title of this last chapter is "Moksha," after all.) First, he learns that the only person aware of his fugitive status harbors no plans to bring him to justice. Bannon tells Andrew that he recently gave up the bounty hunting business, having "been bested by Reb, who was safely now in Chicago" (174). So in physical terms at least, there remains no reason for the narrator to consider himself a slave. Yet even with the knowledge of Reb's escape and with his own freedom all but guaranteed, the narrator feels persistently like chattel, owing to the other fact he learns from their conversation: that his father, George Hawkins, was murdered by Bannon prior to the Soulcatcher's retirement. George's murder devastates Andrew—and not just because it means he has failed to honor his filial pledge to purchase the old man's manumission. What he finds most troubling is that it happened before he had a chance to come to terms with his father over the "inheritance" that was left him. For years Andrew has been struggling to overcome the "way of seeing" that George passed on to him as a child. And now, as an adult about to be formally released from the hold of slavery, he views himself as still enslaved by his father's essentializing rhetoric and the emphasis he always placed on the "*distinctions*" between people of different races and genders (172).

The character of George Hawkins is, by Johnson's own account, a prototype for the black nationalist agenda of the 1960s and 1970s—a man who taught his son that whatever he does in life either "pushes the Race forward, or pulls us back" (21).[28] It was this logic of cultural essentialism, crystallized in the aesthetic of the Black Arts Movement, that Johnson railed against in his doctoral dissertation, arguing that such ideological constraints foreclose "the free investigation of phenomena" in life and in literature (*Being* 26). Thus, at the end of *Oxherding Tale*, his narrator discovers that real freedom is contingent upon liberation from the bondage of an essentially divisive ideology as well. To complete his transformation,

Andrew must abandon his father's teaching and accept the absolute interconnectedness of all being, which in this novel, as I have been suggesting, is equivalent to absorbing the Allmuseri worldview. That revelatory moment, wherein he finally achieves *moksha*, signals the triumph of Reb's phenomenological perspective. It happens in an instant, while Andrew is gazing at "the intricately woven brown tattooes" on the Soulcatcher's body, each one a representation of an individual (animal, plant, human) murdered by Bannon:

> Not tattooes at all, I saw, but forms sardined in his contour, creatures Bannon had killed since childhood: spineless insects, flies he'd dewinged; yet even the tiniest of these thrashing within the body mosaic was, clearly, a society as complex as the higher forms, a concrescence of molecules cells atoms in concert, for nothing in the necropolis he'd filled stood alone, wished to stand alone, had to stand alone, and the commonwealth of the dead shape-shifted on his chest ... their metamorphosis having no purpose beyond the delight the universe took in diversity for its own sake, the proliferation of beauty, and yet all were conserved in this process of doubling, nothing was lost in the masquerade, the cosmic costume ball, where behind every different mask at the party—behind snout beak nose and blossom—the self-same face was uncovered at midnight, and this was my father. (175)

Reminiscent of the way Reb says the Allmuseri elders taught him to "send his *kra* forth to dwell ... in ten thousand hosts" and to observe "intimately" how every organism is connected, even in death, the world inscribed on Bannon enlightens Andrew—all at once—to the diverse unity of being. (49). The will to distinguish between individuals or groups of individuals on the basis of their essential differences has been extinguished. As the grammar of the passage indicates, the narrator now sees only sameness where he was inclined previously to divide. (Note, for example, the disinclination to use commas to separate items in a list: "snout beak nose and blossom.")

Andrew has in this moment, then, fully transcended the desire to position himself uniquely in the world, which Reb associates with nonbeing or being "dead inside." Indeed, like the Allmuseri, he has come alive finally to the radical position-less-ness of the self by perceiving its intrinsic presence in others. In this sense—the sense of achieving new knowledge about what it means *to be*—his transformation thus reflects the Platonic movement toward being that, in Johnson's view, along with the movement toward wisdom, undergirds all confessional narratives since Augustine. It has been necessary to flesh out the various ways that the narrator's journey to freedom incorporates these other two Platonic movements, indeed, in order to establish the correspondence between Andrew's revelatory vision, his *moksha*, and the vision of God that Augustine describes in salvific terms in the *Confessions*. For just as Andrew's Zen liberation involves his instantaneous acclimation to a radically altered perception of the world, Augustine writes that he was saved from sin in a flash of transcendent light, with which his eyes were shocked "so that I might see that what I was seeing is Being" (7.10.16). Up until the instant of his revelation, Augustine's sight was characterized by "weakness," he confesses; it was limited by an inability to perceive the presence of divine nature in all existing things. But after he came to see differently, in this one moment of sudden enlightenment, the *Confessions* demonstrates that he never again doubted what was revealed to him: that God is being itself, the source and creator of every other part of existence.

As Scott MacDonald has recently shown, despite the abruptness of Augustine's salvific vision, his narrative "makes clear" that it actually did not occur "in the twinkling of an eye" as the saint suggests. Rather, "the journey leading to that crucial point was long," MacDonald argues, the result of years spent grappling with the intellectual traditions in which Augustine was embroiled. Specifically, the way Augustine conceived of being had to evolve over decades from Manichean dualism "by way of Platonism to an understanding of the God of Christianity" (20). Without going too far into the philosophical subtleties of MacDonald's argument, it is sufficient for my purposes to note that the *Confessions* portrays its narrator's mature thinking about being—and thus his Christian salvation—as a sloughing off of a "youthful ignorance" that made him "defenseless" to the Manichees' influence. Most notably, Augustine garnered from his study of Plato the "wisdom" to challenge the Manichean principle of evil, an intellectual development that facilitated his apparently instantaneous conclusion that "God is the reality that truly *is*" (31). And so MacDonald's painstaking analysis of the Platonic basis for Augustine's spiritual epiphany confirms how Johnson represents the formal structure of the *Confessions* in chapter VIII of *Oxherding Tale*—as a "movement from ignorance to wisdom, nonbeing to being." But it also, quite significantly, points to another connection between the novel and its Augustinian intertext, one that Johnson seems more reticent to acknowledge. Namely, we find that Andrew's transformation in the final moments of *Oxherding Tale* draws noticeably from the way Augustine ultimately resolved his dispute with the Manichees and thereby reconciled himself with the beliefs of the Catholic Church.

MacDonald explains that the main obstacle to Augustine's salvation, prior to his salvific vision, was a series of questions posed to him in his youth by Manichees, who ridiculed "the Christian belief that God created human beings in God's own image" (21). According to Manichean rationalism, the existence of evil on earth invalidates the idea, fundamental to Catholic theology, that the divine will is omnipotent and incorruptible, for would a good God really choose to create evil? The reality that as a young man Augustine could not adequately defend Catholicism against these doubts—and, in fact, grew susceptible to them himself—becomes the greatest regret of his post-conversion life. Again and again in the *Confessions*, he laments being persuaded by the solution the Manichees proposed for the problem of evil, referring to his dalliance with their dualistic worldview as "the principal and almost sole cause of my inevitable error" (5.10.19). Hence Augustine presents that moment in Milan, when he says his eyes were finally opened to God's unifying power, in terms of deliverance from the sin of false doctrine. Claiming that his vision left "absolutely no room . . . for doubt," he means that seeing God in this way—as being itself—convinced him, once and for all, that the Manichees were wrong to regard the natural world as independent of the divine (7.10.16). In his mature understanding, "evil exists only as a privation of good," because God unifies every part of creation, from the lowest to the most highly developed (3.7.12). Even maligned creatures, such as poisonous snakes whose only purpose seems to be destructive, bear some degree of divine nature, Augustine comes to realize, given that they "come from" God and God "made all things good" without making "all things equal" (7.11.17, 7.11.18). What this indicates, then, is that following his time in Milan, Augustine learned to recognize aspects of true being anywhere he looked. For, as he writes in another text, *On the Catholic and the Manichaean Ways of Life*: "If you look for something strictly contrary to God, you will find absolutely nothing" (qtd. in MacDonald 32).

I would suggest that in finding his father's face "behind every different mask" of the organisms "thrashing within the ... diversity" inscribed on the Soulcatcher's chest at the end of *Oxherding Tale*, Andrew is effectively reenacting the revelation from the *Confessions*—in addition to the Allmuseri-inspired revelation, which the passage more overtly evokes. Indeed, it should be noted that if Andrew were perceiving that vast commonwealth from an exclusively Allmuserian perspective, it would be an image of his own being (his *kra*, as Reb calls it) that he would be locating beneath the masks of all those creatures. So the fact that he sees George Hawkins there instead of himself implicates Augustinian theology in his revelatory vision. Not only does Augustine emphasize the necessity of discovering one's "supremely good Father" in and through the created world, but he also uses strikingly similar imagery to account for the effect of this immutable paternal presence on creation. Consider, for example, how the passage excerpted above continues, as Andrew proceeds to describe the experience of seeing George, over and over, among the "thousand individualities" (175) moving about:

> the profound mystery of the One and the Many gave me back my father again and again, his love, in every being from grubworms to giant sumacs, for these too were my father and, in the final face I saw in the Soulcatcher, which shook tears from me—my own face, for he had duplicated portions of me during the early days of the hunt—I was my father's father, and he my child. (176)

The reference here to love—to a father's love—being returned eternally to Andrew by "the profound mystery of the One and the Many" recalls the way Augustine discusses God's love, in the wake of his conversion. Before the revelation in Milan, Augustine admits in the *Confessions*, he failed to love appropriately, seeking only transient fulfillment of his desires in the material realm. Afterwards, though, he came to understand love in Trinitarian terms: as the gift of the Father, bestowed on earth by the Holy Spirit, who unites every facet of existence through his Son.[29] In this sense, God's love is a "common and immutable good" that can be rejoiced in and shared among diverse members of creation, making—as Augustine has written on numerous occasions in related language—"'one heart' out of many" or "many souls one soul."[30]

Thus, for Augustine, the love of the Father transcends temporal divisions because it is itself indivisible and timeless, the primal unity of everything that exists, has existed, or will exist. We find equivalent logic in the way that Andrew sees George's love for him given back "again and again" in self-sameness by a multitude of life forms "from grubworms to giant sumacs," living and dead, who "too were my father." Note the tense of his phrasing. Andrew is not referring to an ongoing development by which these organisms are becoming more and more like George over time; rather, the use of the indicative past (they "were" George) emphasizes an originary fact about their very being, suggesting that all existence—past, present, and future—is ontologically determined by him. In fact, it should be clear that the process documented in this passage does not actually involve George, or even any of the creatures who appear to be newly assuming his image. The transformation is entirely the narrator's own, a consequence of (finally) seeing something that has been there, as the grammatical tense implies, from the beginning: his father's love revealed in the universe. Once that love is revealed to him in its timelessness, Andrew alights on what unifies, instead of what divides, the complex "society" represented on the Soulcatcher. He perceives George's presence immanent in each different part of creation. And, as I have been arguing, this resonates with how Augustine came to perceive *his* "Father's" presence following the revelatory vision in Milan. Book 7 of the *Confessions* shows him discovering "in the flash of a trembling glance" God's "invisible nature" in all the things of the earth and his sudden understanding that to God all these things "owe their existence" (7.16.22, 7.15.21). The power of Augustine's revelation therefore hinges on the very same shift in perception that Andrew's does. Both men are awakened to the common goodness of the material world when they discover in it the previously hidden (yet always there) love of the father/Father.

With respect to the crisis of faith that drew Augustine away from Catholicism and led to his sojourn with the Manichees, it follows that he would need a vision to establish God's immanence in creation. His failure to recognize that all things derive from God was, as he claimed, the greatest obstacle to his personal salvation. And since a primary motive of the *Confessions* was to attest to its narrator's unwavering belief in Catholic doctrine, the text devotes much attention to the moment Augustine overcame his Manichean doubts by seeing the divine "Father" in everything that exists.[31] But if we grant that Andrew's vision involves a similar kind of perception, there is in *Oxherding Tale* no comparable motivation for it—at least in terms of the narrative's "theological" orientation. What I mean is that the Allmuseri worldview that Andrew very clearly assumes at the end of the novel does not prioritize a paternalistic idea of God in the same way that Catholic theology does. Nothing in what readers learn about Reb's belief system nor about his concept of the Absolute prepares us for the significant role that Andrew's own father plays in his final revelation. Indeed, the position-less-ness that Reb advocates as an Allmuseri is premised on the total renunciation of all personal attachments, paternal or otherwise. Because the Allmuseri believe in a supreme being who does not differentiate between people according to their relationships with one another—"in Allmuseri, all is A. One person was A_1, the next A_2," and so on (97)—they assign no special meaning to the rank of father. This explains why Reb seems less affected by the death of his son, Patrick, than Andrew expected him to be. Although he clearly loved the boy, Reb has long ago abdicated responsibility for Patrick's life or his protection. Paternal feelings implicitly contradict what he learned from the Allmuseri elders about disavowing private possessions and the will to control one's "belongings."[32] Therefore, Reb refuses to assign blame for the brutal loss of his son or even to mourn him in any traditional way, telling Andrew that he sees no reason to dwell on it: "I put his casket in the ground a month ago. You the one still carryin' it around" (61).

In this exchange Reb makes clear that, within the Allmuseri cosmology, fatherhood does not grant him the right to expect his children's wellbeing or to be affected personally by their pain. As I have been suggesting, these sentiments run counter to how Andrew comes to see George at the end of *Oxherding Tale* and the significance he places on finding the eternal love of his father. Even more important, to my mind, is that Reb's words contain a pointed critique of the narrator's need for absolution. Better than anyone else at Leviathan, the Coffinmaker knows Andrew indirectly caused his son's suicide when he showed up there with Master Polkinghorne's permission to work for Flo Hatfield, rendering Patrick redundant. Reb warned Andrew that his plan to earn money for his manumission would result in death, and he scoffed at his yearning for selfhood. Yet despite the narrator's disregard of these admonitions, Reb pronounces him blameless for what happened to Patrick, indicating that his gravest mistake has been "carryin' . . . around" for more than a month the hope of being absolved of culpability. To the Coffinmaker, guilt and forgiveness are always irrelevant constructs. Given his spiritual predisposition toward suffering, he deems it foolish for Andrew to be grasping after his—or anyone else's—mercy. Reb's pedagogical function in the novel, in fact, revolves around helping the narrator embrace the futility of chasing after redemption. That, Andrew learns just before his final revelation, is the way he became free. Reb ultimately eluded capture and completed his journey north, Bannon explains, precisely because he "didn't want *nothin*'" and "didn't care 'bout merit or evil" (173, 174). The Coffinmaker's freedom thus confirms the meaninglessness of the search that Andrew has been pursuing; it demonstrates how misguided he has been to seek "merit" in a world where worthiness, like evil, is not something that can be granted or taken away but *just is*.

All of the lessons Reb has taught him contribute to the narrator's enlightenment by revealing that liberation happens when one stops seeking, when one simply accepts what the universe offers without expectation of anything more. And, of course, there is a sense in which Andrew's vision of paternal love at the end of the novel signifies his newfound openness to this Allmuseri ideal, because he learns to receive—freely and unequivocally—the gift being given to him at the present instant by all the world's creatures. But I would submit that this explanation alone does not account for George's presence in Andrew's revelation, nor for the way that presence fulfills the narrator's desire for reconciliation. It is, after all, in response to a series of desperate questions about George that Bannon bids Andrew to examine the "necropolis" inscribed on his chest, saying "He's heah. . . . Ask him yoself." So in addition to facilitating his break with his father's essentialism, the final revelatory moment of the text also serves to absolve the narrator of the guilt that has haunted him ever since he started passing; it serves as his answer to whether George "died feeling I despised him, or if he . . . died hating me" for pretending to be white (175). The last promise Andrew made to his father, when he said goodbye to him at the gates of Leviathan, was that he would be himself—that he would never deny his blackness, because doing so would be, as George said that day, "like turnin' your back on me and everythin' I believes in" (21). Thus, much of the anguish he feels upon hearing about George's murder is due to his failure to keep this promise and—quite literally—the "sin" of denying his father. That anguish, however, dissolves as a result of his vision, which culminates in the reconciliatory image of the two men joined eternally in mutual understanding ("I was my father's father, and he my child"). Since Reb's beliefs do not sustain either Andrew's feelings of remorse over his relationship with George or his hope of being forgiven by him, it appears the narrator's liberation cannot be explained by Allmuseri logic alone.

Indeed, insofar as it offers the narrator a means of reconciling with George over the sin of denying him, I argue that Andrew's final revelation is structured by the economy of forgiveness laid out in the *Confessions*. To be saved from transgression and set free, Augustine wrote, the sinner must cleave to the Father through the principle of the Holy Spirit, which unites all persons timelessly within the body of his "coeternal Son" (7.21.27). The emphasis Augustinian theology places on "cleaving"—on being conformed to the likeness of God on earth—informs the culminating image of Andrew's vision and helps to explain why he imagines reconciliation with George as an eternal transformation into him, wherein father and child are forever one, indistinguishable from each other for eternity. On the level of the narrator's temporal experience in the text, this fantasy of paternal unification cannot be justified in any way, for Andrew currently lives as a white man and will continue to pass for white (the novel implies) even after his formal emancipation from slavery. He is not really anything like his father, given how radically his existence differs from the life George lived himself and made Andrew promise to live. It seems erroneous to believe, then, that the narrator's father would ever actually absolve him of guilt, since passing fundamentally contradicts the "world-historical mission" of black revolutionaries, which George fervently upheld and, in fact, died trying to protect. As George saw it, even the smallest act of denial threatens the future of the race, and so he could not forgive something that undermines the very idea of history he "been fightin' for" all these years (21).

However, when we think about the culminating image of Andrew's vision in atemporal terms—as a kind of reconciliation with the father/Father that transcends "vicissitudes of time"—then the historical consequences of his passing become irrelevant to him. This kind of reconciliation is exactly what, I am suggesting, the Augustinian supplement provides to the narrator of *Oxherding Tale*. It gives Andrew a way to circumvent the racial structures that determine history, suggesting that George's love for him (like Augustine's idea of God's) is eternally present and not subject to the temporal order. According to Augustine, there exists "a sublime created realm cleaving with such pure love to the true and truly eternal God," wherein man "never detaches" from the Father nor "slips away into the changes and successiveness of time" (12.15.19). It is an idealized space like this one, constituted by "pure love," that I argue Andrew envisions in his final revelation, at the moment he discovers George's face in his own. For him, as for Augustine, liberation occurs when the transcendent love of father interrupts the temporal horizon, changing how one relates to the standard chronology of lived experience. Thus, just before referring to himself as a "freeman" for the first time in the novel, the narrator seems to be glimpsing a new order of existence, outside of human temporality, in which he is timelessly cleaved to George, as his eternal son and father. Reconciling with George in these (Augustinian) terms therefore has the curious, and doubly troubling, effect of divesting Andrew of the historical impact of his actions—his passing for white—while legitimizing his ultimate decision to stay with his wife and to raise their daughter together, fully immersed in the white world.

I indicated earlier that the domestic turn Andrew takes at the end of the novel has proved problematic for critics, who point out its inherent inconsistency with his final revelatory vision of George. They rightly ask why, if the narrator had in fact reconciled himself with his father as the final image suggests, would he not feel compelled to honor that revolutionary legacy by striking out against the very structures that enslaved him in the first place? How can Andrew possibly square George's revolutionary agenda with the tone on which his own narrative concludes—in apparent acceptance of and assimilation to *the way things are*? My answer is that Augustinian theology enables this controversial choice, by offering an imaginative means to bypass the political and social implications of his marriage as well as justifying the faith he puts in love. In other words, the priority the narrator places in the last sentences of the text on his domestic responsibilities—on "rebuilding . . . the world" (176) together with his wife and his daughter, whom he has named after his white mistress/mother—does contradict every aspect of George's ideology, making it irresolvable with the vision of paternal reconciliation he describes in the preceding paragraph. But it is, I argue, perfectly consistent with how Augustine imagines loving *his* "Father" in the *Confessions*. In Augustine's view, the Father's transcendent love is expressed on earth through the purity of the love one shares with others. This principle, integral to the Catholic sacrament of marriage, means that people who are joined appropriately in their reverence for God and for each other abide eternally in that "sublime created realm," which Augustine maintains is independent of historical experience.[33] Andrew's earlier depiction of marrying Peggy makes it clear that he envisions his relationship with her as a timeless union capable of transcending the racial structures specific to his—or any other—moment in history. In fact, their entire wedding ceremony is imbued with strange Catholic overtones that reflect the Augustinian tenor of the love that unites them.

Nominally, of course, their wedding ceremony is Protestant—presided over not by a priest but by a minister, whose "Pelagian" beliefs bespeak an anti-Catholic orientation (138). Yet the decadence of the event, which Peggy calls "the gaudiest thing since the carnival came to town," and the description of the church's "stained glass window awash with sunlight . . . that . . . rippled, ever richer, as it neared the pulpit," are suggestive of Catholicism, rather than the unadorned style commonly found in Protestant chapels. Even more suggestively, Andrew refers to the act of taking his vows in sacramental terms that correspond to how Catholics define marriage. To him, it is a "nearly mystical" event that "gave the abstract form flesh" and "glorified . . . all of us . . . through a ceremony that suspended Time." He goes on:

> The heart knew nothing of hours. Minutes. It moved on a plane above history, error. . . . We stood, I felt, translated, lifted a few feet off the ground, exchanging replies in old, old voices in a different tongue we borrowed from our better selves—the people we were intended to be—in some parallel world, where the absences of this life were presences, the failures here triumphs there, a realm of changeless meaning for which the only portal was surrender. (140)

Apart from his final revelatory vision, this is the only occasion in *Oxherding Tale* where the narrator experiences temporal disjuncture, and I would contend that for that reason alone the two passages inform each other. Moreover, the out-of-place Catholic resonances of the scene and Andrew's reference to a "changeless" space "above history, error" implicitly connects what is happening here—in this instant of timeless presence—to the revelation he has at the end of the novel. The connection is significant, because it implies that the narrator's marriage and the love he shares with Peggy transform him in a similar way to the love he shares with his father. Both "unions" have a transcendent effect that propels the narrator outside of time, granting him eternal distance from the reality of his historical situation and the troubling political implications of his decision to pass.

In the case of the wedding ceremony, these implications are immediately apparent to Andrew. For, right after he and Peggy "fell back into clock time" from their transformative vow-taking, the narrator and his new wife go to a reception filled with well-wishers, some of whom wear the uniform "of the Confederacy." The couple is then treated to a barrage of racist and sexist diatribes from their guests, including an "argument for the necessity of Negro slavery [that] drew from the most recent studies in breeding, from the Old Testament, from history, and from the subordination of one creature by another in the natural world" (141). Quite plainly, therefore, the text demonstrates that their marriage has not really transported Andrew and Peggy to an atemporal realm where love turns all historical "failures" into "triumphs." They remain at this point in the novel very much subject to the racial ideologies of their time—a fact that Andrew laments through an imagined conversation with his father, in which the two men discuss his bride. He knows that George "would reject me" for marrying a white woman, "claiming I had rejected him, and this was partly true." Yet the narrator holds out hope for his eventual approval, since

> I loved my father. What would I not have given for him to be at the wedding? Proud of me. To know he approved of Peggy. Was what I'd done so wrong? So contrary to his cracked vision that, if George lived, he would not forgive me? (142)

According to my reading of his final revelation, Andrew gets what he admits to missing on the day he marries Peggy: he gets George to sanction—indeed, to bless—the union retroactively. And, as I have been claiming, that paternal blessing signifies the last hurdle he believes he must overcome before becoming free.

My point, then, is that the Augustinian supplement "saves" the narrator's marriage by offering him a means of imaginatively fulfilling the desire for forgiveness from his father. But it is vital to recognize that the salvation being offered is also inexorably linked in the text to Andrew's racial compromise—to his problematic assimilation to the entrenched structures of power. That is because the father's forgiveness, as Augustine characterized it in the *Confessions*, does not take place in time; it happens on a plane above temporality, independent of history. While this atemporal view of reconciliation might absolve the narrator of the guilt he feels about marrying Peggy, a woman he seems truly to love, it creates irresolvable tension with regard to what their union signifies in the real time of the novel. In the end, we should not ignore that Andrew's actual liberation, from slavery as well as from the debilitating racist attitudes that followed in its wake, is made possible by his marriage and his continuing ability to pass for white. Without the protection that his domestic situation provides, he would not really be free. And so the danger of the Augustinian supplement—the danger of bracketing off one's self from the vicissitudes of time and history—is manifest in the ambivalence with which the narrative concludes.

It is possible, of course, that Johnson did not intend the conclusion of his novel to be ambiguous and, rather, that he perceives Andrew's "surrender" to domesticity in a wholly affirmative way. For despite the widespread criticism surrounding the last paragraph, there is nothing in it to suggest the narrator's—or even Johnson's—dissatisfaction with the life he chooses to live after slavery. That dissatisfaction has been placed on *Oxherding Tale* entirely from without, by critics arguing (correctly, I think) that Andrew's liberation does not transcend race but merely reinscribes its social and political strictures within the historical context of the narrative. A close look at the language Johnson uses here, though, reveals that these concerns matter very little to the writer of *this* tale: a man who, it seems, has reconciled himself fully to the meaninglessness of all designations of personal identity. In fact, the narrator appears in the final sentences of the text to have become the literary embodiment of what Johnson meant when he wrote in *Being and Race* that "great writers are sexless, raceless, and have no historical moment circumscribing their imagination and curiosity" (45).

. . .

In the preceding pages, I have been attempting to demonstrate that the novel's recourse to Augustinian theology is responsible for its irresolvable ending—because the construct of salvation it supports is atemporal, outside of history. Yet it must be noted that Johnson's text at least gestures toward a historical resolution, implying that the entrenched racial structures in which Andrew is still mired when his narrative ends will at some point be overcome. Indeed, as suggested by the specificity of the date the narrator gives for his daughter's birth (April 23, 1861), the final paragraph prepares us for a *real* future moment when race means nothing and integration is achieved. Andrew's daughter, whose very existence signals a kind of racial reconciliation, represents the hope for that integrationist possibility. This, in combination with the novel's only footnote, amounts to how Johnson imagines a resolution to the racial tension with which the novel concludes. The footnote interrupts the narratological exposition of Andrew's escape from Leviathan, flashing forward to describe what happens to a white guard he meets along the way, a young man full of racist vitriol. After recounting the guard's distasteful remarks, the narrator walks back his negative characterization, saying "I'm hardly being fair to this fellow: he was not a bad sort, considering the day." Then comes the footnote:

> He is fifteen in my account. In two years this boy—James Travis, Jr.—will be wounded at Fort Sumter, fighting with Major Robert Anderson: his nurse will be a black girl, Zelphy Thomes, and James, finding her with child on August 3, 1861, will choose love over bigotry, moving his new family to southern Illinois, where his great-granddaughter, Ellen, an early NAACP activist, will integrate a lunch counter on April 23, 1935. She will die five years later, on the Northeast Side of Carbondale, surrounded by admirers, white and black. (110)

The hopeful tone of this passage points to a future beyond the one depicted in the final paragraph of the novel—a future in which racist structures actually begin to be destabilized, rather than simply bypassed by people like Andrew who can live as white. For most readers, though, this kind of forward-looking hopefulness will ring false, given what we know about the bleak state of race relations in the United States in the years since 1935, when James's great-granddaughter supposedly integrated a lunch counter. I would submit that these small attempts to resolve what I have called the danger of the Augustinian supplement only further implicate Johnson's text in the troubling political consequences of an atemporal view of salvation.

4

Catholicism and Narrative Time, Continued

Divine Prescience in Edward P. Jones's *The Known World*

THE FINAL CHAPTER of my study focuses on temporal disjuncture as well, but in this case I consider manipulations of futurity rather than of the past or present, as in *Stigmata* and *Oxherding Tale*. In fact, I examine here a novel that makes frequent use of the flash-forward technique Johnson deploys only once in his. Edward P. Jones's *The Known World* is a highly acclaimed and Pulitzer Prize–winning portrayal of the little known history of black slaveholders in the United States. Since its publication in 2003, it has been heralded as a "classic" of African American literature and considered "one of the best American novels of the past twenty years" (Eggers). Its success has been attributed partly to how realistically it depicts a facet of the slave system that has gone largely unremarked in the sociological and historical analysis of slavery. But, as I will discuss here, the novel's realism is also a point of contention for critics, many of whom have debated whether or not the "realist" label is appropriate, given the patently antirealist and often disorienting way the novel disrupts chronological time by flashing to a future beyond the limits of the story being told. In what follows, I offer a new perspective on that debate, suggesting that instead of thinking about the novel's temporal structure in terms of realism versus antirealism, we would do better to understand the value that the novel attaches to narrative foreknowledge. I argue that Jones's use of the flash-forward technique is informed to a significant extent by the concept of divine prescience that Augustine developed in his analysis of the biblical story of creation.

As we shall see, the novel engages with Augustinian theology in multiple ways, but most directly by challenging (through its depiction of a character named Augustus) the view of slavery advanced in *The City of God against the Pagans*. Jones's engagement with Augustine, I suggest, reveals itself throughout *The Known World*, especially in the way it represents art and artists. Moreover, the Augustinian subtext of the novel, I will demonstrate, accounts for the surprising presence of Catholic characters and Catholic themes in the narrative. While not Catholic himself, Jones came into contact with Catholicism at several pivotal junctures in his life. As a child, he attended parochial school until his mother (who encouraged him to become a priest) could no longer afford it. Then later, as related in the book *Fraternity* by journalist Diane Brady, he was offered a scholarship to attend the College of the Holy Cross in Massachusetts, where he joined the first cohort of African American students at that institution. Thus Jones would have encountered, in various forms, the Catholic interpretation of Augustine's theology that I contend he deploys in *The Known World* in order to imaginatively disrupt the temporal structures of slavery.

...

The flash-forwards in Jones's novel follow a parallel trajectory to that of the footnote about James Travis Jr. in Johnson's *Oxherding Tale*. They propel the reader out of the chronological—and exceedingly realistic—framework of the text to offer a telescoping glimpse of what happens in the lives of marginal characters and their descendants decades after Emancipation. In some cases, the stories they tell reflect an affirmative view of the future, like Travis's, documenting small triumphs over racial injustice and adversity. For example, readers learn that one of the slaves on the Virginia plantation where Jones's novel takes place will in 1987 have a street in Richmond named after him, commemorating the Home for Colored Orphans that he founded with his wife during Reconstruction. The petition to rename the street, we learn further, was led by the couple's great-granddaughter, who successfully appealed to the "white people who ran the government" to recognize in "official" terms the significant historical contribution made by these former slaves (205). Other instances of this flash-forward technique in *The Known World*, however, point toward a dramatically different futurity, in which the racist logic of slavery does not in fact ever get undermined or overthrown. For every case of personal redemption, there are dozens of stories about enslaved characters that do not end by affirming their freedom—such as Ralph, who chooses to remain loyal to his white mistress even once he is emancipated (162)—along with a number of peripheral references to the interminability of structural racism, which persists far past the conclusion of the novel. At one point the narrator of Jones's novel, an omniscient third-person speaker, interrupts the description of the county sheriff, John Skiffington, to discuss a scholarly history of his term in office that will be produced in 1979. The scholar responsible for that account, our narrator tells us, will stake her academic career on portraying Skiffington as "a godsend" for slaveholders, because he ushered in "years and years" of "peace and prosperity" by way of the night patrols he organized to capture runaway slaves (44, 43).

The fact that a historian will receive tenure from an old-line southern university (Washington and Lee) more than a century after slavery, and in the wake of the civil rights movement, for writing a favorable—if uninspired—portrayal of a man who protected the interests of the slaveholding elite is, of course, an affront to the idea of racial "progress." Moreover, the historian's portrayal of Skiffington, which so baldly contradicts how Jones's narrator portrays the sheriff's influence, exposes a deep fissure between the "authoritative" historiography of this period and what was actually experienced by those who lived it. For these reasons, critics frequently interpret the temporal disjuncture in *The Known World* as antagonistic to claims of historical accuracy more generally. Madhu Dubey, for one, points out that the "disorienting" flash-forwards disrupt "the notion of self-contained time periods," implying that "slavery should not be seen as a closed chapter of US history" but rather as an institution whose injustices persist still ("Neo-Slave" 344). Likewise, Carolyn Vellenga Berman argues that the narrator's "broad foreknowledge" about the characters' futures and about the cultural space their descendants will inhabit fosters a sense of connection between "the private lives of an antebellum plantation" and "a twenty-first-century reading public," suggesting that both communities are "part of the same world" (235). Arguments such as these, which highlight the novel's compression of spatiotemporal distinctions, are at the center of the debate surrounding how to classify *The Known World*: as realist, "pseudorealist," or postmodern fiction.[1]

Indeed, nearly all the scholarship on the novel since its publication in 2003 makes at least some mention of the way the flash-forward technique confounds the otherwise realistic quality of Jones's prose. But whether the temporal shifts merely expand "the parameters of historical realism by manipulating the existing conventions of the genre," or whether they reject those conventions altogether—in a manner usually associated with postmodernism—is a question not easily settled (Spaulding 126). As Maria Seger explains, the critical disagreement over classification comes down to how seriously one takes the omniscience of the narrator.[2] In other words, if we believe that the narrator's knowledge really does exceed what has been written in the official record of slavery, then it is possible to read the narrative as a corrective for prior inaccuracies and omissions. This would mean, as Spaulding contends, that, its expansive view of history notwithstanding, *The Known World* still fits rather comfortably inside the limits of realist fiction, since it adds to—rather than "re-forms"—our understanding of slavery by broadening the historical scope of the narrative to account for the "passage of time as a continuum" (126). Alternatively, though, if we regard the narrator's knowledge as intentionally ironic, focusing on those moments that the third-person speaker "falls short of total omniscience" and "overrelies on documents" about slave history that were previously discredited by the novel's version of events, then, according to Maria Seger, *The Known World* calls into question the very possibility of accurate representation (1190). This, she suggests, is the function of all the examples of erroneous historical reporting that Jones involves in the telling: to parody any attempt to accurately represent the experience of slavery, including the narrator's own, thereby cultivating "similar levels of skepticism" to what we find in classic works of postmodernism and historiographic metafiction (1191).

For many readers, the debate regarding the novel's classification seems beside the point—something external to the story, which only literary critics would be interested in deliberating. Jones himself has intimated as much, insisting in interviews that at the time he was writing *The Known World*, he gave no consideration to the realist view of history that he is now being accused of (or celebrated for) violating. As he told Hilton Als in 2013, the principles of historical realism could not have informed the construction of his narrative, since he was not even cognizant of their implications: "I did things in that novel that I never learned you're not supposed to do. In one paragraph you leap forward ninety years, things like that." Though Jones surely overplays his ignorance of realist conventions, it is clear he wants to deflect scholarly attention away from the issue of representational accuracy. He has repeatedly denied doing extensive research for the *The Known World*, growing "obviously tired"—as Katherine Clay Bassard puts it—in the years following its publication of inquiries into his knowledge of the subject matter. Some of his earliest interviews reveal that he spent more than a decade studying "books about slavery" before starting to write his own (Fleming 254). Yet by 2005 he was quoted as rejecting the premise that he read anything at all on the topic: "There was no research. No. I didn't do any research. . . . Forget the research. It's overrated" (Bassard 409). So what was it that inclined him against acknowledging his familiarity with slave history and historiography?

In partial answer to this question, Bassard reminds us that we should understand "Jones's de-emphasizing of historical research in the context of the tendency to focus too heavily on the 'historical' accuracy or authentication of African American literature as autobiography, sociology, and lived experience and an under-appreciation for the genius of the black imaginary" (409). The reminder is an important one. Undoubtedly Jones would have sensed a tone of condescension from audiences who asked him—over and over again—how his novel compares to the "reality" of slavery. Because of the controversial and largely unknown history of African American slaveholders to which *The Known World* refers, there were multiple calls to justify its account, specifically concerning the statistical information presented in the opening pages. There the narrator says that of the thirty-four free black families presiding in Manchester County, Virginia, prior to the Civil War, "eight of those free families owned slaves," and one black family in particular (Henry Townsend's) owned more slaves than most white residents (7). Readers will want to know, a prominent historian wrote in 2006, the "general plausibility" of these fictional statistics and, in wider terms, about Jones's faithfulness to the historical record (Pressly 81). Thus the novel motivated scholars of history and sociology to reexamine census information from the period, checking whether the narrator's numbers hold up against comparable data.

Thomas J. Pressly probably believed he was giving Jones a vote of confidence when he determined, after analyzing the relevant scholarship, that his book "meets major tests of statistical plausibility for its historical period—whatever may be its degree of success or failure in satisfying the various other literary or aesthetic criteria by which its readers may evaluate it" (86). But, as the "whatever" clause makes plain, Pressly's verification does not amount to an endorsement of the work's artistic value. In fact, he suggests that its accuracy—its realism—might even minimize the approval *The Known World* receives on "various other" scales of analysis, including creativity and authorial vision. By implicitly corroborating Bassard's concerns, then, this and other like-minded attempts to verify the history represented in the novel can negatively affect its reception as literature, as fiction. Perhaps that explains why Jones started backing away from his initial statements regarding historical research and began to stress in interviews instead the significant role the "creative part of the brain" played in the book's genesis. The narrative that has emerged since then about how *The Known World* came to be confirms the extraordinary power of his imagination. Jones says that after "avoiding doing research" for "over ten years" and simply thinking through the story "in his head," he finally sat down to write it "in the final days of December 2001," when he was laid off from his job (Als). A draft of the manuscript was ready a short time later, in March—which signifies a remarkable feat of productivity for any novelist, especially one writing on such a massive scale. *The Known World* is not only long (the longest by far of any of the texts examined in this study) but also intricately woven and complex. So many individual stories pervade its pages that readers often remark on the difficulty of keeping track of all the characters.[3] Yet Jones maintains that he wrote the entire novel in two and a half months, because he had spent a decade imagining these people and the lives they lived.

His imaginative vision of the characters was responsible too, he says, for the temporal disruptions that have fascinated critics and spurred the debate over how to categorize his work. When asked to explain his use of the flash-forward technique, Jones resists the suggestion that the conventions of historical realism determined—in any way—his representation of time. He did not adhere to a standard chronological approach, he admits; but neither did he set out purposefully to undermine it or to prove a point about slave historiography. Rather, he quite strikingly ascribes the structure of the narrative to a mythology of creation, in which the artist—the "creator"—sees beyond the human experience of temporality:

> I always thought I had a linear story. Something happened between the time I began . . . taking it all out of my head and when I finished months later. It might be that because I, as the "god" of the people in the book, could see their first days and their last days and all that was in between, and those people did not have linear lives as I saw all that they had lived. What Tessie the child did one day in 1855 would have some meaning for her 50, 75 years later. She might not be able to look back and see that moment, but her creator could. That, perhaps, is why she says something about the doll her father made for her to Caldonia and Fern in September 1855 that she will repeat on her deathbed, some 90 years later; she might not even remember the first time she uttered those words, but I can't afford to forget if I'm trying to tell the truth. (HarperCollins)

Emerging here, in Jones's characterization of authorial knowledge, is a take on narrative omniscience that frustrates both the realist and the postmodernist readings of his novel. In referring to himself "as the 'god' of the people in the book," Jones cannily sidesteps the question of representational accuracy, harkening back to a premodern conception of art, where "meaning" is revealed from without by an author/narrator not subject to the vagaries of temporal existence. To put this another way: for Jones, telling "the truth" about slavery necessitates a perspective independent of time and history, from which he can document—and make a kind of sense of—even those events that seemed meaningless or impossible to understand in their own historical context. Notably, the work involves more than just remembering what happened in the past from some future moment in the continuum of human experience. For, as the above example shows, memories change and are forgotten over the span of a person's lifetime. Thus it is possible that the character Tessie will die not knowing, not realizing what it meant to be able to tell the woman who owned her in 1855 that the beautiful doll she held in her hands was carved for her by her father, Elias. The memory of that exchange, as well as its significance, "might not even" occur to her on her deathbed, when she looks back at her life "90 years later" and repeats the words she spoke to her mistress almost a century before. Moreover, she will never be aware of the great effort Elias put into carving the doll in her likeness, since it did not turn out to resemble her all that closely. So Tessie lives and dies believing, as her father falsely told her out of embarrassment, that the doll has the face of his mother—a woman whose features he has no actual recollection of, after being forcibly separated from her thirty years earlier. These lost and misremembered "histories" would be all that remains of Tessie, and Elias too for that matter, if their stories were related linearly, Jones suggests. To meaningfully recall that which cannot be known or will soon be forgotten therefore requires the knowledge possessed by a remote narrator, who stands outside of the temporal world his characters inhabit and sees "all that they had lived" all at once, from a point of view absolutely unimaginable to them.

And so, according to Jones, the flash-forwards in the text should not be measured in terms of historical realism, because the transcendent vision they reflect exists independently of lived experience. Neither, though, do these temporal interruptions indicate a postmodern skepticism about the representation of history, given that they affirm, rather than subvert, the creator's authority. Indeed, the way Jones mythologizes his own creative process constitutes an ideal rejoinder to critics inclined to underestimate what Bassard calls "the genius of the black imaginary." As he describes it, the distinctive temporality of *The Known World* comes exclusively from his imagination and the godlike perspective he exercises over the "people" he creates. Whether or not Jones was thinking about the criticism focused on the accuracy of the novel when he made these remarks, it is apparent that, to him, the value of art has remarkably little to do with how realistically it depicts time—for he regards the temporal disjuncture in his narrative as evidence of "some meaning" which transcends linear chronology. Meaning and "truth" in fact reside in those disorientating textual moments, he claims, that pose the greatest challenge to our ordered view of human existence and force us to see the world differently.

To readers who find the flash-forward technique distracting or worse—Alan Cheuse called it "annoying, sometimes even irritating" in his review for the *San Francisco Chronicle*[4]—Jones's interpretation of the novel's temporality offers a pointed response, gesturing toward a totalizing rationale that cannot be explained by the categories of "realism" or "postmodernism" alone—that significantly deviates, in fact, from both categorizations. In the following pages I will explore the terms of the logic Jones uses to defend the narratological flash-forwards, because I contend that that logic has profound implications not only for how *The Known World* is structured but also for how it represents the many artists and works of art that appear within. The novel cultivates a view of aesthetic production that sustains the way its author mythologizes his own creative process. This holds true for a range of imaginative "creations" portrayed in the book: from the widely celebrated, large-scale masterpieces by Augustus Townsend and Alice Night to those destined for far smaller audiences, such as the doll Elias carves for Tessie or even the fantastic stories that the slaves of Manchester County make up for each other to explain the horrors of slavery. Throughout *The Known World*, Jones incorporates into the description of these artworks a mythology similar to the one that has developed around his personal experience of writing the manuscript, especially with regard to the genesis of its temporal landscape. By considering what unites all of these diverse "texts" and their respective representations of time, I can argue that they are informed to a surprising extent by the theory of divine prescience that Augustine developed throughout his works—but primarily in *The City of God*—to explain the biblical myth of creation. Indeed, as I will show, Augustinian theology figures prominently in the novel, informing the great authority its artists wield, as well as the transformative power of their aesthetic imaginations. Furthermore, I argue that an examination of the terms Augustine uses to describe God's creative power yields important insight regarding the strange and seemingly incongruous presence of Catholicism in the narrative—an aspect of the novel I will address in the final section of this chapter.

. . .

Admittedly, Augustinian theology might seem at first glance an unlikely source for Jones's aesthetic perspective. His novel, after all, plainly criticizes the justification for slavery that Augustine proposes in *The City of God*, offering countless examples to refute the idea of enslavement as a divinely sanctioned and ordained remedy for sin. Within the various matrices of human bondage portrayed in *The Known World*, mastery over another individual—however well intentioned or benign—is always destructive. None of the fictionalized slave owners ever achieves, or comes close to achieving, the idealized version of servitude that Augustine calls "that order of peace which prevails among men when some are placed under others" (19.15). Quite to the contrary, the novel teems with stories of "peace" dangerously interrupted by a cadre of shortsighted masters and miserable slaves, whose collective experience underscores the depravity of all forms of slavery. The case of Henry Townsend provides the primary evidence for this point. A former slave himself, Henry at one time vowed "he would be a master different from any other, the kind of shepherd master God had intended." His plan to rule ethically over a plantation of "happy," well-fed slaves—on whom he will look down from a position of charitable goodwill, "like God on his throne looked down on him" (180)—recalls, with striking similarity, the model of ethical mastery elaborated in *The City of God*.[5] But of course, instead of advocating that model as Augustine does, Jones chronicles its inevitable failure, emphasizing the many times Henry left the men and women in his care without enough to eat and had them whipped or disfigured on charges of insubordination. The fact that he does not enjoy and is actually deeply disturbed by these kinds of punishments has no bearing on their outcome. Again and again, the text demonstrates that even the most kindhearted masters commit grievous acts of injustice, as a necessary condition of the status that slave ownership affords them.

The corrupting effects of bondage on masters and slaves alike have been well documented in the literature of slavery. From the sketches of "humane" and "pious" women debauched by "an atmosphere of licentiousness and fear" in Harriet Jacobs's *Incidents in the Life of a Slave Girl* to Toni Morrison's *A Mercy*, which recounts the moral degradation of the reluctant slave owner Jacob Vaark, there are in our popular imagination numerous accounts of otherwise compassionate individuals compromised by their affiliation (direct or indirect) with such a depraved institution.[6] What makes *The Known World* unique and sets it apart from other texts that destabilize the notion of ethical mastery that Augustine promotes in *The City of God* are its free black characters, who appear as vulnerable as whites to the corrosive influence of owning slaves. In the words of one critic, Jones's novel deconstructs the "historical dialectic between benevolent and commercial black slaveowning," suggesting that everyone involved in the purchase of slaves—including those participating for purely philanthropic reasons—contributes to the system's immorality and corruption (Bassard 412). Sadly, this means that even Augustus Townsend, whose carpentry work has allowed him to buy himself and then his family out of bondage, is not immune to the consequences. Although he sought only to free Mildred and Henry from their master, William Robbins, the narrative implies that Augustus unwittingly fortifies slavery in Manchester County in two ways: first, by increasing the wealth of its largest proponent (Robbins, who benefits financially from both sales, in particular Henry's) and, second, by not legally freeing his son. For reasons of convenience and political expediency, Augustus chooses to assume ownership of Henry himself rather than seeking his formal manumission. This was a common practice at the time, which allowed the families of freed slaves to live together when they would otherwise have been forced to leave the state.[7] But despite how reasonable his decision seems in context, as Bassard astutely points out, by becoming Henry's master, Augustus ironically "replicates the social hierarchy" that he had intended to transcend, thereby confirming for his son the inexorability of the slave system to which their family remains subject (415).

In one sense, then, the character of Augustus is a vehicle for Jones to explore and ultimately critique the notion, articulated in *The City of God,* that "the father of a family should draw his own precepts from the law of the city, and rule his household in such a way that it is brought into harmony with the city's peace" (19.16). When Augustus does exactly this—effectively letting the "law" of the plantation determine his relationship with his wife and son—he makes them all complicit in slavery's expansion. Not only will being his father's slave help Henry justify his own slaveholding interests one day—he tells his parents, "Nobody never told me the wrong of that" (137)—but it also forces Henry to look elsewhere for paternal companionship and support, bringing him ever closer to William Robbins, who encourages his lust for mastery. Thus the novel implicates Augustus and the Augustinian theology that his name evokes in Henry's meteoric rise to power as well as in his mistreatment of slaves. In one revealing scene, which occurs just after Henry confesses to buying his first bondsman, Augustus banishes his son from his land, telling him he "would never suffer a slaveowner to set foot on it"; then, when the younger man refuses to heed his father's warning, Augustus hits him across the back, saying, "Thas how a slave feel! . . . Thas just how every slave every day be feelin" (138). Ostensibly this physical response is meant to awaken Henry's empathy for the person he has recently purchased, Moses, and to encourage him to set Moses free. Augustus's violence therefore satisfies *The City of God*'s criteria for a father's justifiable use of force. "If anyone in the household is an enemy to domestic peace because of disobedience," Augustine writes, "he is corrected by a word, or by a blow, of by whatever other kind of punishment is just and lawful . . . but this is for the benefit of the person corrected, so that he may be readmitted to the peace from which he has sundered himself" (19.16). Augustus—who is far from a violent character[8]—likely viewed his own outburst in similar terms: as a means of correcting Henry's grievous error and reminding him of his moral obligation to the black community.

The problem, though, is that as a slave owner himself—legally, if not in practice—Augustus possesses neither the authority nor the moral capital to convince his son of the "wrong" of what he has done. In fact, by referring to Henry as "slave" and caning him, he merely reveals his own hypocrisy in the matter, further compromising whatever parental influence he once had. So it could be argued that Augustus's recourse to violence is not consistent with the aims laid out in *The City of God*, because it limits the father's "domestic rule" (19.16) rather than extending it. And yet we find upon examination of the scene's aftermath that it actually accords perfectly with Augustinian logic, perversely confirming the "harmony" between Henry Townsend's household and the wider civic organization. In other words, even though the blow Augustus strikes does not reestablish Henry's obedience to his biological "master," it does—in full accordance with Augustine's principle of righteous mastery—bring the younger man's personal values in line with the presiding laws of land. For immediately after being hit by his father, Henry seeks refuge with his *original* owner, William Robbins, where he resolves once and for all to participate as fully as possible in the plantation economy. Indeed, it is there, sitting on Robbins's porch the day Augustus banishes him from his childhood home, that Henry first realizes "how much he wanted" to lord it over a whole empire of slaves, governing them according to the example that Robbins and the other "Caesars" of Manchester County set (141).[9] In this way, therefore, Jones exposes the dark underside of Augustinian theology, highlighting the various means by which the discussion of just rule from *The City of God* could be used—and, in fact, *was* used—to sanction slavery in general and the physical abuse of slaves in particular. Much like Toni Morrison's critique of the Pauline epistles in *Beloved* (which I discuss in chapter 1), *The Known World* relentlessly undermines any suggestion of the divinely ordained nature of servitude, showing that enslavement can never be benevolent or redemptive, regardless of its context.

To be sure, Morrison and Jones engage comparable justifications for slavery in their novels, since Augustine's theological position on this matter derives largely from Paul's letters. In the chapters of *The City of God* that concern the condition of servitude, Augustine refers directly to 1 Corinthians and Ephesians, where he reminds readers that "the apostle admonishes servants to be obedient to their masters ... so that, if they cannot be freed by their masters, they can at least make their own slavery to some extent free" (19.15). Here and throughout book 19, Augustine bases his interpretation of divine enslavement upon the very same—conservative—pole of Pauline theology that I claim Morrison condemns in her fiction (via Baby Suggs's sermon, for example). By calling attention to the inherent inconsistencies of the Augustinian concept of ethical mastery, *The Known World* is, by extension, incriminating Paul's teachings on slavery as well, in a manner analogous to *Beloved*. But just as Morrison's novel stops short of a total repudiation of Pauline Christianity (and ultimately privileges through the construct of rememory those aspects of Paul's epistles that emphasize communal sharing and redemption), I want to argue that Jones's engagement with Augustine is more ambivalent than a surface-level reading would suggest. On this point, it is important to note, I am not alone. Political scientist Stephen Marshall makes the case in a brilliant article that *The Known World* both "contests" and "embraces" the account of servitude put forth in *The City of God*. Specifically, he contends that while Jones's text remains intensely critical of the defense of violence from Book 19, it simultaneously proposes an Augustinian solution—his notion of "exilic virtue"[10]—for the "problem of slavery" that it depicts. Marshall even goes so far as to say that the "heroic" slaves whom the novel celebrates for confronting violence with "an indomitable self-discipline, which simply refuses the master/slave relation as such" exemplify the "personal cultivation" that Augustine advances in *The City of God* (179, 176).

As the only extant scholarship on *The Known World* to focus explicitly on the novel's Augustinian subtext, Marshall's article establishes a useful framework for exploring the ambivalence at its core and runs parallel to my own. I will be suggesting that precisely because Jones mounts such a rigorous challenge to Augustine's analysis of slavery, *The City of God* informs every aspect of his characters' defiance of enslavement. Moreover, I view the art produced by slaves in *The Known World* as what Marshall calls "a philosophically profound critique" of "the order of servitude" that Augustine defends. Near the end of his essay, Marshall offers the compelling proposition that one of the novel's artists, Alice Night, successfully "transcends" the condition of slavery altogether through songs and material productions that "repudiate" the human "lust for mastery" and (in the words of W.E.B. Du Bois) "'grope toward some unseen power'" instead.[11] I agree with this assessment but want to expand it to include not only the artwork of other slaves represented in the text but also the text itself. However—and this marks my significant departure from Marshall—whereas he perceives Alice's art in terms categorically opposed to "Augustine's or any particular religion's" theology, I argue that her aesthetic vision and the aesthetic vision prioritized by Jones more generally actually incorporates the theological stakes of *The City of God*, specifically with regard to the concept of divine prescience (181).

. . .

What is it, then, that connects Alice's artistry to the way Augustine describes God's eternal "idea" of the world in *The City of God*? I begin with this question because of the central role her character plays in defining the novel's broader approach to art. Alice is often said to represent "the author in the text" on account of "her knowledge" and "her capacity for invention" (Berman 237). Moreover, multiple critics have cited the two mixed-media pieces she creates along with the enigmatic songs she writes as indicative of the "transformative" or "transcendent"—some have even suggested *salvific*—power Jones assigns to aesthetic creation.[12] And *The Known World* provides much to support these kinds of interpretations. For we discover in the final pages of the novel that the confounding lyrics Alice could always be heard singing around Master Henry's property were not unintelligible ramblings, as everyone believed; rather they were part of an extensive code she developed to map out the geography of the plantation. In a very real sense, her lyrical verses can be said to transcend the order of slavery, since they are what deliver Alice and the two other slaves she eventually runs away with to freedom. Along similar lines, the "grand" wall hangings, which are displayed for patrons of the restaurant/safe house she operates in Washington, D.C., effect life-altering experiences. Calvin explains in a letter home to his sister Caldonia, Alice's former mistress, that when he happened upon the "massive miracle" she had produced, he sank to his knees and began for the first time ever to confront an unacknowledged part of his past: "that I, no matter what I had always said to the contrary, owned people of our Race" (385–86). As a direct result of the personal revelation brought about by the artwork, Calvin postpones, possibly forever, his lifelong "need to be in New-York" (383) and commits himself to the service of fugitive slaves, helping them find safety in the North.

Given the transformations it facilitates and the miraculous—almost inexplicable—nature of its content, Alice's art has a mystical quality that the scholarship overwhelmingly associates with an "alternative" (that is, non-Western) spirituality. In addition to Marshall, who ascribes her aesthetic vision to an "openness to diverse sources of religious insight" and a polytheistic conception of the universe (he refers to "her *gods*' divinity"—plural), many scholars also have emphasized what differentiates Alice from the dominant Western paradigms explored elsewhere in the novel (181).[13] Clearly she conforms to the worldview neither of the slaves nor of the slaveholding class, a fact that everyone in Manchester County blames on an injury she suffered when kicked in the head by a mule. Alice tells a vivid story of that incident, which people point to in order to explain how she "lost her mind" (3), and she is held to a different standard than those she lives among. No one expects her to be able to communicate rationally or to adhere to the normalizing rules of plantation culture. This means that as long as she completes her fieldwork efficiently, Alice has leave to do what she pleases. Henry and Moses, his overseer, permit her to wander freely at night, and she suffers no penalty for "doing things that sometimes made the hair on the backs of the slave patrollers' necks stand up" (12). All of her antics—including the chants she sends up "as if . . . to reach the rafters of heaven" (75) and the nonsensical predictions she makes about the future—are deemed products of an addled brain and thus not quashed with the same force that nonconformist actions typically incur from masters wary of insubordination.

But, as the narrator establishes early on, Alice's insanity is simply a façade, a performance she stages to excuse behavior that would have resulted in severe punishment for any other slave. Three pages into the novel, for example, we learn that there were no mules on the farm where Alice lived prior to Henry's, where she supposedly sustained the wound that "sent all common sense flying out of her." On that plantation, "in a faraway county whose name only she remembered," Alice could not have been injured, at least not in the way she describes, because her owner at the time "was terrified of mules and would not have them on his place" (4). Then, a bit later in the narrative, it is revealed that "on a day before the mule kicked her in the head, an African woman who spoke very little English had told her that some angels were hard of hearing, that it was best to speak real loud when talking to them" (76). Implicitly, these fragments about Alice's past link her to a cosmology and a mode of truth-telling that run counter to the realist, rationalist strain of the text. Not only does the account she gives of her personal history appear to be fictional, but it seems she was also influenced by a set of beliefs that fall outside the bounds of Western religious traditions (as suggested by the reference to her companionship with "an African woman"). And so Jones gives critics like Marshall credible evidence to support an argument for reading Alice against the grain of "dogmatic" Christianity because her perspective so radically diverges from nearly everyone else's we meet in *The Known World*—and certainly all those individuals identifying in the novel as Christian.[14] Indeed, the sole character who has been shown to complement Alice's unconventional approach to religion and spiritual insight is the narrator him/herself.[15] Yet if we consider what really connects the two figures, their resemblance, I argue, has much more to do with traditional Western Christianity—and specifically the tenets of Augustinian theology—than criticism thus far has acknowledged.

Beyond the fairly obvious comparisons that can be made on the level of artistic representation—they both confuse truth and fiction; they both blend genres and modes of articulation; they both incorporate supernatural elements—Alice and Jones's narrator take a similar God's-eye view of Manchester County, which in turn determines the temporal scope of their respective narrations. Earlier I discussed how *The Known World* flashes forward at odd intervals to reveal what happens to marginal characters at the hour of their death. Likewise, we read that one of the ways Alice terrorizes the slave patrollers who guard the perimeters of Henry's plantation is by giving them "the day and time God would take them to heaven, would drag each and every member of their families across the sky and toss them into hell with no more thought than a woman dropping strawberries into a cup of cream" (12). Although the patrollers dismiss these ramblings as mad, her prophecies are analogous in their specificity and the telescoping detail they provide to the novel's own forward-looking glances. Just as Alice claims to know when exactly and how the people around her will die, so too does the narrator describe with remarkable precision the circumstances surrounding each future event. For instance, in referring to the slave child Patrick, the narrative notes not just that he would be killed someday by his girlfriend's jealous husband but that his murder would occur "when he was forty-seven," during the same week he gambled away "$53 and owed one evil man $11 more" (68–69). This kind of particularization indicates foreknowledge that is, like Alice's, simultaneously sweeping and intimate. It reflects a vision of the world that does not conform easily to the human experience of temporality. For that reason, in both cases, audiences tend to receive these temporal disruptions skeptically, because omniscience of any sort exceeds the limits of lived reality. (Think of the reviewer Alan Cheuse, who objected to the novel's flash-forward technique on the grounds that it distracts from the narrator's realist pretense. His complaint recalls the slave patrollers' about Alice, in the sense that he also finds the "interjected references to all the tomorrows that follow" the temporal borders of the narrative defamiliarizing and "annoying.")

Despite the negative reactions it can conjure, however, *The Known World* ultimately validates Alice's omniscience—as well as its own—by means of the letter Calvin writes to Caldonia. The document, which is afforded a privileged place at the end of the novel, serves to honor and to confirm the value of art that represents "what God sees when He looks down on Manchester" (384). It is, after all, due to the startling aesthetic experience of witnessing the entire county and its people represented from above that Calvin says he was inspired to transform his life. In particular, he notes how affected he was by the one piece depicting "every single person" who ever lived on his brother-in-law's plantation: all of them, including long-dead slaves risen from their graves, standing together as they never could have in reality, outside the cabins they once occupied, with faces "raised up as though to look in the very eyes of God" (385). Something about this tapestry and its capacity for compressing so many distinct historical moments, so many distinct stories of life and death, on the same narrative plane awaken, Calvin tells his sister, "matters in my memory that I did not know were there until I saw them on that wall" (386). He becomes incapable of denying any longer his complicity in the fate of each individual, living and dead, enslaved by a system that benefited him. Seeing those individuals portrayed according to Alice's expansive vision of them—and without regard for linear continuity or history—disrupts whatever provisional reason Calvin has used previously to justify slavery (the obligation he felt to maintain his mother's property until her death, for example). As a number of critics have observed, then, his reaction to the wall hangings legitimizes the "indulgence" required by any work that stakes claims about its characters "from a distance" and "across discontinuities" of space and time (Berman 237). And, by extension, Calvin's letter tacitly endorses the disruptive temporality of Jones's writing too, by emphasizing the transformative potential of art that transcends temporal existence and takes an omniscient view of the world.

Notably, even the words Calvin uses to describe Alice's artistry—he dubs each of her productions a "Creation" with a capital C and refers to one as a "massive miracle"—resonate with the way the author himself has mythologized the production of his novel. In the long passage quoted above from his interview with HarperCollins, Jones also makes clear that he prefers the term "creator" to artist or writer and, quite strikingly, defends the nonlinearity of his text by likening his authorship to being "the 'god' of the people in the book." Jones's tendency to associate aesthetic vision with the divine comes through so powerfully, in fact, that when reviewing the author's most recent story collection for the *New York Times*, Dave Eggers remarked: "Jones is at his best when he plays God. As an omniscient narrator, he has a most assured grasp of the world he writes about." The same could be said for Alice Night, whose "grasp of the world" and vast knowledge of her environs quite literally determines the fate of the people she saves from slavery. While surely countless factors influence how authors speak about their writing publicly (and we know that Jones has had to work harder than most to be recognized for the powers of his imagination), the congruence of his public statements on the novel with Calvin's epistolary celebration of Alice is conspicuous. Both draw upon the language of the Bible—and the creation myth from the Book of Genesis specifically—to answer for lapses in realism, as well as to explain narrative omniscience. Indeed, and more specifically still, I want to suggest that what emerges in these two accounts of aesthetic creativity is an idea of the artist that complements (and mines considerable influence from) the Augustinian reading of Genesis, in particular, wherein Augustine defines God's "perfect" and "eternal" knowledge of the world.

The Book of Genesis, of course, makes frequent appearances in Jones's novel, and other critics have noticed that Calvin's letter plainly alludes to the biblical story of creation. It seems that everyone who inhabits the fictional space of Manchester County draws inspiration in one form or another from that master text—or from one of its many interpretations, such as *Paradise Lost*. An early scene depicts Caldonia offering to read to Henry, just before he dies, "A bit of Milton? Or the Bible?" (5–6). These are, she implies, the sole books they own, since when he confesses to being tired of both, her only other option is to sing to him. In fact, we learn later via the recollections of his former teacher, Fern Elston, that Henry was deeply sympathetic to Milton's revisionary portrait of the Devil and particularly to that character's proclamation "that he would rather rule in hell than serve in heaven." As Fern recalls, Henry "thought only a man who knew himself well could say such a thing, could turn his back on God with just finality" (134–35). This rather simplistic understanding of Satan's choice clearly inspires Henry's own approach to slavery, as does his belief—also motivated by a misreading of Genesis—that "God gave" a portion of Creation to him (6). In addition to Henry, many other residents of Manchester look to Genesis for guidance on how to manage their slaveholding interests. For instance, Reverend Valtims Moffett advises his property-owning congregants to avoid overtaxing themselves with anxiety about unhappy slaves because those sorts of worries would not be pleasing to the Lord, especially on the Sabbath. As justification for his words, Moffett refers to how "God put such emphasis on Sunday, on resting" in Genesis 2 (89). Sheriff Skiffington, too, vows to rest every Sunday according to the example set by the Lord, and he likewise uses other passages from Genesis to help him contend with the guilt he feels about working to support slave owners and owning a slave himself (though he does not regard Minerva as such). The story of Lot, especially, reminds him that all things—even those he finds "disturbing," like slavery—are "part of God's plan" and not to be questioned by man (161, 162).

Through the allusions that I have just described, and others as well, Jones conveys the malleability of Genesis, revealing how readily its contents could be manipulated by supposedly pious individuals seeking divine justification for deplorable acts. But when Calvin alludes to the story of creation as a way of communicating to his sister the miracle of the artwork he views in Washington, his reference to Genesis takes another form entirely. Instead of using the biblical text to justify Alice's actions or to suggest that God sanctioned her escape from slavery—two gestures one would think he might make, given that Caldonia was still lawfully her owner and could travel north at any point to reclaim that stolen property—Calvin portrays the runaway as a creator-god herself: someone whose knowledge of the land is so complete that she need not fear legal retribution from aggrieved slaveholders or anyone else with the law on their side. In fact, his letter makes no mention of Alice's fugitive status at all, nor does he attempt to disguise her location or to shield her in any manner from the threat of his sister's vengeance. His singular concern about writing to Caldonia is that their correspondence will expose *him* and *his* past associations with slavery. Consequently, Calvin closes the document by asking that when she replies to him by mail, care of the hotel owned by Alice, she "recall my fear of being cast out and please write my name on the envelope as humbly as you possibly can" (386). What his request implies is that Alice has created a new order of existence—a new world—in Washington that operates independent of the antebellum justice system and according to a set of "laws" totally of her own design. Calvin considers himself fortunate to have access to everything she has built, saying, "I am happy when I get up in the morning, and I am happy when I lay my head down at night," and yet he views his inclusion in this paradise as temporary, since it is contingent on remaining in Alice's good graces. Thus, in language reminiscent of the Fall of Man in Genesis, he agonizes over the possibility that she will cast him out for his sins, like Adam and Eve from the Garden.

To Calvin, then, Alice's creative vision comprises not just the art she produces but also the many lives she has given form and meaning to through her work. As he sees it, this renders her as powerful as a deity—the reason why, I think, he refers to her with the kind of awe and reverence that the Bible reserves for God alone. The power Alice wields is indeed "miraculous" in Calvin's estimation, because of the sheer magnitude of all she has been able to accomplish in the short time after leading Priscilla and Jamie out of slavery. In just a few years she has become well known and respected throughout the city as an artist as well as the visionary owner of a hotel where "Senators and Congressmen lodged" but that is also "hospitable" to fugitive slaves (384). For people who knew her on the Townsend plantation, when she was deemed a madwoman, the totality of what she has created would have seemed impossible. But, as Calvin discovers the moment he reads the words "Alice Night" at the bottom right-hand corner of the wall hanging, her "exquisite" aesthetic masterpieces as well as the boardinghouse she runs were part of the plan from the beginning: the end result of an all-encompassing idea that was hatched long before, with the story she made up and told to anyone who would listen about a mule that kicked her in the head. Therefore, just as Jones says he spent nearly a decade walking around thinking about the characters in *The Known World* before putting anything on paper, Alice also devoted large portions of her life to imaginatively mapping out the "Creation" she would one day make real.

Significantly, the foreknowledge that both artists gained about their respective projects during these long periods of solitary planning informs the temporal structure of the art they turn out. Alice's wall hanging, as I have said, brings together each person and every inch of the land she came to know while slaving on—and preparing her route off—Henry's plantation. All the information she collected over the years is represented from a single sweeping perspective that compresses the passage of time. Similarly, Jones ascribes the telescoping feature of *The Known World* and the narrator's omniscience to all he learned about his characters' lives (their "first days and their last days") as the design for the novel developed in his head. Having a protracted period of planning, when he was able to picture in his mind the entirety of the plot, explains too, Jones says, the relative speed with which he produced the manuscript, once he sat down to attend to it. Indeed, even the impetus to finally start writing was, like the impetus for Alice to strike out from the plantation, sudden—yet also completely arbitrary. Jones has said that being laid off from his job gave him an excuse to write without any distraction but that the book would have been written anyway, given how rigorously he had thought it through; talking to Maryemma Graham in 2008, he was quick to insist on this point: "The world should not think, 'Oh he lost his job and that spurred him on to write a novel'" (426). Likewise, although Alice left when she did to help Priscilla and Jamie, her escape route had been prepared for a while and she was ready to leave at a moment's notice, whenever a reason for leaving presented itself. Thus she could respond to Moses's request the day after he made it, knowing exactly where to lead his wife and his son so that they would remain safe. Whether that request came months earlier, months later, or not at all, though, Alice obviously had already amassed all the knowledge necessary to bring her plan to fruition—knowledge that she would then use to create her "wondrous" art.

My purpose then in highlighting the similarities between the author's own creative process and that of his character Alice is to pinpoint Jones's abiding concern with the way artists relate to time. In the interviews he has given about *The Known World* as well as in the text itself, Jones places special emphasis on how long various works of art take to construct, as though to signal the temporal contingencies of aesthetic production. For example, at one point early in the novel, his narrator tallies the length of time Augustus spends building each piece of furniture in his repertoire: "He could make a four-poster bed of oak in three weeks, chairs he could do in two days, chiffoniers in seventeen days" (14). This measuring of Augustus's wood carving in chronological terms recalls the precision with which Jones describes the period of drafting his manuscript (he tells nearly every interviewer the date he started writing and when the first draft was completed). Not only do such details underscore the material processes involved in creating masterpieces, but they also reinforce the mythology that Jones tends to associate with art making more generally—reminding readers, once again, of the biblical story of creation. In the same manner that the miracle of Genesis is compounded by the astonishing speed with which God created the universe, so too does Jones invoke temporality to stress the miraculousness of artistic enterprise. (Carving in just two days, as Augustus can, a chair whose beauty brings "sinners to tears" is indeed a miraculous feat, comparable perhaps to producing a Pulitzer Prize–winning novel in only two and a half months or to, say, making the earth and all its denizens in just under a week.) And yet, despite Jones's interest in establishing a timeline for each of the projects represented in the narrative, there emerges a very clear—and seemingly contradictory—sense that the individuals responsible for those projects are themselves entirely unaffected by the hours or days or weeks it takes to produce them: that their vision of the work resists temporal limits and thus cannot be measured by any standard concept of time.

Unlike other characters who rigidly attend to the clock, letting it dictate every facet of their lives, the artists of *The Known World* are not beholden to temporality in the same way. They evince a capacity for looking beyond the immediate context of daily existence, from a perspective far removed from time's vicissitudes. This is what distinguishes them from someone such as Moses, whose overseer responsibilities require him to track, meticulously, the passing hours in the day in order to optimize the productivity of the growing season. While Moses berates Elias for staying up late to carve the doll for Tessie and is constantly after Alice to return to her cabin at night (so they will both be ready to work in the morning), these two are always too consumed by whittling or by singing to heed his warning about the fast approaching dawn. Along similar lines, the narrator says at one point of Augustus that "as usual" he judged incorrectly how long it would take to deliver his furniture to clients in other counties, and often "he and the mule were about a day late getting home to his wife" (210–11). Their inability—or unwillingness—to abide by chronological time and the temporal logic of the plantation puts all three of these artists at risk of dangerous consequences: Elias and Alice because of what Moses will do to them if they do not meet the morning bell, and Augustus because his habitual lateness has inclined Mildred not to contact the authorities to report his absence as early as she should (8). However much they might suffer, though, for being out of sync with the chronology that everyone else in Manchester County adheres to, the novel never supports the suggestion, made by some in the community, that this indicates a cognitive deficiency or lack of mental acuity on their parts. Quite to the contrary, Jones implies that the tendency of artists to perceive time differently only increases their authority, rendering them ever more like the Creator-God of Genesis. For, as I discussed above, it is Alice's unique viewpoint—her ability to transcend temporal conventions and to represent distinct historical moments in one sweeping vision—that gives her art its transformative power and, according to Calvin's letter, signifies the "miracle" of her "Creation."

Indeed, I want to suggest that the way Alice and other artists in the text experience time corresponds not just in broad terms to the Old Testament myth of a divine creator but actually, and with remarkable specificity, to Augustine's influential reading of Genesis, which argues that God cannot be measured by any existing temporal standard. As John Cavadini has explained, Augustine devoted so much attention in his theological writings to the biblical story of creation because of his commitment to demonstrating "the uniqueness and the superiority of God's mind" as well as its inherent incomprehensibility (37). In contradistinction to the philosophers of the period who sought to articulate precisely why and for what reason God created the world when he did, Augustinian theology is premised on the impossibility of ever being able to reconcile "His eternal knowledge" with human temporality.[16] Thus a point Augustine stresses throughout *The City of God* is the difference between how the Lord regards time and how the rest of "us" do:

It is not with God as it is with us. He does not look ahead to the future, look directly at the present, look back to the past. He sees in some other manner, utterly remote from anything we experience or could imagine.... He sees all without any kind of change.[17] (11.21)

Here, and elsewhere in the treatise, Augustine maintains that attempts to understand God's vision and the creative act willed by it in terms of our linear, mutable lives are futile, since the creator "sees all" at once, from an omniscient perspective impervious to temporal changes. This argument, like the one he makes about temporality in book 11 of *Confessions*, hinges on the absolute inadequacy of human ways of seeing, relative to the Lord's. One of Augustine's primary goals, then, in *The City of God* is to establish the supremacy of God's sight—its timeless and immutable prescience. With regard to the Genesis story, in particular, he does that by arguing that, at the instant of creation (and eternally before), God foresaw every individual creature who inhabits the earth—past, present, and future. Therefore, Augustine claims, no part of this infinite multitude was ever outside the Lord's purview: "He has not produced them without order or foresight; nor has he foreseen them only at the last moment, but by His eternal knowledge" (12.19).

Augustine's claims regarding God's timelessness, and his reading of Genesis more broadly, were of course highly significant for Christian theology, informing, among other things, how different strands of Western Christianity have interpreted the providential design of creation. Indeed, Augustine's contention that God "sees all" helped to shape both the Catholic and the Protestant doctrines of predestination, which (though divergent in some important ways I will consider below) mutually affirm the divine prescience of historical events. For the idea that the world's creator "does not occupy time" and, in fact, could foresee the sum of human existence prior even to the making of the first man means that history in all its particularity was intended by God and contained within his plan (11.21). Hence, in *The City of God*, Augustine takes pains to show that God's intentionality encompasses the most disastrous or seemingly irrational happenings—such as the sack of Rome by the Visigoths in 410, which was the immediate catalyst for his book. (Letters from the period confirm that Augustine undertook the writing to dispute the charge that God had abandoned Rome or been otherwise powerless to prevent the tribulations that the empire endured.)[18] Christians, he argues, must have faith that their temporal experience has been divinely ordered and that the meaning of their suffering as well as their triumphs will be revealed at their deaths. In line with this theological position, *The City of God* took the controversial stance that the emperors ruling Rome at any given moment—the "godly and ungodly alike"—were each granted their authority by the Lord. As Augustine puts it: "He Who gave power to Marius also gave it to Gaius Caesar. . . . He Who gave it to Vespasii, father and son, the gentlest of emperors, also gave it to Domitian, the cruelest," and "all these things" please "the one true God" equally, inasmuch as they were foreseen in the earth's creation (5.21). Thus Augustine uses Genesis to advocate for history's ultimate goodness, and he tells his fellow Christians to wait, as piously and patiently as possible, for the coming revelation.

Clearly this is not a view of history that Jones's novel endorses in any tangible, political sense. Again and again readers witness the dangers of accepting without question the intentionality of the created world in the way that Augustine counsels. The character most closely associated with Augustine's analysis of Genesis, Sheriff Skiffington, gets exposed at the end of the narrative as a religious hypocrite of the worst kind: the type of Christian so convinced of the righteousness of God's eternal vision that he refuses to challenge any part of the established order, even when the slaveholders (whom he tellingly calls "Caesars") force him to commit acts of injustice. Skiffington's final act, the murder of Mildred, underscores the stark moral and ethical consequences of an Augustinian theology of creation. This would suggest that Jones rejects out of hand the principle of divine prescience on which that theology is based.

Yet, at the same time, I am tracing through my examination of Alice and the other artists in the novel what amounts to a mythology of aesthetic production that—paradoxically—affirms how *The City of God* depicts creative enterprise. Like Augustine's Creator-God, Jones's art makers approach their work with an intention and a knowledge that transcends all forms of temporality. We find this not only in the omniscient perspective of Alice's wall hangings but also in her ability to account for the unique life of each individual, human and otherwise, that lived on the Townsend property—as Calvin says, "There is nothing missing. . . . I suspect that if I were to count the blades of grass, the number would be correct" (385)—an extraordinary ability that evokes the infinite scope of God's sight as

Augustine defines it. What is more, Jones correlates the mysterious and apparently nonsensical behavior Alice exhibits during slavery to the absolute supremacy of her mind. Just as Augustine teaches that only God can foreknow the purpose of every event that occurs throughout time, even those that resist rational explanation, Jones's text implies that Alice alone foresees the ultimate purpose of her own mystifying actions; they were all, as it turns out, part of her all-encompassing design, revealed at the conclusion of the novel.

Therefore it is possible, I am arguing, to read the narratological structure of *The Known World* and the history it represents in terms consistent with Augustine's historical theology, since the plot reveals in its completion the fullness of the creator's prescience. Notably, by "creator" here, I refer to Alice as well as to Jones. For in the same way that Alice's God's-eye perspective on creation gives meaning to her supposedly irrational past (including her story about being kicked by a mule), so too does the omniscience of Jones's narrator reveal the intentionality behind the more confounding aspects of his text. So I would submit that when Jones imagines the artist as God, who creates with timeless purpose, he is calling upon the very same concept of providential design that he critiques relentlessly elsewhere in the novel—via characters like Sheriff Skiffington and even Augustus, both of whom are reticent to disrupt the authority of the created order. But rather than quietly accepting things as they are and waiting for the revelation of divine justice (in the fashion counseled by *The City of God*), Jones's artists use their atemporal perception to transcend slavery in the here and now. In the final section of this chapter, I will consider a few more of the ways they do this, ultimately accounting for the Catholic imagery associated with their eternal vision of the world.

. . .

Undoubtedly, Alice's wall hangings produce the most tangible changes in the social order of the novel—effecting Calvin's decision to take up the antislavery cause and transforming the way audiences regard the agency of slaves. Other artworks, though, have a transformative effect as well, albeit not always with such spectacular results. We might think of the doll Elias carves for Tessie, for example: a modest and deeply personal expression of his paternal affection, which does not turn out how he wanted it to look. In spite of its perceived limitations, however, the doll affords his daughter the opportunity to challenge in a small yet meaningful exchange with her mistress the assumption that slaves cannot possess property or be cared for by anyone except their owners. When Tessie proclaims to Caldonia and the other slaveholders within earshot, "My daddy made it for me," she is tacitly diminishing their authority over her, to an extent that even she is not cognizant of at the moment (350). The fact that a piece of artwork is what enables this gesture of defiance implies something significant, I am suggesting, about not just the value of the piece itself but also of the vision of the artist who created it. In other words, the narrative attributes the doll's worth to the effort and love Elias put into carving it—and, specifically, to his attempt to accomplish what Alice advises him to do with his art: "just make it good, make it to last" (78). This bit of advice counts as one of the few sensible phrases Alice speaks in the text, and it is certainly the only statement of any kind she offers about artistry. Not surprisingly, then, given the argument I have been making about her godlike prescience, Alice's words indicate that artists should not be bound by the limits of human temporality and should strive instead for a lasting—eternal—purpose whose goodness surpasses the measure of linear time.

Glancing back at the quoted HarperCollins interview and Jones's own comments on the nonlinearity of the novel, we perceive that he, like Alice, locates the purpose of Elias's artwork outside the bounds of temporal existence. That is why, Jones says, he needed to abandon the chronological approach of his narrative and flash forward to the instant of Tessie's death in order to reveal it: because only by disrupting temporality in this way could he communicate the doll's historical "meaning" for Tessie and for generations of her ancestors. It requires an omniscient perspective, unbounded by the vicissitudes of time, to see that the toy created by an enslaved man for his daughter will outlast them both, well into the twentieth century—long enough to be passed down to her great-grandchildren, who recover it from the attic at Tessie's bidding on the day she dies. The temporal disruptions in the novel thus affirm and give expression to the eternal vision that Alice counsels Elias to bring to his art, demonstrating that the doll does indeed stand as a lasting symbol of goodness, unaffected by the passage of time. On multiple levels, then, and across distinct periods of history, Jones associates the doll with a sense of timelessness, which—quite literally—transcends the order of slavery. From the moment of its inception, when Elias was too consumed with carving to heed Moses's instructions about the growing lateness, until the hour of Tessie's death, when she repeats the proclamation of ownership she made to Caldonia ninety years earlier, the doll constitutes an enduring threat to the slaveholders' authority. And, significantly, the threat it presents is one that ultimately cannot be contained, since it lasts longer, at least in material form, than slavery itself—far past the historical point at which the institution concluded and into the timeless space beyond.

To the slaveholders in *The Known World*, the idea of timelessness is destabilizing, even incapacitating. Throughout the novel, Jones makes a point of demonstrating that every aspect of plantation culture depends on a rigorous adherence to the "clock's hour and minute hands" (46). Any deviation from linear chronology signals a serious problem for those in power. Thus William Robbins believes that losing "whole bits of time" to his mental "storms" makes him "vulnerable" to the abolitionists, while Clara Martin blames her slave's perceived disobedience on the fact that time "has no meaning anymore" (25–26, 152). Without the certainty of chronological experience to rely on, Jones suggests, the slaveholders' way of life becomes impossible to sustain. It is for that reason, I am arguing, that the artist's atemporal perception figures so prominently in the narrative, both in form and in content. Because their sight is not limited by clock time and their attention turns persistently toward the eternal, Jones's artists have the ability to imagine a realm in which the established structure of slavery no longer holds. The creations they make are, in fact, materially linked to that realm, as they upset the traditional balance of power and enable acts of resistance against the prevailing order. (Think of the way Alice's wall hangings inspire Calvin to bring runaway slaves to freedom or how Tessie's doll helps her defy her mistress's authority.) Over and over again, in this manner, the novel correlates the artist's timeless vision to the liberation of slaves, implying that seeking after the eternal can enable actual freedom.

This secular premise, of course, has a theological counterpart in Augustine's writing. In *The City of God*, as in all his treatises, salvation necessitates one's faith in an eternity beyond the temporal world. For that reason, Augustinian theology maintains that any person wishing to be liberated from suffering must be able to envision the possibility of lasting redemption, as a step on that journey. Although, in accordance with his views on divine prescience, he believed the ultimate fate of every individual was foreknown by God, he also held firmly to the position that God wills all human beings to be saved—even though some of them are not, because they focus too much on "temporal things" (1.10). This apparent contradiction gave rise to a fundamental divergence between Protestant and Catholic doctrines of predestination, as I indicated earlier. While Protestants, following John Calvin, tend to stress Augustine's claim that God alone predestines who will receive salvation and that humans cannot save themselves, Catholics historically have emphasized the portions of Augustine's teaching that suggest humans can choose either to accept or reject God's salvific promise according to their own free will.[19] The official stance of the Catholic Church on this matter, which Jones would surely have heard as a child in parochial school and while studying at Holy Cross, is that being saved requires *both* the grace of divine favor and the willing assent of individuals to participate in the eternal goodness of the Lord. In other words: as opposed to Calvinist strands of Protestantism, Catholicism upholds the part of the Augustinian logic of predestination that makes salvation contingent on a person's willful decision to seek redemption. According to the Catholic interpretation of Augustine, people who direct their attention away from "fleeting temporal" experience and toward "an endless eternity" can be redeemed from suffering, through the grace of God (3.20).

A parallel logic, I am suggesting, informs the correlation Jones draws in his novel between an artist's atemporal perspective and the possibility of real-life liberation from slavery. We find it operating, for example, in the story the narrator tells of the slave girl Ophelia, who "disappeared" from the home of her licentious master "without an explanation that satisfied everyone." Most of the white people in Manchester County attribute the disappearance to "her jealous and possibly murderous mistress," but the slaves in town have a different perspective. The alternative theory they whisper among themselves goes as follows:

> Ophelia had met Jesus' mother one late afternoon on the main road people took to get to Louisa County and that Mary, hearing Ophelia sing, had decided right then that she didn't want heaven if it came without Ophelia. Mary asked Ophelia about coming with her and eating peaches and cream in the sunlight until Judgment Day and Ophelia shrugged her shoulders and said, "That sounds fine. I ain't got nothin better to do right at the moment. Ain't got nothin to do till evenin time anyway." (40)

When compared with the premise that Ophelia was murdered by her owner out of jealousy over the transgressive (and most certainly unwanted) affair she had with the woman's husband, the account above appears entirely unrealistic, to say the least. Yet realism, I would submit, serves no purpose in this case. Rather the implicit function of the tale the slaves tell one another is to sustain hope for Ophelia's salvation. Refusing to believe that the life of this "very self-confident fourteen-year-old slave girl" (40) ended in an utter lack of agency, they create an entirely fictitious narrative—a work of art—which imaginatively saves her from enslavement. And, importantly, this creation bears the hallmarks that I have attributed to the novel's other artworks, in that it incorporates an atemporal perspective that challenges the structure of the slave system. Note that Ophelia's decision to eat "peaches and cream in the sunlight until Judgment Day" gets figured as a conscious rejection of the linear chronology of the plantation, as she chooses a timeless future with Mary over whatever duties she has "right at the moment" as well as what she had to do later in the day, at "evenin time." The story thus stands as testament to the ultimate meaninglessness of the plantation clock, further destabilizing—with every retelling—the slaveholders' authority.

In fact, what is so threatening about the story the slaves tell each other is that it contradicts, in strikingly similar language, the message of righteous obedience they have received "Sunday after Sunday" from Reverend Moffett. A man paid by slaveholders to provide religious justification for the institution by which they live, Moffett closes each sermon by reminding the congregation "that they should obey their masters and mistresses, for heaven would not be theirs if they disobeyed," and then he punctuates the point with this image: "One day I want to sit with yall and eat peaches and cream in heaven. I don't wanna have to lean over and look way way down and see yall burnin in them fires of hell" (87). The Ophelia narrative directly opposes Moffett's view of salvation, suggesting that the privilege of eating peaches and cream in the eternal realm does not depend on how closely a slave adheres to the order of the plantation system, but rather on a willingness to see beyond the system's fleeting temporal existence. As her fellow slaves imagine it, Ophelia's fate resides in her willful decision to seek redemption on her own terms by turning away from temporality and accepting the salvific grace offered to her by Mary.

I have been arguing that this way of thinking about salvation corresponds much more readily with the Catholic doctrine of predestination than it does with a traditional Protestant doctrine such as Moffett preaches, and this likely accounts for the strange role that Mary plays in the story. For it is strange indeed that slaves who live Manchester County, Virginia, where Protestantism is not just the majority religion but also the denomination of their only official preacher, would invoke the name of "Jesus' mother" to explain the liberation of one of their own. The veneration of Mary as a heavenly figure capable of performing miracles and providing supernatural assistance to people in need is a distinctly Catholic phenomenon, not something that falls within the Protestant system of belief. Mary's presence in the story about Ophelia signals, I think, a departure from Protestantism's traditional interpretation of predestination—particularly the idea that human beings are incapable of saving themselves. In other words, the Catholic overtones of the Ophelia narrative imply that a slave has at least some agency in her own salvation, even if the ultimate power to save her resides in (Mary's) divine nature.

An equivalent point is made in another scene of a slave's liberation, where Catholicism again intrudes on the narrative in an unexpected way and structures how the narrative imagines freedom. I am referring to the story of Rita, whose harrowing journey the narrator relates shortly after recounting the different explanations for Ophelia's disappearance. Like Ophelia, Rita is one of a number of slaves who went missing around the same time, prompting widespread apprehension among slave owners about "what Robbins had begun to call 'a hemorrhaging of slaves'" (41). And, in Rita's case at least, their fears were justified, since her escape realizes an ingenious—and eventually successful—attempt to leave slavery behind. With Augustus's help, the narrator explains, she absconded from Robbins's plantation in broad daylight, on the same afternoon Henry was officially sold to his father. A few days later, after hiding out with the Townsends, she is packed into a container of walking sticks and shipped without anyone else's knowledge to Augustus's merchant in the North, where she emerges travel weary and sore but alive—and presumably free. The tale is, as anyone familiar with fugitive slave narratives would surely notice, nearly identical to one told in *The Life of Henry Box Brown*, which also features a daring escape from slavery by way of the U.S. Postal Service. Even small details, such as the words painted on the container that holds Rita, "THIS SIDE UP WITH EXTREME CARE" (52), and the handlers' blatant disregard for those instructions at various stops along the way, bear a remarkable similarity to Box's famous account.[20] Clearly, then, Jones had the Box story in mind when he imagined Rita's salvation from slavery.

Rather than focusing on the similarities between these two narratives, though, I want to examine the changes Jones made to Brown's story when he appropriated it for his novel. I have in mind, specifically, Jones's choice to ship the box containing Rita to New York, instead of to Philadelphia as in Brown. The change in venue results in the box being opened not by members of the Philadelphia Anti-Slavery Society but by an Irish immigrant named Mary with no connection to the abolitionist cause. Because the vignette is otherwise so faithful, in ways both major and minor, to the details of Henry Brown's escape, these two divergences call attention to themselves. Most obviously, they provide an opening for introducing into Jones's narrative a description of Mary's miserable emigration to the United States. The narrator devotes pages to Mary's immigrant story—almost as many as those spent detailing Rita's journey. One could even argue that Jones provides more information about Mary than about the slave whom she rescues. We learn, for example, that both her first husband and her infant daughter died on the ship out of Cork Harbor and were given burials at sea, during which her older son performed multiple recitations of the Lord's Prayer and the Hail Mary. We also learn that Mary's breast milk "stopped flowing" the day after her daughter's death and that it never returned, even after she had three more children and prayed to "Mary the mother of Jesus to intercede with God on her behalf" and help her feed her babies (51).

Faced with such seemingly extraneous pieces of Mary's personal history, critics have attributed this and other references to people from Ireland in *The Known World* to "the associations between slaves and the Irish in the popular imagination" (Giemza 41). In other words, they would contend that Jones uses the sad tale of her emigration experience in a general sense to express some fundamental commonality, perhaps, in how African Americans and Irish immigrants have been disenfranchised in the United States.[21] But Mary's character, to my mind, has more *direct* relevance to the way the novel imagines slavery than the criticism would suggest—that her background actually underscores how significantly Jones's secular interpretation of salvation is informed by Catholicism's doctrine of predestination. The fact that Rita's freedom depends on the mercy of an Irish Catholic woman whose name and life story link her to "the mother of Jesus" is of central importance to the entire vignette, especially when we consider that Henry Brown's rescuers were all men, and the one he credits with actually receiving him in Philadelphia, James Miller McKim, was a Presbyterian minister. Jones's decision to change the gender and the religious orientation of the person responsible for opening the box demands interpretation. Not only does the characterization of Rita's rescuer forge an imaginative connection to the Ophelia narrative, since both slaves are "saved" by women named Mary with strong ties to Catholicism, but it also signals, once again, a turn away from the traditional Protestant view of salvation.

Attending to Jones's revisionary incorporation of Catholicism, I am arguing, illuminates the role of the artist in the realization of a slave's liberation. For, just as in the Ophelia narrative, when Mary determines "right then and there" on account of the young girl's beautiful songs to take her away from slavery, it appears that Rita too will be saved by art. In fact, the art that likely secures her freedom is, like the other works in the text, a piece indicative of its creator's eternal vision. The creator in this case, though, is not Rita but Augustus, whose act of aesthetic creation makes her liberation possible. For, however much he remains beholden to the order of slavery in his personal life, when it comes to his art, Augustus reveals a creative capacity for seeing beyond it. He not only invents the plan to send Rita by mail to his merchant in New York, he also carves the walking stick that Mary's son "had been waiting for all along" (53). Notably, the stick that so captivates the boy is itself a symbol of both artistic and divine prescience: a figurative retelling of the Book of Genesis, which relates individuals from different historical periods to the first man and woman supposedly created by God, suggesting that they were all part of his providential design. It depicts Adam and Eve at its base, and they are "holding up" a long line of their descendants—"fourteen or more other figures," from Cain and Abel to George Washington and even the artist's idea of the current "king and queen of England"—all of whom appear together in an atemporal view of human history (47). The piece thus recalls, with its sweeping perspective that transcends the passage of time, Alice Night's "miraculous" wall hangings, and I am suggesting that its ultimate effect is quite similar to those wall hangings as well. Both works, in the imaginative way they disrupt temporality, bring about the actual liberation of slaves, thereby confirming the transformative power of art.

Coda

WHETHER OR NOT ONE READS temporal disjuncture in *The Known World* as pessimistic about the future of race relations in the United States, it would be hard to deny that the novel privileges art as a means for transcending the suffering of slavery. In this manner, like *Stigmata* and *Oxherding Tale*, Jones's work suggests that disruptions in narratological time can have actual real-world consequences, transforming how audiences perceive their relationship to the existing order. That is, in effect, how the contemporary slave narratives of Jones, Perry, and Johnson determine the *value* of aesthetic creation: in terms of the artwork's ability to challenge the conventions of Western temporality by imagining a space unbeholden to the linear, progressive view of history through which the system of slavery was rationalized and sustained. In fact, given the way that the tropes of rememory and spirit possession also disrupt temporal conventions in the representations of the slave experience by Morrison, Forrest, and Gaines, it could be said of these antirealist devices more broadly that they enact a collective and destabilizing critique of the ideologies undergirding the rationalizing impulse of the antebellum period. Altogether, then, as I have been contending throughout the preceding chapters, the effort to revise the traditional historiography of slavery is commensurate in these texts with a drive toward irrationality, which is often expressed—strangely enough—through the language of Catholicism.

The Catholic margin thus emerges in the contemporary narrative of slavery as a site of oppositional discourse, wherein alternative ways of remembering the past are realized. And yet the alternative historiography that Catholicism, in a sense, makes possible also implicates the religion and the institutions it gave rise to in the very structures these texts set out to undermine. For, as we saw in *The Known World*, at the same time that a

Catholic logic of salvation informs how slaves imaginatively transcend suffering, Catholic theology—following Augustine and, by extension, Saint Paul—is simultaneously responsible for the conditions that caused them to suffer in the first place. Consequently, it would be erroneous to infer from my reading that Catholicism operates in Jones's novel, or in any of the texts in this study, as an unproblematic or "pure" mode of dissent. Quite to the contrary, I have attempted here and throughout *Sacraments of Memory* to demonstrate the deeply conflicted way the contemporary narrative of slavery deploys its Catholic margin.

Notes

Introduction: Toward a Reading of the Catholic Margin
in Contemporary Narratives of Slavery

    1. On Catholicism in Dunbar-Nelson's fiction, see Kristina Brooks as well as Haddox 41–44. A recent article in *Callaloo* by Madhuri Deshmukh traces Claude McKay's "road to Catholicism," and Giles addresses the topic briefly in the final chapter of his book (518–19). In fact, McKay is one of the two African American writers, along with Leon Forrest, whom Giles associates with Catholic culture.

    2. Douglass famously noted in his *Narrative of the Life* that he used the "mighty speeches on and in behalf of Catholic emancipation" to help define his own antislavery position, while Harriet Jacobs compared her white master to the Catholic leaders responsible for the Inquisition in order to emphasize his cruelty (84). (On Catholicism in Jacobs, see Franchot 104–5.) The extreme divergence in how these two authors deploy Catholicism for a common purpose (abolition) indicates the variable nature of the Catholic margin and the variety of uses to which it is put in different texts.

    3. The structure of Parks's play, she has said, was informed by the Stations of the Cross: a series of images depicting the Passion of Christ, which are displayed in Roman Catholic churches and often used in prayer ceremonies held during Lent and on Good Friday. See Geis 58.

    4. The term "neo-slave narrative" was coined in 1987 by Bernard Bell, who used it to refer to fictional accounts of slavery that take the first-person form and assume the narrative structure of the antebellum autobiographies of fugitive slaves. Ashraf Rushdy used the term in a similar way in his 1999 landmark study of the genre. But in 2004, Arlene Keizer proposed that "contemporary narratives of slavery" be used instead, as a way to signify the many different styles and forms of address used in fiction about slavery. She points out, for example, "how few contemporary narratives of slavery are written in the first person" (3). For the most part, in this study, I follow Keizer's preferred terminology, though I am not as concerned as she is with maintaining a rigid distinction between the two generic labels. That is because, in the years since Keizer's book was published, the term "neo-slave narrative" has been more widely applied and is now used to refer to a greater variety of texts than Bell and Rushdy originally intended it to represent (see Valerie Smith's essay "Neo-Slave Narratives," for example). Therefore, I will at times use the two terms interchangeably for the sake of convenience.

5. Contemporary narratives of slavery began to appear in large numbers after 1966, following the publication of Margaret Walker's *Jubilee*, which is generally regarded as the first "neo-slave narrative" in the United States. However, as Rushdy and Valerie Smith note, Arna Bontemps's *Black Thunder* was published three decades before Walker's novel, in 1936, and it "anticipates much of the cultural work that later texts in the genre perform" (Smith, "Neo-Slave" 170). With the exception of Bontemps's novel, though, fictional accounts of slavery were not being produced until the late 1960s, and they really exploded after the mid-1970s.

6. For further discussion of the historical context in which these questions surfaced, see Dubey, "Neo-Slave Narratives."

7. Spaulding makes a very similar case in the introduction to his study, which focuses on the postmodern aspects of contemporary slave narratives.

8. Nathaniel remembers, specifically, how the "Pope blessed" Mussolini's actions, anointing the heads of his soldiers "as a fire-worshiping idolator" (65).

9. On religion as a "dynamically constituted" category of discourse, see also Eytan Bercovitch's "The Altar of Sin," along with Ferraro's *Feeling Italian*; Mizruchi's *The Science of Sacrifice* and her introduction to *Religion and Cultural Studies*, which she edited; Orsi's *The Madonna of 115th Street*; and Jonathan Smith's *Imagining Religion*.

Chapter 1. Toni Morrison's Sacramental Rememory

1. See Wyatt for an argument that relates Denver's insatiable hunger to a primal desire to speak words that cannot be spoken (i.e., the words that would describe her mother's infanticidal act).

2. For example, Valerie Smith claims that Beloved "dissolves when [her community] forgets and swallow[s] her all away" (352).

3. See United States Congress of Catholic Bishops, *General Instruction of the Roman Missal*, esp. chapter 2, section III, part C.

4. On the "unprecedented spread" of Protestant Christianity among African Americans in "the closing years of the eighteenth and the early decades of the nineteenth centuries," see Raboteau, 107–43.

5. Specifically, Valkeakari's study briefly considers how in *The Bluest Eye* the Catholic sacrament of confession "resonates" (96).

6. See, for example, Raboteau's often-cited study of slave religion, wherein the author claims that slaves "in the British colonies of North American were not likely to be exposed to [Catholicism] unless they lived in Maryland, the only colony with a sizable Catholic presence" (112).

7. As recently as 11 May 2012, Morrison referred to herself as Catholic during an interview by Tom Ashbrook.

8. Patterson aligns the rise of fundamentalist Christianity with "the great religious awakening" (elsewhere called the Second Great Awakening) that spread through the slaveholding states during these years and "culminated in the religious conversion of the South from classical Protestantism to revivalist fundamentalism" (73).

9. See Patterson 72.

10. The precise number of conversions among the slave population is impossible to deter-

mine, given that the majority of them occurred en masse during tent revivals. Raboteau cites church records of African American membership as "one index—a rather stringent one—to the influence of Christianity upon the life of the slave." He goes on to note that "Du Bois quoted a figure of 468,000 black church members in the South in 1859" (209).

11. A number of critics have taken Crouch to task for precisely this failure. See, for example, Paul Gilroy's famous response to Crouch's review in the concluding pages of *The Black Atlantic*.

12. This and all subsequent biblical quotations are from the English Standard Version.

13. Patterson regards the brand of Protestantism that developed in the slaveholding American South as "Rome's closest counterpart in the modern world," arguing that it played "the identical role . . . in the slave system" that Catholicism had for the ancient Romans, "eighteen hundred years" earlier (76).

14. A few lines later in the novel, the mark on Sethe's mother is referred to as a "circled cross" (73).

15. For an explanation of the way that Protestants have historically minimized the doctrine of transubstantiation as well as other "mysteries" of the Mass, see Berger 111–13.

16. The scars on Sethe's back, a consequence of the slavemaster's whip, resemble those from scourging, which Jesus endured during the Passion. Although not a cross itself, a number of critics have also seen the image of the chokecherry tree as an embodied link to Jesus, specifically the abrasions he endured while carrying the wooden cross to the site of his crucifixion at Calvary. See Atlas, esp. 55; Griesinger, esp. 690; Otten 94.

17. In addition to the passages from Romans in which Paul commands his followers to live according to "what we do not see," the apostle is himself famously associated with blindness. As told in Acts 9, his conversion to Christianity happened as a direct result of being temporarily blinded by God on the road to Damascus. There it is written of Paul that "although his eyes were opened, he saw nothing. . . . And for three days he was without sight" (9.8–9). This resonates quite clearly with the way Morrison describes Sethe's eyes in the woodshed—eyes that I've argued are likewise turned toward God. As we shall soon see, it also resonates with her description of another set of eyes: those of the slavewomen depicted in *A Mercy*.

18. Priests wear vestments of purple and rose and light candles of the same color specifically during the last days of Lent and Advent, when the church emphasizes the need to atone for one's sins in preparation for meeting the Lord at Easter and Christmas respectively. See Glazier and Hellwig 174; Broderick 123.

19. Neither Nathaniel Bacon nor Bacon's Rebellion is explicitly named in the text, but in a series of discussions she had while promoting the novel, Morrison was forthright about her interest in the conflict and the way it influenced her depiction of this period of American history. See, for example, her interview with National Public Radio's Lynn Neary.

20. See Foner 100; Cooper 9.

21. Tessa Roynon points out that the anti-Catholic poem in which these lines originate, "Exhortation to His Children," by the Protestant martyr John Rogers, was included in a number of primers published in both London and Boston during the second half of the seventeenth century (596).

22. This is not the first time that Morrison has employed the trope of an elementary school primer to highlight the extent to which pedagogical tools can inculcate in children

particular attitudes and prejudices. Almost four decades before *A Mercy*, in *The Bluest Eye*, she includes excerpts from a Dick-and-Jane-style storybook to suggest the ways that young African American girls are taught to regard themselves as ugly and unworthy of love.

23. As an example of the lengths to which Protestant masters would go to address the inherent contradiction that the liberating conception of Pauline theology posed for slaveholders, Patterson points to the Anglican masters in the Caribbean, who "avoided the problem altogether by abandoning religion or making a mockery of it, both for themselves and for their slaves" (72). One might argue that Jacob Vaark's disinclination to practice formal aspects of Protestantism and his decision to promote an "unchurched" existence on his farm (among his family and his slaves) would suggest that he too recognizes the incompatibility of his slaveholding with his religion.

24. Although Jacob does not take the anti-Catholic sentiment as far as do his brethren in England who sought to expunge all Catholics from the land, he does understand why "they had been excluded from Parliament back home" and makes it clear that "other than on business he would never choose to mingle or socialize with the lowest or highest of them" (23).

25. In referring to the house as "befitting a squire," Rebekka's words may imply an association between the new construction and medieval feudalism. This association evokes a popular portrayal of American slavery that proliferated among northern abolitionists and proslavery southerners alike, equating the plantation system with antimodern, feudalistic ideals. Thomas F. Haddox has emphasized the ways that this "'medievalist' ideology ultimately required a religious grounding," arguing that it implicitly correlates plantation slavery with Catholicism (48).

26. Numerous critics have commented on the biblical imagery on display in Jacob's gate, including Valerie Babb, who regards the serpents as symbolic of Vaark's desire to create an American Eden and his eventual "fall from grace," which she links to his participation in the sugar trade, "his deal with the devil" ("E Pluribus Unum?" 155).

27. On the structure of slave narratives, see Olney, esp. 152–53. On literary realism and the slave narrative, see Andrews.

28. A good example is Zauditu-Selassie's chapter on *Beloved*, 145–67.

29. See Pérez-Torres, "Between Presence and Absence," and also Spaulding 61–76.

30. Postmodernism and African spirituality are both typically perceived to be antithetical to Western religious belief in general and Christianity in particular. Accordingly, critics who align Morrison's novels with either tradition tend to argue against any Christian interpretation of her work. This has contributed to the widespread critical reluctance to concede how Catholicism shapes her concept of rememory.

31. Since evangelicals were largely responsible for publishing and promoting slave narratives, their tastes dictated the genre's form. As Gould notes, "Evangelical groups like the Methodists and Baptists, who emphasized the central importance of the individuals 'new birth' . . . took an interest in black autobiographies because of their spiritual value in disseminating religious ideas and thereby converting souls. These groups often assumed the role of publisher—the agent financing and taking risk on publication" (14–15).

32. On the ways that slave autobiographies "portrayed religion in the slave South as a perversion of true Christianity," see Bruce 30–31.

33. Yolanda Pierce defines spiritual autobiography as "a written document in which a convert to Christianity details his or her experience in recognizing the true light of Christian doctrine." She goes on to say that the antebellum slave autobiographers "overwhelmingly adopt[ed] the spiritual autobiography form in their accounts of bondage" in order to justify their own pursuit of freedom (92).

34. See McBrien 9–10.

35. See Berger 112.

36. The term "analogical imagination" comes from theologian David Tracy's book of the same name. Greeley's analysis of the Catholic worldview draws heavily upon Tracy's claims, and in fact his 2000 sociological study *The Catholic Imagination* is dedicated to Tracy, whom he calls "theologian of the Enchanted Imagination."

37. For an explanation of the Protestant dialectical imagination, see Tracy 405–8.

38. In fact, one of the most refreshing aspects of Giles's argument is that he does not limit his survey to practicing Catholics; instead, he considers the way "cultural Catholicism" has shaped the aesthetics of even those writers who have attempted to distance themselves from the church into which they were born. This approach broadens the discussion of the Catholic countertradition in American literature to include texts that are ambivalent about or even explicitly antagonistic toward Catholicism.

39. See Morrison's interview with Schappell (87).

40. Giles's oversight is especially significant, given his recurrent references to Morrison's work. Yet none of these references accounts for Morrison's longstanding personal relationship to Catholicism. At one point Giles even invokes Morrison in support of a tenuous claim for a fundamental divergence in the way that "blacks" and Catholics characterize their respective (and the implication is *separate*) modes of existence: "if blacks exert pressure toward the recognition of difference, Catholics exert pressure toward the recognition of similarity, analogy, universalism" (29). It is noteworthy that a study so attuned to the pluralistic nature of the Catholic experience overlooks how Morrison's work represents both modes of existence simultaneously. Indeed, I would suggest that Giles's lapse is part of a wider critical inability to see Christian themes in Morrison's fiction—and the fiction of most African American authors—as anything other than Protestant.

41. See McBrien 820–23.

42. *Decree on Ecumenism*, Vatican II, qtd. in McBrien 828.

43. In her interview with Marsha Darling about *Beloved*, Morrison explained that she understands the resistance her characters felt to remembering the slave experience: "They don't want to talk, they don't want to remember, they don't want to say it, because they're afraid of it—which is human. But when they do say it, and hear it, and look at it, and share it, they are not only one, they're two, and three, and four, you know. The collective sharing of that information heals the individual—and the collective" (248).

44. In the chapters assigned to her toward the end of the novel, she speaks of an unnamed woman who "chews and swallows me" (252).

45. The idea that the sacrament of the Eucharist could bring "judgment, not grace" in cases where division is present comes from Paul's First Letter to the Corinthians 11.17–34.

46. Elsewhere in the novel, Florens refers to writing in terms typically reserved for speech. She calls the linguistic symbols scratched onto the surface of rocks "stone talk" (6), and she believes that the words she carves into Jacob's house "will talk to themselves" after

she is gone (161). This purposeful conflation of written and spoken articulation throughout Florens's narrative reinforces the possibility of reading it as a ceremonial act of confession, a sacrament of which she would have no longer been able to partake properly, given the dearth of priests at the Vaark property. What is more, the fact that Florens conveys her story in secret, sequestered in a small, dark "talking room" (161), emphasizes the confessorial nature of the telling. The room resembles a Catholic confessional, where the faithful go to speak—and, ultimately, to be absolved of—their sins.

47. Although Catholic confessions are mediated by priests, the Church makes clear that only God can forgive sins. With respect to this arrangement then and the way it imaginatively structures Florens's narrative, her *unintended* readers (those of us who managed to access the writing in spite of her plan to burn it) could be said to occupy a priestly role. We bear witness to the appeal but remain powerless to absolve her or grant mercy.

48. For an argument linking Florens's "excessive devotion" to that of other women characters in Morrison's fiction, see Vega-González.

Chapter 2. A Sacred Communion: The Catholic Side of Possession in *The Autobiography of Miss Jane Pittman* and *Two Wings to Veil My Face*

1. Reed's collection *Conjure* contains poems titled "Neo-HooDoo Manifesto" and "The Neo-HooDoo Aesthetic," which critics tend to regard as his first statements about the relationship between spirit possession and African American literature (see Rushdy 126–27 and Schmitz). His concept of HooDoo writing bears heavily not only on *Flight to Canada* but on his other works of fiction, including *Yellow Back Radio Broke-Down* (1969) and *Mumbo Jumbo* (1972), and nonfiction as well, such as *Shrovetide in Old New Orleans* (1978).

2. In the connection he draws between textual possession and Vodou ceremonies, Rushdy is relying primarily on the analysis of Haitian Vodou that Colin Dayan provides in *Haiti, History, and the Gods*. The interior quote here is from Dayan, "Voudon" 19.

3. Among those who believed Jane Pittman to be a real person, Marcia Gaudet includes former New York governor Hugh Carey, who "included her on a list of historical black women"; a number of "national news magazines [that] asked Gaines for a picture of Jane to publish along with reviews of the book"; and the study *Folklore and Literature in the United States*, which "lists Jane Pittman in the author index" (24).

4. In this argument, Dubey explicitly builds upon similar claims made by Rushdy in *Neo-Slave Narratives* 31–42, 91–92.

5. Dubey argues it was only *after* "the task of historical recovery seemed to be relatively far along" that antirealist slave narratives began to appear, and "in fact, the expansion of the historical archive formed a necessary condition of possibility for their emergence" (783).

6. Dubey, for one, associates the trope of spirit possession with the second wave of neo-slave narratives—those that followed the earlier, realist versions such as *Miss Jane Pittman*. She argues that this trope "resonates powerfully in speculative fictions of slavery, amplifying their antihistoriographic impulse" (789).

7. Throughout her narrative, Jane uses the term "mulatto" to refer specifically to descendants of European settlers, in a way that distinguishes them from other African Americans

whose ancestors were "white, but not Creole white. Poor white—no quality" (157). Thus, for Jane, "mulattoes" are always already associated with Catholicism, since as a group they tended to celebrate their historical links to the French and Spanish colonizers, including their religion. For the sake of consistency, in my discussion of the novel, I will follow this meaning of the term.

8. Haddox's fascinating analysis of literary portrayals of *plaçage* includes texts by George Washington Cable, Grace King, Alice Dunbar-Nelson, and William Faulkner, all of which he argues have anti-Catholic resonances. Although the motivation for criticizing the church is different for each of these authors, Haddox points out that they "explore the associations" of Catholicism with the rise of the "mulatto" class in New Orleans (10).

9. For examples of the various roadblocks Catholic bishops in the South set up to prevent their congregants from joining the struggle for civil rights, see Gallagher.

10. In his speeches and letters, King regularly references the nonparticipation of Catholic priests and bishops in the struggle for racial justice. For example, in "The Experiment of Love," King points out that of all the Christian denominations, only Catholics refused to send priests to participate in the Montgomery bus boycotts, even though "many of their parishioners took part" (17).

11. The precise date the novel concludes is not clear, though most critics follow Babb in citing "the mid-1960s" as its end point (*Ernest Gaines* 96). I would argue that somewhere between April 1962 (when Leander Perez was excommunicated by the Catholic Church, an event mentioned in the narrative [216]) and the Freedom Summer of 1964 (when the civil rights movement in Louisiana gained considerable momentum) is even more accurate, since Jane indicates that the protest she joins in the final scene is one of the first of its kind in her part of the state. This means that Jane's narrative terminates *just before* the moment in March 1965 that for historians signaled the Catholic Church's full support of civil rights: the participation of nuns and priests in the Selma-to-Montgomery March (see McGreevy 152–60).

12. In her essay "Speculative Fictions of Slavery," Dubey also uses the term "haunt" to refer to a mode of articulation that "refutes not only the rational and detached stance of modern historiography, but also its linear and progressive temporality" (788–89). Here she is explicitly drawing upon the way that scholars such as Avery Gordon and Hershini Bhana Young have previously used the term.

13. The prominent anthropologist Melville J. Herskovits noted, in his observations of spirit possessions in Haiti, that a possessed person "often exhibits a complete transformation in his personality; facial expression, motor behavior, voice, physical strength, and the character of his utterances are startlingly different from what they were when he is 'himself'" (67).

14. For a summary of Tillich's definition of "the Protestant principle," see Giles 186. See also Berger 111–12.

15. In the portion of his study quoted here, Giles is referring specifically to *The Great Gatsby*, arguing that Fitzgerald's title character effectively tries to "transubstantiate" his beloved in this way, as he "seeks to redeem the accident of Daisy's time on earth" (186–87).

16. In making this claim about Catholicism, Giles draws from and expands the argument Sacvan Bercovitch proposed about Puritanism in the groundbreaking study *The Puritan Origins of the American Self*.

17. As Clarke Garrett affirms in his study *Spirit Possession and Popular Religion*, the Roman Catholic Church does not accept that humans can be possessed by any spirit other than God or the devil: "If the spirits are not God's and good, they must be evil" (7). This necessarily negates the possibility of humans becoming possessed by ancestral spirits.

18. Rushdy takes the term "Hoodoo aesthetic" or "Hoodoo writing" from Ishmael Reed, whose novel *Flight to Canada* is at the center of his analysis.

19. Of Leon Forrest's complexity, Edward P. Jones once said that it prevented him from finishing the first novel in the Bloodworth Trilogy (of which *Two Wings to Veil My Face* is the last): "You get to the book, and ask where's the story, where are these people, and what is he doing? Everything in me rebels against that. If these are real human beings imagination-wise, then you can use plain language to tell what they are doing and saying" (Graham 428).

20. See Dubey, "Speculative" 787–89, and Rushdy 125–31.

21. See Taylor-Guthrie 226–27.

22. Berry is quoting Clifford Longley's article "A Spiritual Land with Little Time for Church" from the *Daily Telegraph*, Friday, 17 December 1999.

23. Berry uses the term "post-religion" to refer to that "paradoxical (and notoriously difficult to define) cultural and economic phase" that succeeded modernity, in which "not only orthodox religion but even the more general concept of 'value' appears to have reached a critical impasse" due to, among other things, "the dissemination of increasingly populist cultural forms" and modes of knowledge (168–69).

24. For analysis of the racial discrimination prevalent in Catholic churches in Chicago, where Forrest grew up, see McGreevy.

25. For example, a single passage from *Two Wings* brings together allusions to the Jewish—or, possibly, Islamic—rite of circumcision ("our old ways must be discarded, as the foreskin of flesh") with references to Blake and Paul Robeson (211). Another interweaves quotations from Christian liturgy ("oh Kyrie eleison, oh Christe eleison") with *Macbeth*'s "tomorrow and tomorrow" speech (295).

Chapter 3. Catholicism and Narrative Time: Transcending the Past and the Present in *Stigmata* and *Oxherding Tale*

1. On the scholarly consensus regarding historiographical skepticism in contemporary narratives of slavery, see Dubey, "Speculative."

2. Rushdy cites an interview in which Reed indicates that "his art 'aims to sabotage history' and that he wanted to conduct an ongoing 'artistic guerilla warfare against the Historical Establishment'" (Reed in O'Brien 179, qtd. in Rushdy 110).

3. In her entry "Neo-Slave Narratives" in *A Companion to African American Literature*, Dubey claims: "Some variant" of Yerby's "pessimistic view of US racial history impels most novels of slavery published since the 1970s, especially those that break from narrative realism" (344).

4. Examples of contemporary slave narratives that deploy various time-bending devices to indicate the ongoing presence of slavery in contemporary culture include Octavia E. Butler's *Kindred* (1979), Jewelle Gomez's *The Gilda Stories* (1991), Steven Barnes's *Blood Brothers* (1996), and James McBride's *A Song Yet Sung* (2008). Through descriptions of time travel, vampires, possession, and paranormal visions these novels support the "pessimistic senti-

ment" of race relations in the United States, which Dubey associates with "all speculative fictions of slavery" ("Speculative" 793).

5. Though Lizzie's last name has obvious resonances with W.E.B. Du Bois's, Perry insists she was thinking of her own family's history when she chose it (see Duboin).

6. Evelyn Coleman in "Advance Praise for *Stigmata*," on the cover of the novel's first Hyperion edition.

7. For a discussion of the lengths to which fugitive slave authors had to go to prove their capacity for rational thought, see Olney. Lee discusses the ambivalence with which Douglass in particular often approached the rationalist imperative in his writing (95–109). I also consider the rationalist imperative of slave autobiography in chapter 1.

8. In *My Bondage and My Freedom*, Douglass refers to the child-slave "as happy as any little heathen under the palm trees of Africa," thus purposefully detaching his younger self from the older (and more rational) adult author (35).

9. See Sundquist 83–93.

10. It is notable that the footnote about Sandy was inserted in the *Narrative* a number of pages *after* Douglass's description of the root's apparent success. In other words, it seems as though Douglass used the footnote to walk back the suggestion he gave earlier in the autobiography that Sandy's magic actually helped him overpower Covey. Whereas he previously wrote that he was "half inclined to think the *root* to be something more than I at first had taken it to be," in the amending footnote he refers to Sandy's claims of success as "superstition . . . very common among the more ignorant slaves" (111, 119).

11. For example, toward the end of the novel, Sarah's Aunt Eva states in an aside that Lizzie is "one of you," suggesting that her supernatural claims about time travel and spirit possession have precedent among the women in their family (218).

12. In addition to Passalacqua's article, see Duboin and also Sievers.

13. In fact, Perry's second novel does this very thing. The redeeming force in *A Sunday in June* is Miz Willow, a roots worker trained in the traditional African practice by Ayo before her death. Just as Father Tom does for Lizzie in *Stigmata*, Willow uses her spiritual training to help two characters, Eva and Mary Nell, contend with the burden of their supernatural vision and learn how to use it in a productive manner.

14. In 1998, when *Stigmata* was published, Padre Pio had recently passed the second of four stages in the process of canonization in the Roman Catholic Church. The process began in 1982, the year an investigation into his candidacy for sainthood was officially opened, and concluded in 2002, when John Paul II declared him a saint.

15. Sociologist Michael P. Carroll notes that although "some stigmatics have been Protestant, the overwhelming majority have been Catholic" and that "the correlation between the stigmata and Catholicism" still persists today, whereas such a correlation has fallen away in the Protestant tradition (80–81). Thus, the Catholic Church's ongoing policy of honoring stigmatics, like its doctrine of transubstantiation and the ritualistic performances of the Stations of the Cross celebrated during Lent, speaks to the rather exceptional means by which the body in Catholicism mediates memory.

16. As Richard Kearney puts it, "Augustine underscores the fact that it is in the very midst of our experience of temporal dispersal that our desire for some eschatological reconciliation emerges" (149).

17. My use of the term "education" here is not meant to suggest that Lizzie receives

formal theological training from Father Tom; there is nothing in the novel to suggest that she does. I intend merely to highlight how similar the effect of learning about stigmatics was for Perry and for her character Lizzie.

18. For readings of the influence of Eastern philosophy and religion on Johnson's fiction, see Little, Selzer, and Storhoff.

19. Derrida describes the Western philosophy of temporality as a "succession of 'nows,' where we have a horizon of the future, the coming, the next now, the coming now" ("Composing" 23).

20. See, for example, how closely the chapter's description of the formal history of American slave narratives resembles what Johnson wrote about this same topic in the introduction to *Oxherding Tale* that was appended to later editions of the novel (xiv).

21. For example, in his famous essay on the slave narrative form, "'I Was Born': Slave Narratives, Their Status as Autobiography and Literature," James Olney discusses the ways that the genre both incorporates and overturns the conventions of the Augustinian confessional mode.

22. In this chapter the essayist notes that Puritan Narratives, like Augustine's *Confessions*, were autobiographical testimonies of having "accepted Christ" (118).

23. See Pierce, whose scholarship traces the themes of spiritual enlightenment and Christian salvation in fugitive slave narratives.

24. For a thorough account of how Johnson's novel dramatizes the *Ten Oxherding Pictures*, see Gleason. His article provides a chapter-by-chapter analysis of the narrative's fictional retelling of each of the images, which considers in impressive detail the way *Oxherding Tale* both confirms and reinvents its twelfth-century intertext.

25. In his analysis of the novel's dramatization of the *Ten Oxherding Pictures*, Gleason points out that the model Johnson explicitly drew from (an illustration series based on the earlier Chinese pictures by the fifteenth-century Zen artist Kuo-an Shihyuan) "describes a progressive movement toward enlightenment" (714). Each picture in the series, Gleason contends, brings the oxherder closer to his enlightenment depicted in the last image. And so he reads Andrew's journey in similar terms: as part of a cumulative progress toward liberation, in which every interaction along the way (with Flo, with Reb, with Dr. Undercliff, and so on) contributes to his ultimate "deliverance from the bondage of Samsara (both life and death)" (716).

26. For further discussion of the Zen values that inform Reb's worldview, see Little 93–95 and Rushdy 199–200. Johnson himself has also confirmed that the character stands for these values, saying in a 1987 interview, "Reb is the Zen Buddhist in the novel, and a lot of reviewers don't realize that. They don't know enough about other cultures to recognize him as such. He doesn't operate out of desire, he operates out of duty. It's duty that is the foundation for all his behavior" (O'Connell 25).

27. It should be noted, however, that Rushdy does not believe Andrew actually achieves that liberation at the end of the novel. He argues that the narrator's decision to pass for white fundamentally contradicts Allmuseri teaching, because it reveals a desire for self-possession which Reb denies. In Rushdy's reading, Reb is thus the only character who fully satisfies the novel's "vision" of freedom by becoming "a revolutionary to the degree that he becomes unpositioned in the material world and manages to make his possession of property a means of further unpositioning himself" (199). Although Andrew makes im-

portant and tangible strides toward a similar goal, Rushdy claims that he remains mired in the social order which Reb manages to escape. My reading of the end of *Oxherding Tale* also finds Andrew complicit in the power structures of a racist society. But, as I will explain, the reasons for Andrew's complicity have more to do with how he defines temporal salvation (by way of Augustine) than with his desire to possess property.

28. In the introduction to *Oxherding Tale*, Johnson refers to George Hawkins as a tragic figure: a "black nationalist . . . forever suffering from the pains caused by racial dualism" (xvii).

29. On Augustine's understanding of love as a divine gift, bestowed by the Holy Spirit, see Meconi, who notes: "It is an Augustinian commonplace that the Holy Spirit is the Gift of the Father and the Son, the Love between the Lover and the Beloved, the Glue who unites persons eternally (221).

30. See Augustine's *Tractates on the Gospel of John* (39.5), for example, quoted in Ayres.

31. On Augustine's contemporary reasons for writing the *Confessions*, see Meconi and Stump 6. See also Henry Chadwick's introduction to his translation on the text, xii–xiii.

32. For a discussion of the Allmuseri philosophy of ownership and personal possessions, see Rushdy 199.

33. For more on how Augustine defines love between persons, see Meconi 221–223 and Ayres 71–76.

Chapter 4. Catholicism and Narrative Time, Continued: Divine Prescience in Edward P. Jones's *The Known World*

1. The label "pseudorealist" is argued for by Maria Seger, who contends that the novel both accedes to and resists the "norms of realism" (1182).

2. See Seger, esp. 1188–91.

3. Anecdotally, the customer reviews for *The Known World* on Amazon.com reveal that readers often struggle to keep up with the sheer number of names (of people, of places) and to understand the relevance of some minor characters to the larger narrative. I will admit to using a list to track their appearances myself, as it can be overwhelming to remember when characters have been mentioned previously by the narrator and in what context. The effort it takes to *read* the novel with any hope of remembering "who did what and when" makes it all the more astonishing that Jones was able to *write* their stories so quickly, and with so much detail, in less than three months' time.

4. I am indebted to Tim A. Ryan for drawing my attention to Cheuse's review of *The Known World*. Ryan quotes from the review at length in the chapter devoted to Jones (205).

5. In his discussion of slavery in book 19 of *The City of God*, wherein he lays out the ideal of benevolent mastery, Augustine reminds readers "the first just men were established as shepherds of flocks, rather than as kings of men. This was done so that in this way also God might indicate what the order of nature requires, and what the desert of sinners demands" (19.15). Augustine's point—that slaveholders should rule over their slaves and all those in their care with humility and a sense of justice—resounds in Henry's (doomed) plan to practice a "different" kind of slavery and is especially resonant in his use of the term "shepherd master."

6. The quotes from *Incidents in the Life of a Slave Girl* come from that book's famous

chapter "Sketches of Neighboring Slaveholders," wherein Jacobs recounts a number of stories of the "all-pervading corruption produced by slavery" (51). One of the most shocking accounts tells of a slaveholder's daughter who "selected one of the meanest slaves on his plantation to be the father of her first grandchild. She did not make her advances to her equals," Jacobs explains, "nor ever to her father's more intelligent servants. She selected the most brutalized, over whom her authority could be exercised with less fear of exposure" (52). In slave society, this sketch and the many others like it suggest that men and women of all ranks—masters as well as slaves—are subject to "the unclean influences every where around them" (51).

7. As the narrator explains early in the novel, at the time Augustus bought his own freedom from Robbins, there was a law stating "that any freed person who had not left Virginia after one year could be brought back into slavery." Because he wanted to remain close to his family and eventually purchase them out of bondage, Augustus petitioned the state to be allowed to stay in Manchester County—a petition that was granted, due in large part to his skills as a carpenter. Yet we learn that, after buying his wife, "Augustus did not seek a petition for Mildred . . . because the law allowed freed slaves to stay on in the state in cases where they lived as someone's property, and relatives and friends often took advantage of the law to keep loved ones close by. Augustus would also not seek a petition for Henry, his son, and over time, because of how well William Robbins, their former owner, treated Henry, people in Manchester County just failed to remember that Henry, in fact, was listed forever in the records of Manchester as his father's property" (15–16).

8. At only one other place in the text do we see Augustus raise his hand in anger. Then, too, the violence is directed against Henry: he shakes his son and pushes him to the ground after the boy has been repeatedly—and unapologetically—late for visits with his parents, during the years William Robbins still owned him. In both instances, then, Augustus uses physical force in a manner consistent with Augustinian theology. He is exercising his "duty" as a father: punishing Henry's disobedience and reminding him of his filial obligations to "domestic rule." But notably, here as in the scene discussed above, his violence has an effect other than what he intended. It ends up confirming Robbins's power and the ethics of plantation life, rather than his own parental authority. Indeed, upon hearing that Augustus "did something" to Henry, Robbins tells him and Mildred, "I won't have you touching my boy, my property," and prohibits them from visiting him for a month (19). Since they are defenseless against him, Augustus and Mildred have no choice but to abide by Robbins's decree. Therefore, although it does not happen the way he wanted, Augustus's show of force accomplishes exactly what *The City of God* says it should: it bolsters "the integrity of the whole of which it is a part," bringing into "harmony" the law of the household with the law of the land (19.16).

9. Although Henry does not use the term "Caesars" to refer to Robbins and other wealthy slaveowners in Manchester County, other characters do, most notably Sheriff Skiffington throughout the novel.

10. According to Marshall, Augustine's notion of "exilic virtue" is a defense against the "temptations" of mastery, which suggests that "to live the best life possible in a political system whose corrosive values justify extreme domination, one should live as a 'pilgrim'— that is, one who is in a state of exile. In practice, this means willfully submitting oneself

to the order of servitude as a means of cultivating the self" (176–77). In Marshall's reading of Jones's novel, the model of exilic virtue inspires "three outstanding examples of slaves repudiating the lust for mastery" (178). The examples he gives are: Celeste and Elias, "who establish relations of familial intimacy under condition of natal alienation" (178); Augustus, who in the last moments of his life chooses to walk peaceably toward death having "seen the folly of his own decline into the lust for mastery when he attempted to coerce his son through violence" (179); and Alice Night, who makes art that "transcends the lust for mastery by transcending the lust for servitude" (181).

11. The internal quote is from Du Bois's "pioneering observations" on slaves' sorrow songs, found in his *Writings* (New York: Library of America, 1986), 538. Following Du Bois's analysis, Marshall says, "commentators . . . interpreted the music and art of slaves as profound and articulate protest against the experience of enslavement." Because Marshall is particularly concerned with the way Alice Night's artwork critiques mastery—as opposed to the condition of servitude—he extrapolates from Du Bois's interpretation of the sorrow songs to suggest that *The Known World* "poignantly insists that rather than, or perhaps in addition to, protesting slavery, the art of slaves articulates a philosophically profound critique of the problem of mastery" (181).

12. Regarding the various scholarly interpretations of Alice's artwork: Seger discusses its ability to elicit "a positive emotional and visceral reaction" in viewers which, in turn, transforms their worldview (1189–90); Bassard refers to her wall hanging as "immanent and transcendent" (418); and Donaldson writes that in her sculpture/tapestry "lies salvation" (281).

13. These types of readings—which emphasize Alice's divergence from "traditionalist," "white," or "European" conceptions of the world—are so common, in fact, that one critic, Tim A. Ryan, felt compelled to challenge an interpretation of her character that is "organized around such simple oppositions" (206). However, even Ryan's deconstructivist analysis does not take into account, as mine will, the way her artwork is informed by Western Christianity. He focuses instead on how her tapestries "echo," in their representation of specific and local stories, "the project of contemporary historiography" (207).

14. With the exception of a few Catholics whose presence in the novel I will try to account for in turn, the vast majority of characters in *The Known World* are Protestant, as we would expect from a novel set in Virginia in the years following the Second Great Awakening. In fact, in a private correspondence with me, Jones indicated that the slaves and slaveholders depicted in the novel "were, no doubt, all Protestants." What is more, everyone on Henry Townsend's plantation attends regular Sunday services officiated by Reverend Moffett, whose preaching, the narrator remarks, "had but one theme—that heaven was nearer than anyone realized and that one step away from the righteous path could take heaven away forever. . . . His ending words were that [the slaves] should obey their masters and mistresses, for heaven would not be theirs if they disobeyed" (87). Thus we discover in the particular brand of Protestantism proffered by Moffett a striking similarity to the conservative pole of Pauline theology that I discussed in chapter 1 in terms of fundamentalist Christianity.

15. Among the critics who draw comparisons between Alice and the narrator of *The Known World* are Seger, Berman, and of course Marshall.

16. Cavadini demonstrates that one of Augustine's main purposes in writing *The City*

of God is to reveal "the insufficiency even of philosophy to provide an adequate account of what seems to be an almost uniquely philosophical topic, God's eternal knowledge" (37).

17. Here, instead of the Dyson translation of *The City of God* elsewhere used in this chapter, I am quoting from the translation that Cavadini uses in his essay, which he notes is an adjusted version of Henry Bettison's 1972 edition.

18. For a discussion of the political impetus for *The City of God*, see Dyson's introduction, especially xi–xv.

19. Eleonore Stump provides an informative summary of Augustine's teaching on the role human beings play in their own salvation as well as the "insoluble" contradictions that such teaching give rise to (171–81).

20. The words on Brown's container, which he repeats a number of time throughout his narrative, read "This side up with care"—almost exactly the same phrase inscribed on Rita's container.

21. Giemza compares *The Known World* with other novels by contemporary African American writers that, he says, portray blacks and Irish as "strange kin" in the United States. Examples he points to include *The Autobiography of Miss Jane Pittman* and Morrison's *Sula*, as well as Richard Wright's *Black Boy* and *Native Son*.

Bibliography

Als, Hilton. "The Art of Fiction No. 222: Edward P. Jones." Interview. *Paris Review* 207 (Winter 2013): 140–72.
Andrews, William L. "The Representation of Slavery and Afro-American Literary Realism." *African American Autobiography: A Collection of Critical Essays*. Ed. William L. Andrews. Englewood Cliffs, NJ: Prentice Hall, 1993. 77–89.
Ashbrook, Tom. Interview with Toni Morrison. *On Point*, 11 May 2012. http://onpoint.legacy.wbur.org/2012/05/11/toni-morrison.
Atlas, Marilyn Judith. "Toni Morrison's *Beloved* and the Reviewers." *Midwestern Miscellany* 18 (1990): 45–57.
Augustine. *The City of God against the Pagans*. Trans. R. W. Dyson. Cambridge: Cambridge University Press, 1998.
———. *Confessions*. Trans. Henry Chadwick. Oxford: Oxford University Press, 1991.
Ayers, Lewis. "Augustine on the Triune Life of God." Meconi and Stump 60–77.
Babb, Valerie. "E Pluribus Unum? The American Origins Narrative in Toni Morrison's *A Mercy*." *MELUS* 36.2 (Summer 2011): 147–64.
———. *Ernest Gaines*. Boston: Twayne, 1991.
Bassard, Katherine Clay. "Imagining Other Worlds: Race, Gender, and the 'Power Line' in Edward P. Jones's *The Known World*." *African American Review* 42.3/4 (Fall-Winter 2008): 407–19.
Bell, Bernard W. *The Afro-American Novel and Its Tradition*. Amherst: University of Massachusetts Press, 1987.
Bercovitch, Eytan. "The Altar of Sin: Social Multiplicity and Christian Conversion among a New Guinea People." Mizruchi, *Religion* 211–35.
Bercovitch, Sacvan. *The American Jeremiad*. Madison: University of Wisconsin Press, 1978.
———. *The Puritan Origins of the American Self*. New Haven, CT: Yale University Press, 1975.
Berger, Peter L. *The Sacred Canopy: Elements of a Sociological Theory of Religion*. Garden City, NY: Doubleday, 1967.
Berman, Carolyn Vellenga. "*The Known World* in World Literature: Bakhtin, Glissant, and Edward P. Jones." *Novel: A Forum on Fiction* 42.2 (2009): 231–38.
Berry, Philippa. "Postmodernism and Post-religion." *The Cambridge Companion to Postmodernism*. Ed. Steven Connor. Cambridge: Cambridge University Press, 2004. 168–81.
Blake, Jeanie. "Interview with Ernest Gaines." 1982. Lowe 137–248.
Blassingame, John W. *The Slave Community: Plantation Life in the Antebellum South*. New York: Oxford University Press, 1972.

Boccia, Michael. "An Interview with Charles Johnson." 1996. McWilliams, *Passing* 192–205.
Brady, Diane. *Fraternity*. New York: Spiegel & Grau, 2012.
Broderick, Robert C., ed. *The Catholic Encyclopedia*. Rev. ed. Nashville: Thomas Nelson, 1987.
Brooks, Joanna. *American Lazarus: Religion and the Rise of African-American and Native American Literatures*. New York: Oxford University Press, 2003.
Brooks, Kristina. "Alice Dunbar-Nelson's Local Colors of Ethnicity, Class, and Place." *MELUS* 23.2 (Summer 1998): 3–26.
Brown, Henry Box. *Narrative of the Life of Henry Box Brown, Written by Himself*. 1851. Oxford: Oxford University Press, 2002.
Bruce, Dickson D., Jr. "Politics and Political Philosophy in the Slave Narrative." Fisch 28–43.
Burns, Charlene. "'Soul-Less' Christianity and the Buddhist Empirical Self: Buddhist-Christian Convergence?" *Buddhist-Christian Studies* 23 (2003): 87–100.
Byerman, Keith. *Remembering the Past in Contemporary African American Fiction*. Chapel Hill: University of North Carolina Press, 2005.
Caputo, John D., and Michael J. Scanlon, eds. *Augustine and Postmodernism: Confessions and Circumfession*. Bloomington: Indiana University Press, 2005.
Carroll, Michael P. *Catholic Cults and Devotions: A Psychological Inquiry*. Kingston, ON: McGill-Queen's University Press, 1989.
Cavadini, John C. "God's Eternal Knowledge According to Augustine." Meconi and Stump 37–59.
Cawelti, John G. "Leon Forrest at the University of Kentucky: On *The Bloodworth Orphans*." Interview with Forrest. 1988. Williams 13–26.
Cheuse, Alan. "When a Former Slave Becomes Master." Rev. of *The Known World*, by Edward P. Jones. *San Francisco Chronicle*, 14 September 2003.
Cixous, Hélène. *Stigmata: Escaping Texts*. 2nd ed. London: Routledge, 2005.
Coleman, James W. "Charles Johnson's Quest for Black Freedom in *Oxherding Tale*." *African American Review* 29.4 (Winter 1995): 631–44.
Cooper, William J., Jr. *Liberty and Slavery: Southern Politics to 1860*. New York: Knopf, 1983.
Crouch, Stanley. "Aunt Medea." *New Republic*, 19 October 1987, 38–43. Rpt. in *Toni Morrison: Beloved*. Ed. Carl Plasa. Columbia Critical Guides. New York: Columbia University Press, 1998. 26–30.
Darling, Marsha. "In the Realm of Responsibility: A Conversation with Toni Morrison." 1988. Taylor-Guthrie, *Conversations* 246–54.
Dayan, Joan [Colin Dayan]. *Haiti, History, and the Gods*. Berkeley: University of California Press, 1995.
———. "Voudon, or the Voice of the Gods." *Sacred Possessions: Vodou, Santería, Obeah, and the Caribbean*. Ed. Margarite Fernández-Olmos and Lizabeth Paravisini-Gebert. New Brunswick, NJ: Rutgers University Press, 1997. 13–36.
Derrida, Jacques. "Composing 'Circumfession.'" Caputo and Scanlon 19–27.
———. *Of Grammatology*. Trans. Gayatri Chakravorty Spivak. Corrected ed. Baltimore: Johns Hopkins University Press, 1997.
Deshmukh, Madhuri H. "Claude McKay's Road to Catholicism." *Callaloo* 37.1 (2014): 148–68.
Desmangles, Leslie G. *The Faces of the Gods: Vodou and Roman Catholicism in Haiti*. Chapel Hill: University of North Carolina Press, 1992.

Donaldson, Susan V. "Telling Forgotten Stories of Slavery in the Postmodern South." *Southern Literary Journal* 40.2 (2008): 267–83.
Douglass, Frederick. *My Bondage and My Freedom*. 1855. New Haven, CT: Yale University Press, 2014.
———. *Narrative of the Life of Frederick Douglass*. 1845. New York: Penguin Classics, 1982. Print.
Dubey, Madhu. "Neo-Slave Narratives." *A Companion to African American Literature*. Ed. Gene Andrew Jarrett. Malden, MA: Wiley-Blackwell, 2010. 332–46.
———. "Speculative Fictions of Slavery." *American Literature* 82.4 (2010): 779–805.
Duboin, Corinne. "Confronting the Specters of the Past, Writing the Legacy of Pain: An Interview with Phyllis Alesia Perry." *Mississippi Quarterly* 62.3–4 (Summer-Fall 2009): 633–53.
Dunn, Richard S. *Sugar and Slaves: The Rise of the Planter Class in the English West Indies, 1624–1713*. Chapel Hill: University of North Carolina Press, 1972.
Eggers, Dave. "Still Lost in the City." Rev. of *All Aunt Hagar's Children*, by Edward P. Jones. *New York Times*, 27 August 2006.
Ferraro, Thomas J. *Feeling Italian: The Art of Ethnicity in America*. New York: New York University Press, 2005.
Fisch, Audrey, ed. *The Cambridge Companion to the African American Slave Narrative*. Cambridge: Cambridge University Press, 2007.
Fleming, Robert. "Just Stating the Case Is 'More Than Enough': PW Talks with Edward P. Jones." *Publishers Weekly* 250.32 (11 August 2003): 253–54.
Foner, Eric. *Give Me Liberty! An American History*. 3rd ed. New York: Norton, 2011.
Forrest, Leon. *Two Wings to Veil My Face*. New York: Random House, 1983.
Franchot, Jenny. *Roads to Rome: The Antebellum Protestant Encounter with Catholicism*. Berkeley: University of California Press, 1994.
Gaines, Ernest J. *The Autobiography of Miss Jane Pittman*. New York: Dial, 1971.
———. "Miss Jane and I." *Callaloo* 24.2 (Spring 2001): 608–19.
Gallagher, Charles R. "The Catholic Church, Martin Luther King Jr., and the March in St. Augustine." *Florida Historical Quarterly* 83.2 (Fall 2004): 149–72.
Garrett, Clarke. *Spirit Possession and Popular Religion: From the Camisards to the Shakers*. Baltimore: Johns Hopkins University Press, 1987.
Gaudet, Marcia. "Miss Jane and Personal Experience Narrative: Ernest Gaines' *The Autobiography of Miss Jane Pittman*." *Western Folklore* 51.1 (January 1992): 23–32.
Geis, Deborah R. *Suzan-Lori Parks*. Ann Arbor: University of Michigan Press, 2008.
Genovese, Eugene D. *Roll, Jordan, Roll: The World the Slaves Made*. New York: Pantheon, 1974.
Giemza, Bryan. "Turned Inside Out: Black, White, and Irish in the South." *Southern Cultures* 18.1 (Spring 2012): 34–57.
Giles, Paul. *American Catholic Arts and Fictions: Culture, Ideology, Aesthetics*. Cambridge: Cambridge University Press, 1992.
Gilroy, Paul. *The Black Atlantic: Modernity and Double Consciousness*. London: Verso, 1993.
Glazier, Michael, and Monika K. Hellwig, eds. *The Modern Catholic Encyclopedia*. Rev. ed. Collegeville, MN: Liturgical Press, 2004.
Gleason, William. "The Liberation of Perception: Charles Johnson's *Oxherding Tale*." *Black American Literature Forum* 25.4 (Winter 1991): 705–28.

Gould, Philip. "The Rise, Development, and Circulation of the Slave Narrative." Fisch 11–27.
Graham, Maryemma. "An Interview with Edward P. Jones." *African American Review* 42.3/4 (Fall-Winter 2008): 421–38.
Greeley, Andrew. *The Catholic Imagination*. Berkeley: University of California Press, 2001.
Griesinger, Emily. "Why Baby Suggs, Holy, Quit Preaching the Word: Redemption and Holiness in Toni Morrison's *Beloved*." *Christianity and Literature* 50.4 (2001): 689–702.
HarperCollins. "Edward P. Jones on *The Known World*." 2003. Book Interview link at www.harpercollins.com/9780060557546/the-known-world.
Haddox, Thomas F. *Fears and Fascinations: Representing Catholicism in the American South*. New York: Fordham University Press, 2005.
Herskovits, Melville J. *Man and His Works: The Science of Cultural Anthropology*. New York: Knopf, 1948.
Ingram, Forrest, and Barbara Steinberg. "On the Verge: An Interview with Ernest J. Gaines." 1973. Lowe 39–55.
Jacobs, Harriet A. *Incidents in the Life of a Slave Girl, Written by Herself*. 1861. Ed. Jean Fagan Yellin. Cambridge, MA: Harvard University Press, 1987.
Jameson, Fredric. *Postmodernism, or, The Cultural Logic of Late Capitalism*. Durham, NC: Duke University Press, 1991.
Johnson, Charles. *Being and Race: Black Writing since 1970*. Bloomington: Indiana University Press, 1988.
———. *Oxherding Tale*. 1982. New York: Scribner, 2005.
Jones, Bessie W., and Audrey Vinson. "An Interview with Toni Morrison." 1985. Taylor-Guthrie, *Conversations* 171–87.
Jones, Edward P. *The Known World*. New York: Amistad, 2003.
June, Pamela B. *The Fragmented Female Body and Identity: The Postmodern, Feminist, and Multiethnic Writings of Toni Morrison, Theresa Hak Kyung Cha, Phyllis Alesia Perry, Gayl Jones, Emma Pérez, Paula Gunn Allen, and Kathy Acker*. New York: Peter Lang, 2010.
Kearney, Richard. "Time, Evil, and Narrative: Ricoeur on Augustine." Caputo and Scanlon 144–58.
Keizer, Arlene R. *Black Subjects: Identity Formation in the Contemporary Narrative of Slavery*. Ithaca, NY: Cornell University Press, 2004.
King, Martin Luther, Jr. "The Experiment of Love." *A Testament of Hope: The Essential Writings and Speeches of Martin Luther King, Jr.* Ed. James Melvin Washington. 1986. San Francisco: Harper, 1991. 16–20.
Laguerre, Michel Saturnin. "The Ghetto as Internal Colony: Socio-Economic Adaptations of a Haitian Urban Community." PhD diss., University of Illinois at Urbana-Champaign, 1976.
Lee, Maurice S. *Slavery, Philosophy, and American Literature, 1830–1860*. Cambridge: Cambridge University Press, 2005.
Levine, Lawrence W. *Black Culture and Black Consciousness: Afro-American Folk Thought from Slavery to Freedom*. New York: Oxford University Press, 1977.
Little, Jonathan. *Charles Johnson's Spiritual Imagination*. Columbia: University of Missouri Press, 1997.
Lowe, John, ed. *Conversations with Ernest Gaines*. Jackson: University Press of Mississippi, 1995.

MacDonald, Scott. "The Divine Nature: Being and Goodness." Meconi and Stump 17–36.
Marshall, Stephen. "Taking Liberty behind God's Back: Mastery as the Central Problem of Slavery." *Polity* 44.2 (April 2012): 155–81.
McBrien, Richard P. *Catholicism*. Rev. ed. San Francisco: Harper, 1994.
McGreevy, John T. *Parish Boundaries: The Catholic Encounter with Race in the Twentieth-Century Urban North*. Chicago: University of Chicago Press, 1996.
McHale, Brian. *Postmodernist Fiction*. New York: Methuen, 1987.
McWilliams, Jim. "An Interview with Charles Johnson." 2003. McWilliams, *Passing* 271–99.
———, ed. *Passing the Three Gates: Interviews with Charles Johnson*. Seattle: University of Washington Press, 2004.
Meconi, David Vincent. "Augustine's Doctrine of Deification." Meconi and Stump 208–30.
Meconi, David Vincent, and Eleonore Stump, eds. *The Cambridge Companion to Augustine*. 2nd ed. Cambridge: Cambridge University Press, 2014.
Mizruchi, Susan L., ed. *Religion and Cultural Studies*. Princeton, NJ: Princeton University Press, 2001.
———. *The Science of Sacrifice: American Literature and Modern Social Theory*. Princeton, NJ: Princeton University Press, 1998.
Monda, Antonio. "The Search Is More Important Than the Conclusion." Interview with Toni Morrison. *Do You Believe? Conversations on God and Religion*. Trans. Ann Goldstein. New York: Vintage, 2007. 115–22.
Morey, Ann-Janine. "Margaret Atwood and Toni Morrison: Reflections on Postmodernism and the Study of Religion and Literature." *Journal of the American Academy of Religion* 60.3 (1992): 493–513.
Morrison, Toni. *Beloved*. 1987. New York: Vintage, 2004.
———. *A Mercy*. New York: Knopf, 2008.
———. *Playing in the Dark: Whiteness and the Literary Imagination*. Cambridge, MA: Harvard University Press, 1992.
———. "The Site of Memory." 1987. *What Moves at the Margin: Selected Nonfiction*. Ed. Carolyn C. Denard. Jackson: University of Mississippi Press, 2008. 65–80.
———. "Unspeakable Things Unspoken: The Afro-American Presence in American Literature." *Michigan Quarterly Review* 28 (Winter 1989): 1–34.
Neary, Lynn. Interview with Toni Morrison. National Public Radio webcast, 27 October 2008. www.npr.org/2008/10/27/95961382/toni-morrison-a-mother-a-stranger-a-mercy.
O'Brien, John. *Interviews with Black Writers*. New York: Liveright, 1973.
O'Connell, Nicholas. "Charles Johnson." Interview. 1987. McWilliams, *Passing* 16–33.
Olney, James. "'I Was Born': Slave Narratives, Their Status as Autobiography and as Literature." *The Slave's Narrative*. Ed. Charles T. Davis and Henry Louis Gates Jr. Oxford: Oxford University Press, 1985. 148–74.
Orsi, Robert Anthony. *The Madonna of 115th Street: Faith and Community in Italian Harlem, 1880–1950*. New Haven, CT: Yale University Press, 1985.
Otten, Terry. *The Crime of Innocence in the Fiction of Toni Morrison*. Columbia: University of Missouri Press, 1989.
Parks, Suzan-Lori. *The America Play, and Other Works*. New York: Theatre Communications Group, 1995.
———. "Elements of Style." *America Play* 6–19.

———. "Possession." *America Play* 3–5

Passalacqua, Camille. "Witnessing to Heal the Self in Gayl Jones's *Corregidora* and Phyllis Alesia Perry's *Stigmata*." *MELUS* 35.4 (Winter 2010): 139–63.

Patterson, Orlando. *Slavery and Social Death: A Comparative Study*. Cambridge, MA: Harvard University Press, 1982.

Pérez-Torres, Rafael. "Between Presence and Absence: *Beloved*, Postmodernism, and Blackness." *Toni Morrison's "Beloved": A Casebook*. Ed. William L. Andrews and Nellie Y. McKay. New York: Oxford University Press, 1999. 179–203.

Perry, Phyllis Alesia. *Stigmata*. New York: Hyperion, 1998.

———. *A Sunday in June*. New York: Hyperion, 2004.

Pierce, Yolanda. "Redeeming Bondage: The Captivity Narrative and the Spiritual Autobiography in the African American Slave Narrative Tradition." Fisch 83–98.

Pressly, Thomas J. "*The Known World* of Free Black Slaveholders: A Research Note on the Scholarship of Carter G. Woodson." *Journal of African American History* 91.1 (Winter 2006): 81–87.

Raboteau, Albert J. *Slave Religion: The "Invisible Institution" in the Antebellum South*. New York: Oxford University Press, 1978.

Raynaud, Claudine. "*The Autobiography of Miss Jane Pittman*: Generic Twists and Trappings." *Études Anglaises* 58.4 (2005): 440–55.

Reed, Ishmael. *Conjure; Selected Poems, 1963–1970*. Amherst: University of Massachusetts Press, 1972.

———. *Flight to Canada*. New York: Random House, 1976.

———. *Shrovetide in Old New Orleans*. Garden City, NY: Doubleday, 1978.

Rowell, Charles H. "This Louisiana Thing That Drives Me: An Interview with Ernest J. Gaines." 1976. Lowe 86–98.

Roynon, Tessa. "Her Dark Materials: John Milton, Toni Morrison, and Concepts of 'Dominion' in *A Mercy*." *African American Review* 44.4 (Winter 2011): 593–606.

Rushdy, Ashraf H. A. *Neo-Slave Narratives: Studies in the Social Logic of a Literary Form*. New York: Oxford University Press, 1999.

Ryan, Tim A. *Calls and Responses: The American Novel of Slavery since "Gone with the Wind."* Baton Rouge: Louisiana State University Press, 2008.

Ryrie, Charles Caldwell. *The Grace of God*. Chicago: Moody, 1963.

Schappell, Elissa. "Toni Morrison: The Art of Fiction." Interview. *Toni Morrison: Conversations*. Ed. Carolyn C. Denard. Jackson: University of Mississippi Press, 2008. 62–69.

Schmidt, Bettina, and Lucy Huskinson, eds. *Spirit Possession and Trance: New Interdisciplinary Perspectives*. London: Continuum, 2010.

Seger, Maria. "Ekphrasis and the Postmodern Slave Narrative: Reading the Maps of Edward P. Jones's *The Known World*." *Callaloo* 37.5 (Fall 2014): 1181–95.

Selzer, Linda Furgerson. *Charles Johnson in Context*. Amherst: University of Massachusetts Press, 2009.

Sievers, Stefanie. "Embodied Memories—Sharable Stories? The Legacies of Slavery as a Problem of Representation in Phyllis Alesia Perry's *Stigmata*." *Monuments of the Black Atlantic: Slavery and Memory*. Ed. Joanne M. Braxton and Maria I. Diedrich. New Brunswick, NJ: Transaction, 2004. 131–39.

Smith, Jonathan Z. *Imagining Religion: From Babylon to Jonestown*. Chicago: University of Chicago Press, 1982.
Smith, Valerie. "'Circling the Subject': History and Narrative in *Beloved*." *Toni Morrison: Critical Perspectives Past and Present*. Ed. Henry Louis Gates Jr. and K. A. Appiah. New York: Amistad, 1993. 342–55.
———. "Neo-Slave Narratives." Fisch 168–88.
Spaulding, A. Timothy. *Re-forming the Past: History, the Fantastic, and the Postmodern Slave Narrative*. Columbus: Ohio State University Press, 2005.
Storhoff, Gary. *Understanding Charles Johnson*. Columbia: University of South Carolina Press, 2004.
Stump, Eleonore. "Augustine on Free Will." Meconi and Stump 166–88.
Sundquist, Eric J. *To Wake the Nations: Race in the Making of American Literature*. Cambridge, MA: Belknap Press of Harvard University Press, 1993.
Surányi, Ágnes. "The Bible as Intertext in Toni Morrison's Novels." *Toni Morrison and the Bible: Contested Intertextualities*. Ed. Shirley A. Stave. New York: Peter Lang, 2006. 116–28.
Taylor-Guthrie, Danille, ed. *Conversations with Toni Morrison*. Jackson: University Press of Mississippi, 1994.
———. "Sermons, Testifying, and Prayers: Looking Beneath the Wings in Leon Forrest's *Two Wings to Veil My Face*." *Leon Forrest: Introductions and Interpretations*. Ed. John G. Cawelti. Bowling Green, OH: Bowling Green State University Popular Press, 1997. 216–32.
Tracy, David. *The Analogical Imagination: Christian Theology and the Culture of Pluralism*. New York: Crossroad, 1981.
United States Congress of Catholic Bishops. *General Instruction of the Roman Missal*. 2011. www.usccb.org/prayer-and-worship/the-mass/general-instruction-of-the-roman-missal/.
Valkeakari, Tuire. *Religious Idiom and the African American Novel, 1952–1998*. Gainesville: University Press of Florida, 2007.
Vega-González, Susana. "Orphanhood in Toni Morrison's *A Mercy*." *Toni Morrison's "A Mercy": Critical Approaches*. Ed. Shirley A. Stave and Justine Tally. Newcastle upon Tyne: Cambridge Scholars, 2011. 119–36.
Warren, Kenneth W. "The Mythic City: An Interview with Leon Forrest." 1992. Williams 43–62.
Williams, Dana A., ed. *Conversations with Leon Forrest*. Jackson: University Press of Mississippi, 2007.
Wyatt, Jean. "Giving Body to the Word: The Maternal Symbolic in Toni Morrison's *Beloved*." *PMLA* 108.3 (1993): 474–88.
Yerby, Frank. *A Darkness at Ingraham's Crest: A Tale of the Slaveholding South*. New York: Dial, 1979.
Zauditu-Selassie, K. *African Spiritual Traditions in the Novels of Toni Morrison*. Gainesville: University Press of Florida, 2009.

Index

African spirituality, 49, 120, 198n30
Allmuseri worldview in *Oxherding Tale*, 144, 145, 147, 152
American Catholic Arts and Fictions (Giles), 1, 53
Anachronisms, 110
Analogia entis, 52–55
Analogical imagination, 52–55
Antirealism, 6, 200n5
Aquinas, Thomas, 52–53
Art: connection of God's eternal "ideal" of world and, in *The Known World*, 173–77; as protest against enslavement, 207n11; and time and creation in *The Known World*, 177–85; transformative power of, in *Stigmata*, 130–31; transformative power of, in *The Known World*, 185–87, 192
Augustinian theology: and conception of time, 113, 182–83; and connection of artistry and God's eternal "idea" of world in *The Known World*, 173–85; and ethical mastery in *The Known World*, 169, 170–73, 205n3; exilic virtue in, 206–7n10; intentionality of God in, 183–84; *The Known World* and Jones's engagement with, 160–61, 168; and *Oxherding Tale*, 112, 135–40, 148–52, 154–56, 205n29; salvation in, 187–88; and *Stigmata*, 112, 126–29, 131
Authorial knowledge, in *The Known World*, 165–67, 175–77
Autobiographies: by fugitive slaves, 3–5; realist structure of, 48–49, 52; spiritual, 51
Autobiography of Miss Jane Pittman, The (Gaines): and Catholic complicity in hierarchy among African Americans, 71–75; Catholicism and break from reality in, 107–8; connection between Catholicism and hoo-doo in, 83–84; date of, 201n11; historiographical approaches in, 86; Jules's approach to history in, 79–80, 82; moments of possession in, 77–78; narrative structure of, 85–86; possession and experience of slavery in, 80–81; possession and Jane's denial of hoo-doo in, 78–79; possession of Jane's narration in, 75–77, 86–87, 91; realism of, 69–71, 200n3; supernatural inclination of Catholic characters in, 84–85; temporality and temporal disjunctures in, 80–83, 109

Babb, Valerie, 198n26, 201n11
Bacon's Rebellion, 32–33, 198n19
Baraka, Amiri, 2
Bassard, Katherine Clay, 164, 167, 170, 207n12
Being, and nonbeing in *Oxherding Tale*, 143, 144, 145, 147–49
Being and Race: Black Writing Since 1970 (Johnson), 132, 137–38, 139
Bell, Bernard, 195n4
Beloved (Morrison): biblical allusions in, 23–25; and blindness, 29, 197n17; Catholicism as feature of history of slavery in, 17–18, 26–28; characters' resistance to remembering slave experience in, 199n43; critical reception of, 22–24; embodied horror of slavery rebranded as salvation and dignity in, 28–30; Eucharistic resonances in, 13–15, 55–61; excessiveness of, 22–25; image of chokecherry tree in, 197n16; lack of attention to Catholic themes in, 16–17; and Morrison's suspicion of Christianity, 15–16; narratological strategy of, 46–47; pervasiveness of Catholicism in, 30–31; rememory in, 45–47, 54–55; similarities between *Stigmata* and, 114–15; temporal disjunctures in, 109
Benevolent mastery, 25–26, 169, 171–72, 205n3
Bercovitch, Sacvan, 95, 201n16
Berger, Peter, 51–52, 82

218   Index

Berman, Carolyn Vellenga, 162
Berry, Philippa, 94–95, 202n23
Bible, allusions to, in *Beloved*, 23–25
Black Arts Movement, 2, 132, 146
Black Thunder (Bontemps), 196n5
Blindness, 29, 197n17
Bluest Eye, The (Morrison), 198n22
Bontemps, Arna, 196n5
Brown, Henry Box, 190–92
Buddhism, 133, 134–35, 139, 144–45, 204n26
Byerman, Keith, 90, 106

Carey, Hugh, 200n3
Carroll, Michael P., 203n15
Catholicism: function of, in examined texts, 10–11; grace in, 51–53; interpretation of historical time in, 80–83; predestination in, 188, 189–90, 191–92; racism undergirding institutions run and supported by, 7–8; and shaping of slave culture, 17–18; and slave literacy, 61–62
Cavadini, John, 182, 207–8n16
Les Cenelles, 71–72
Cheuse, Alan, 167, 176
Chokecherry tree, 197n16
Christianity: fundamentalist, 19–21, 25–26, 28, 196n8; and institutionalization of slavery, 19–26, 178; Morrison's suspicion of, 15–16; shaping of antebellum narratives of slavery by, 3–4
City of God (Augustine): and connection of artistry and God's eternal "idea" of world in *The Known World*, 173–85; and creative power in *The Known World*, 168; God's perception of time in, 182–83; intentionality of God in, 183–84; justification for slavery in, 168, 169, 170–73; purpose of, 207–8n16; salvation in, 187–88
Civil rights, 74–75, 201n10
Cixous, Hélène, 126, 127
Coleman, James W., 133
Confession, 62–63, 97, 143, 200nn46–47, 202n23
Confessions (Augustine): forgiveness in, 154, 158; influence of, on Johnson, 136–38; and love in *Oxherding Tale*, 154–56; and revelation in *Oxherding Tale*, 148–51; significance of, to fugitive slave narrators, 141; stigmata and embodied memory in, 126; time in, 113, 127, 129
Conjure (Reed), 200n1

Contemporary narratives of slavery, 2–3, 4–7, 109–10, 195n4, 196n5, 202–3n4. *See also* Slave narrative(s)
Conversion: among slave population, 196–97n10; of Paul, 197n17; and slave literacy, 61–62; and spiritual inclusivity in *Stigmata*, 121–22
Creation: and artistry in *The Known World*, 177–85; Catholic views on grace and, 52–53
Creoles, and Catholic complicity in hierarchy among African Americans, 71–75
Cross, encircled, 27–28
Crouch, Stanley, 22–23

Darling, Marsha, 50, 60
Dayan, Colin [Joan], 68, 97–98, 200n2
Derrida, Jacques, 140, 204n19
Desmangles, Leslie, 83
Donaldson, Susan V., 207n12
Douglass, Frederick, 6, 116, 136, 141, 195n2, 203n8, 203n10
Dubey, Madhu: on antirealist slave narratives, 200n5; on dehumanizing racial logic of Enlightenment and *A Mercy*, 39–40; on discourses undermined by contemporary narratives of slavery, 5; on *Miss Jane Pittman*, 75; on paranormal literary devices, 80, 107; on post-1970s "speculative" slave narratives, 79, 80; on realist narratives, 69–70; on temporal disjunctions in *The Known World*, 162; on trope of possession and neo-slave narratives, 200n6; use of term "haunt," 201n12; on Yerby's pessimistic view of US racial history, 202n3
Du Bois, W.E.B., 173, 197n10, 207n11
Dunbar-Nelson, Alice, 2
Dunn, Richard S., 61

Eggers, Dave, 177
Elementary school primers, 35–36, 197–98n22
"Elements of Style" (Parks), 67
Embodied memory: in *Beloved* and *Stigmata*, 114–15; in *Confessions*, 126; legitimization of, in *Stigmata*, 115–18
Encircled cross, 27–28
Enlightenment rationalism, 5, 11, 19, 21–23, 40
Ethical dualism, 25–26, 28–30, 38–39
Ethical mastery, 25–26, 169, 171–72, 205n3
Eucharist: actions recalling, in *Beloved*, 13–15,

Index 219

55–61; actions recalling, in *Two Wings*, 98–99, 105; Catholic perception of, 55
Evangelicals, 50–51, 199n31
Evil, 149
"Exhortation to His Children" (Rogers), 197n21
Exilic virtue, 172, 206–7n10

Fatherhood: and Allmuseri worldview in *Oxherding Tale*, 152; and forgiveness in *Oxherding Tale*, 153–55, 157–58; and fortification of slavery, 169–71
Felix culpa, 126, 127
Feudalism, 40, 42, 198n25
Flâneuse/flâneur, post-religious, 94
Flash-forwards, 110, 160, 161–68, 176
Flight to Canada (Reed), 68, 110
Forgiveness: in Augustinian theology, 138; in *Beloved*, 31; in *A Mercy*, 62–63, 66, 200n47; in *Oxherding Tale*, 153–55, 157–58
Forrest, Leon, 7, 95–97. See also *Two Wings to Veil My Face* (Forrest)
Franchot, Jenny, 11
Fugitive slave authors: as bound and silenced, 21–24; influence of white readership on, 3–5
Fundamentalist Christianity, 19–21, 25–26, 28, 196n8
Futurity, in *The Known World*, 161–64, 165–68, 175–77

Gaines, Earnest, 70, 82, 85–86. See also *Autobiography of Miss Jane Pittman, The* (Gaines)
Garrett, Clarke, 202n17
Gaudet, Marcia, 200n3
Genesis, 177–79, 183, 184
Genovese, Eugene, 3, 21
Giemza, Bryan, 208n21
Giles, Paul, 1, 53, 54, 81–82, 195n1, 199n38, 199n40, 201n15
Gilroy, Paul, 5, 6, 197n11
Gleason, William, 133–34, 138–39, 204n24, 204n25
God: intentionality of, 183–84; and *Oxherding Tale*'s intertextual engagement with Augustine, 149–52; and temporality and creation, 182–83
Gould, Philip, 50–51, 199n31
Grace, 51–53
Graham, Maryemma, 180
Great Gatsby, The (Fitzgerald), 201n15

Greeley, Andrew, 52, 53, 199n36
Guilt: in *The Known World*, 178; in *Oxherding Tale*, 153–55, 157–58

Haddox, Thomas F., 71–72, 198n25, 201n8
Haitian Vodou, 83
Hansberry, Lorraine, 67
Herskovits, Melville J., 201n13
Hoo-doo, in *The Autobiography of Miss Jane Pittman*, 78–79, 83–84, 87
"Hoo-doo writing," (Reed), 67–68, 200n1
House, and theological transformation of Jack Vaark in *A Mercy*, 40–44

Incidents in the Life of a Slave Girl (Jacobs), 205–6n6
Individualism, 144–45
Infanticide, 28–30, 57–58
Intercession of saints, 82–83
Irish immigrants, 192, 208n21

Jacobs, Harriet, 195n2, 205–6n6
Jameson, Fredric, 95, 132
Johnson, Charles, 132, 134, 135, 204n26. See also *Being and Race: Black Writing Since 1970* (Johnson); *Oxherding Tale* (Johnson)
Jones, Edward P., 161, 164, 166, 177, 180–81, 186, 202n19. See also *Known World, The* (Jones)
Jubilee (Walker), 196n5

Kearney, Richard, 203n16
Keizer, Arlene, 195n4
King, Martin Luther Jr., 74, 201n10
Known World, The (Jones), 160–61; Augustus's petition in, 206n7; classification of, 162–64; complexity of, 165, 205n3; connection of artistry and God's eternal "ideal" of world in, 173–85; corrupting effects of bondage in, 168–69; flash-forward technique in, 161–64, 165–68; fortification of slavery in, 169–71; intertextual engagement with Augustine in, 160–61, 168, 169, 170–73; narrative omniscience in, 165–67; planning for, 180; as pseudorealist, 205n1; realism and plausibility of, 160, 164–65, 167; religion of characters in, 207n14; research for, 164, 165; scholarly interpretations of Alice's artwork in, 207nn12–13; time and liberation in, 187–92; transformative power of art in, 185–87, 192; violence of Augustus in, 170–71, 206n8

220 Index

Laguerre, Michel Saturnin, 97–98
Latin Mass, 56–57, 99–101
Levine, Lawrence, 3
Liberation and liberty: infanticide and otherworldly, in *Beloved*, 29; in *Oxherding Tale*, 135, 138–39, 143, 145, 146, 148, 153–55, 157–58, 204–5n27; and salvation in *The Known World*, 188–91; slavery yoked to concept of, 19, 21–22
Literacy, correlation between religion and, 61–62
Literary postmodernism, 49
Literary realism: and evangelical Protestant audience, 52; of *The Known World*, 160, 162–65, 167; of *Miss Jane Pittman*, 69–71, 75, 200n3; in *Miss Jane Pittman* and *Two Wings*, 91, 107–8; of Morrison works, 48–49; Parks on, 67; and trope of spirit possession, 68, 91
Little, Jonathan, 139
Loa/Lwa, 68, 83
"Logic of the supplement," 140
Loss: memory of, 56–58; of selfhood, 63–65
Love: and *Oxherding Tale*'s intertextual engagement with Augustine, 150–51, 154–56, 205n29; self-destructive, 63–65
Lwa/Loa, 68, 83

MacDonald, Scott, 148–49
Magic, Morrison on writing as, 52
Manichees, 148, 149
Marriage, 156–57
Marshall, Stephen, 172–73, 174, 206–7nn10–11
McBrien, Richard P., 55, 59
McHale, Brian, 92
McKay, Claude, 2, 195n1
Meditation, 127, 134–35
Memory: embodied, in *Beloved* and *Stigmata*, 114–15; embodied, in *Confessions*, 126; legitimization of embodied, in *Stigmata*, 115–18; of loss, 56–58; Morrison's approach to, 48–49; in slave narratives, 48–49. *See also* Rememory
Mercy, A (Morrison), 31–32; ambivalence regarding redemptive potential of Catholic sacraments in, 61–66; Catholicism as feature of history of slavery in, 17–18; confessional nature of storytelling in, 199–200n46; disintegration of distinction between Catholic and Protestant justifications of slavery in, 37–39; ideology of Jacob Vaark in, 32–35; Jacob Vaark's revulsion for Catholicism in, 35–37; lack of attention to Catholic themes in,

16–17; Rebekka's acceptance of slaveholding practices in, 43–44; rememory in, 47–48; self-destructive love as enslavement in, 63–65; theological transformation of Jack Vaark in, 40–44; undermining of traditional race-based slavery narratives in, 39–40
"Miss Jane and I" (Gaines), 85
Moksha, 132, 133, 138, 139, 143, 147, 148
Morey, Ann-Janine, 16
Morrison, Toni: on characters' resistance to remembering slave experience, 199n43; Christian interpretation of work of, 198n30; critique of Enlightenment rationality, 11, 19, 21–23, 40; on fugitive slave autobiographies, 4; interest of in Bacon's Rebellion, 198n19; on Latin, 56, 57; on recovering lost past, 5; religious background of, 17, 54, 199n40; rememory and memory of slavery, 46, 48–49; suspicion of Christianity, 15–16; and trope of elementary school primer, 197–98n22; on writing, 52. *See also Beloved* (Morrison); *Bluest Eye, The* (Morrison); *Mercy, A* (Morrison); *Playing in the Dark* (Morrison); "Site of Memory, The" (Morrison)
My Bondage and My Freedom (Douglass), 203n8

Narrative of the Life of Frederick Douglass (Douglass), 136, 141, 195n2, 203n10
Narrative of the Life of Henry Box Brown, The (Brown), 190–92
Narrative omniscience, in *The Known World*, 165–67, 175–77
Neo-slave narratives, 2–3, 4–7, 67–68, 195n4, 200n6
New Testament, allusions to, in *Beloved*, 23–25
Nonbeing, and being in *Oxherding Tale*, 143, 144, 145, 147–49
No-self-ness, 142, 143, 144–45

Olney, James, 48, 204n21
Oxherding Tale (Johnson), 131–35; alternative temporality of, 110–12; Andrew's transformation in, 141–49; Gleason on, 204nn24–25; hope for racial reconciliation in, 158–59; intertextual engagement with Augustine in, 135–40, 148–52; literary ancestry of, 140–41; love and Andrew's domestic turn in, 155–58; redemption and liberation in, 152–55; temporal disjuncture in, 156–58

Padre Pio, 125–26, 203n14
Parks, Suzan-Lori, 67, 68, 107–8, 195n3
Passalacqua, Camille, 123
Patterson, Orlando: on American theology of slavery, 38; on masters' abandonment of religion, 198n23; Morrison's recontextualization of, 39; on rise of fundamentalist Christianity, 196n8; on slave religion, 17, 18–20, 21, 25–26, 30, 31–32; on Southern Protestantism, 197n13
Pauline epistles and theology: allusions to, in *Beloved*, 16, 29; American theology of slavery premised upon, 38, 39; Catholic interpretation of, in Morrison works, 18; and fellowship in Eucharist, 60; justification for slavery in, 24–26; metaphorical language of slavery in, 20, 64; and Paul's association with blindness, 29, 197n17; Protestant interpretation of, 36–37
Pérez-Torres, Rafael, 49
Perry, Phyllis Alesia, 112. See also *Stigmata* (Perry); *Sunday in June, A* (Perry)
Pierce, Yolanda, 199n33
Plaçage, 71–73, 201n8
Playing in the Dark (Morrison), 18–19
Possession. See Spirit possession
"Possession" (Parks), 67
Postmodernism, 49, 81, 85, 90, 92, 94–95, 163, 198n30
"Post-religion," 202n23
Post-religious *flâneuse* or *flâneur*, 94
Predestination, 183, 188, 189–90, 191–92
Present, threefold, Augustine's construct of, 127–28
Pressly, Thomas J., 164–65
Protestantism: disintegration of distinction between Catholic and Protestant justifications of slavery in *A Mercy*, 37–39; grace in, 51–52, 54; and institutionalization of slavery, 20–21, 198n23; interpretation of historical time in, 80–83; interpretation of Pauline theology, 36–37; predestination in, 188, 189–90; and Rebekka's acceptance of slaveholding practices in *A Mercy*, 44; and religious knowledge of Denver in *Beloved*, 14–15; and sensibilities of slave narrative audience, 50–51, 199n31; in slaveholding American South, 197n13; and slave literacy, 61–62

Quilt, in *Stigmata*, 118–20, 121–22, 124, 130

Raboteau, Albert, 3, 83, 196n6, 197n10
Raynaud, Claudine, 86
Realism. See Literary realism
Reconciliation, 62–63, 153–55, 157–59
Redemption, and liberation in *Oxherding Tale*, 153–55, 157–58. See also Salvation
Reed, Ishmael, 68, 87, 107–8, 200n1, 202n2. See also *Flight to Canada* (Reed)
Rememory: in *Beloved*, 45–47; in *Beloved* and *Stigmata*, 114–15; and Catholic analogical imagination, 54–55; Catholic interpretation of, 49–50; and Eucharistic resonances in *Beloved*, 55–61; in *A Mercy*, 47–48; Morrison's religious background and development of, 53–54; and realist structure of slave autobiographies, 48; scholarly views on, 49
Rogers, John, 197n21
Rome, sacking of, in 410, 183–84
Roynon, Tessa, 197n21
Rushdy, Ashraf: on *Flight to Canada*, 68; on lies sustaining white America's view of past, 2–3; and neo-slave narratives, 195n4; on *Oxherding Tale*, 145, 204–5n27; on temporal landscape of *Flight to Canada*, 110; on textual possession and Vodou ceremonies, 200n2; on trope of possession and neo-slave narratives, 87, 106
Ryan, Tim A., 207n13

Sacramentality: in *Beloved*, 52–53, 55–61; in *A Mercy*, 61–66; and Morrison's approach for remembering traumatic past, 45
Saints, intercession of, 82–83
Salvation: and ambivalence regarding redemptive potential of Catholic sacraments in *A Mercy*, 61–66; of Augustine, 148–49; in ethic of redeemed sinner, 26; and Eucharistic resonances in *Beloved*, 58–61; and forgiveness in *Oxherding Tale*, 157–58; of fugitive slave narrators, 141; and infanticide in *Beloved*, 28–29; and intertextuality of Augustine and *Oxherding Tale*, 138, 139–40; and liberation in *The Known World*, 187–92; slavery rebranded as, 28. See also Redemption, and liberation in *Oxherding Tale*
Seger, Maria, 163, 205n1, 207n12
Self-destructive love, 63–65
Selfhood, loss of, 63–65
Selzer, Linda Furgerson, 139

Shared experience: in *Beloved*, 46–47, 57–58, 114–15; in *A Mercy*, 47–48; in *Stigmata*, 114–16
"Site of Memory, The" (Morrison), 21–22
Slave literacy, correlation between religion and, 61–62
Slave narrative(s): antirealist, 200n5; Catholicism and counter-culture in, 6–7; evolution of, 137; influences on, 136; Morrison's desire to redeem, 50; possession in, 67–68; Protestant sensibilities of audience of, 50–51, 199n31; realist structure of, 48–49, 52; salvation of authors of, 141; temporal disjunctures in, 109–10, 202–3n4. *See also* Contemporary narratives of slavery; Fugitive slave authors
Slavery: art as protest against, 207n11; Catholicism and shaping of, culture, 17–18; Christianity and institutionalization of, 19–26, 178, 205n3; circular sense of time associated with, 80–81; concept of liberty yoked to, 19, 21; endurance of, 110; fortification of, 169–71; justifications for, 24–26, 28–30, 38–39, 169, 171–72, 178, 205n3
Slavery and Social Death: A Comparative Study (Patterson), 19, 21, 25–26, 30
Smith, Valerie, 54–55, 59
Social mobility: and circular time in *Stigmata*, 120; of Creoles in *Miss Jane Pittman*, 71–72; and cultural resistance to non-Western modes of knowledge in *Stigmata*, 121
Soliloquies (Augustine), 135
Sorrow songs, 207n11
Spaulding, A. Timothy, 90, 109, 138, 163
Spirit possession: in African American literature, 67–68; Catholic doctrine regarding, 202n17; and embrace of past's complexity in *Two Wings*, 105–7; and experience of slavery in *Miss Jane Pittman*, 80–81; filtered through Catholic sacramentality in *Miss Jane Pittman* and *Two Wings*, 107–8; Gaines's use of, 70; Herskovits on, 201n13; and Jane's denial of hoo-doo in *Miss Jane Pittman*, 78–79, 87; and Jules's approach to history in *Miss Jane Pittman*, 79–80, 82; and linguistic appropriation of religious experience in *Two Wings*, 97–98; linked to Catholicism in *Two Wings*, 88, 98–100; in *Miss Jane Pittman*, 70–71, 77–78; of narration in *Miss Jane Pittman*, 75–77, 86–87, 91; of narration in *Two Wings*, 88–92, 102, 104; neo-slave narratives and, 200n6; Parks on, 67; political thrust of, 97–98; Rushdy on trope of, 106; and supernatural inclination of Catholic characters in *Miss Jane Pittman*, 84–85; trope of, as postmodern device, 92
Spiritual autobiography, 51, 199n33
Spiritual slavery, 63–65
Stations of the Cross, 126, 195n3, 203n15
Stigmata (Perry), 112–13; alternative temporality of, 110–12, 113–14; Augustinian theology and, 126–29, 131; Catholicism's impact on narrative of, 124–26; conversion and spiritual inclusivity in, 121–22; legitimization of embodied memory in, 115–18; new narrative form in, 118–20; non-Western worldview validated by Catholicism in, 122–24; similarities between *Beloved* and, 114–15; temporality and cultural resistance to non-Western modes of knowledge, 120–21; transformative power of art as primary theme of, 130–31
Stigmata and stigmatics, 112, 113, 123, 125–26, 203n15
Stigmatexts, 126, 127
Sunday in June, A (Perry), 120–21, 131, 203n13
Sundquist, Eric, 116
Surányi, Ágnes, 16

Taylor-Guthrie, Danille, 92–93
Temporality and temporal disjuncture: and Augustinian theology in *Stigmata*, 129; in contemporary slave narratives, 109–10, 202–3n4; and cultural resistance to non-Western modes of knowledge in *Stigmata*, 120–21; Derrida on, 204n19; and event of forgiveness, 158; in *The Known World*, 160, 161–64, 165–68, 175–77, 186–87; in *Oxherding Tale*, 110–12, 113–14, 131–32, 133, 135, 156–58; in *Stigmata*, 110–12, 113–14, 119–20. *See also* Time
Threefold present, Augustine's construct of, 127–28
Time: and Augustine's construct of threefold present, 127–28; *Beloved* and convergence of, 59; circular sense of, associated with slavery, 80–81; in *Confessions*, 129; conflation of, in slave narratives, 109; *The Known World* and artists' relation to, 180–82; and liberation in *The Known World*, 187–92; portrayal of, in *Oxherding Tale*, 133; promotion of non-Western approaches to, 111; Protestant versus Catholic interpretation of historical, 81–83; and trans-

formative power of art in *The Known World*, 186–87. *See also* Temporality and temporal disjuncture

Time-travel, 110, 120

Tracy, David, 199n36

Transubstantiation, 28, 126, 201n15, 203n15

Traumatism, 127

Two Wings to Veil My Face (Forrest), 87–88; allusions to other religions in, 202n25; awareness of racist history undergirding Catholic institutions in, 7–8; Catholicism and break from reality in, 107–8; disorientation due to historical knowledge in, 102–4; embrace of past's complexity in, 105–7; fluidity of religious belief in, 92–95; fluidity of religious discourses in, 95–97; historiographical approaches in, 90–91; link between Catholicism and possession in, 88, 98–100; possession and linguistic appropriation of religious experience in, 97–98; possession of narration in, 88–92, 102, 104; quest for historical knowledge and turn away from Catholicism in, 100–102; transformation of stories in, 104–5

Valkeakari, Tuire, 16, 196n5

Vatican II, 56, 57, 74, 96

Virtue, exilic, 172, 206–7n10

Vodou, 68, 83. *See also* Hoo-doo, in *The Autobiography of Miss Jane Pittman*; "Hoo-doo writing," (Reed)

Walker, Margaret, 196n5

Works Progress Administration interviews, 69

Worthiness, in *Oxherding Tale*, 153

Yerby, Frank, 110, 202n3

Zen Buddhism, 133, 134–35, 139, 144–45, 204n26

ERIN MICHAEL SALIUS is assistant dean of Metropolitan College and director of Summer Term at Boston University.

www.ingramcontent.com/pod-product-compliance
Lightning Source LLC
Chambersburg PA
CBHW020836160426
43192CB00007B/681